D1155639

Learner Language
and
Language Learning

MULTILINGUAL MATTERS

1. "Bilingualism: Basic Principles"
   HUGO BAETENS BEARDSMORE

2. "Evaluating Bilingual Education: A Canadian Case Study"
   MERRILL SWAIN AND SHARON LAPKIN

3. "Bilingual Children: Guidance for the Family"
   GEORGE SAUNDERS

4. "Language Attitudes Among Arabic-French Bilinguals in Morocco"
   ABDELÂLI BENTAHILA

5. "Conflict and Language Planning in Quebec"
   RICHARD Y. BOURHIS (ed.)

6. "Bilingualism and Special Education"
   JIM CUMMINS

7. "Bilingualism or Not: The Education of Minorities"
   TOVE SKUTNABB-KANGAS

8. "An Ethnographic/Sociolinguistic Approach
   to Language Proficiency Assessment"
   CHARLENE RIVERA (ed.)

9. "Communicative Competence Approaches to Language Proficiency
   Assessment: Research and Application"
   CHARLENE RIVERA (ed.)

10. "Language Proficiency and Academic Achievement"
    CHARLENE RIVERA (ed.)

11. "Pluralism: Cultural Maintenance and Evolution"
    BRIAN BULLIVANT

12. "Placement Procedures in Bilingual Education: Education and
    Policy Issues"
    CHARLENE RIVERA (ed.)

13. "The Education of Linguistic and Cultural Minorities
    in the OECD Countries"
    STACY CHURCHILL

14. "Learner Language and Language Learning"
    CLAUS FÆRCH, KIRSTEN HAASTRUP and ROBERT PHILLIPSON

MULTILINGUAL MATTERS 14

Learner Language and Language Learning

CLAUS FÆRCH, KIRSTEN HAASTRUP
ROBERT PHILLIPSON

In collaboration with
Esther Glahn and *Knud Bæk Kristiansen*

MULTILINGUAL
MATTERS LTD

PE
1128
.A2
F33x

Learner Language and Language Learning
1. udgave 1. oplag 1984
© 1984 by Gyldendalske Boghandel,
Nordisk Forlag A.S., Copenhagen
Fotografisk, mekanisk eller anden gengivelse
eller mangfoldiggørelse af denne bog
eller dele deraf er ikke tilladt
ifølge gældende dansk lov om ophavsret
Bogen er sat med Baskerville
og trykt hos Nørhaven Bogtrykkeri a/s, Viborg
Omslag og tilrettelægning: John Back
Printed in Denmark 1984

Learner Language and Language Learning
All Rights Reserved. No part of this work may be
reproduced in any form or by any means without
permission in writing from the Publisher.

This co-edition published in 1984 by
Multilingual Matters Ltd.,
Bank House, 8a Hill Road,
Clevedon, Avon BS21 7HH
England

in conjuction with Gyldendal Boghandel,
Nordisk Forlag A.S., Copenhagen

British Library Cataloguing in Publication Data

Faerch, Claus
Learner language and language learning. –
(Multilingual matters; 14)
1. English language – Study and teaching –
Foreign speakers – Case studies 2. English
language – Study and teaching – Danish speakers
I. Title   II. Haastrup, Kirsten
III. Phillipson, Robert   IV. Series
428'.2'4'0710489   PE1128.A2
ISBN 0-905028-28-7

DABNEY LANCASTER LIBRARY
LONGWOOD COLLEGE
FARMVILLE, VIRGINIA 23901

Preface

This book is primarily intended for students of English who need a basic introduction to foreign language pedagogy. It should also be of immediate relevance to teachers of English at all educational levels.

The authors have been attached to PIF (*Project In Foreign Language Pedagogy*) since the mid-70s. The project has brought together a considerable number of researchers, teachers and students who share a wish to develop research into foreign language learning and teaching in Denmark. This book is one product of the investigations undertaken by the project and the teaching related to it. We should like to express our warm thanks to the many colleagues and students who have influenced our thinking over the years and commented on various drafts of the book.

The book itself has been written and rewritten over a period of several years. Knud Bæk Kristiansen has been a member of the book production team throughout its many phases. The final text owes much to his perceptive and constructive criticism. Esther Glahn participated in the early stages of shaping the overall structure of the book, and has made useful comments on many of the draft chapters. Birgitte Sneum typed the innumerable draft versions of the book with superb competence and has patiently converted our joint work into impeccable form.

Finally, we would like to acknowledge the support we have received from the following funding sources for the research on which the book is based: The Danish Research Council for the Humanities; the Department of English, the Department of Applied and Mathematical Linguistics and the Humanities Faculty of the University of Copenhagen; the Institute for Danish, English, French and German, Roskilde University Centre.

DABNEY LANCASTER LIBRARY

1000121754

Abbreviations and transcription conventions

L1   first language, mother tongue
IL   interlanguage
L2   a second or foreign language

grades 6   sixth ⎫
         8   eighth ⎬ class of the Folkeskole
      10   tenth ⎭

1gs   first ⎫
                 ⎬ year, languages line, of the Gymnasium
3gs   third ⎭

–   short pause
– –   longer pause
( )   explanatory information in learner texts
[ ]   phonetic transcription of the relevant word
" "   indicates Danish or Danish-based word in learner text

The phonetic symbols used are, for English, the same as in Davidsen-Nielsen 1975, and for Danish, those of the International Phonetic Alphabet.

Spoken language is transcribed either with each speaker's turn in succession:

   A   bla
   B   bla
   A   bla bla   (see for instance text 2)

or with speakers' contributions on parallel horizontal lines, this making it possible to indicate whether speakers overlap with each other

   A   bla   bla bla
   B   bla   (see for instance text 1).

In the pronunciation chapter, intonation is marked in the

$^{v}{}_{e}{}_{r}$tical axis, and s t r e s s by spacing.

Table of contents

Preface *5*

Abbreviations and transcription conventions *6*

Chapter one: Introduction *7*
1.1 "Learner English" as a variety of English *7*
1.2 Learner language within foreign language pedagogy *9*
1.3 Learner language, foreign language pedagogy, and the teacher of English *14*
1.4 The structure and content of the book *15*

Part I: LEARNER LANGUAGE *19*

Chapter two: Varieties of communication *21*
2.1 Basic concepts for the analysis of communication *22*
    2.1.1 Communicative event *23*
    2.1.2 Setting *24*
    2.1.3 Participants – communicative roles *24*
    2.1.4 Participants – social roles and status *25*
    2.1.5 Contact and channel *26*
    2.1.6 Message *27*
    2.1.7 Code *27*
2.2 Face-to-face communication *28*
2.3 One-way communication *32*
2.4 Characteristics of educational communication *35*

Chapter three: Pragmatics *40*
3.1 Language functions *40*
3.2 Acting by means of language – speech acts *45*
3.3 Questions of politeness – speech act modality *54*

I

Chapter four: Discourse   *60*

4.1 Coherence: initiating and responding acts   *60*
4.2 Coherence, cohesion and variation   *62*
4.3 Discourse phases   *66*
4.4 Turn-taking   *69*
4.5 Gambits   *71*
4.6 Repair work   *72*

Chapter five: Vocabulary   *77*

5.1 What is a word?   *77*
5.2 How to analyse richness of vocabulary in learner
     language   *80*
     5.2.1 Lexical variation   *80*
     5.2.2 Lexical density   *84*
5.3 Some principles for the selection of vocabulary   *85*
     5.3.1 Frequency   *86*
     5.3.2 Availability   *87*
     5.3.3 Coverage   *87*
5.4 The structure of learner vocabulary   *88*
     5.4.1 Relating L2 words directly to their referents   *89*
     5.4.2 L1 – IL vocabulary   *90*
     5.4.3 Relating L2 words to familiar L2 words   *94*
5.5 Lexical inferencing   *96*
5.6 What does it mean to know a word?   *98*

Chapter six: Grammar   *103*

6.1 Analysis of errors in written texts   *104*
6.2 Analysis of errors in speech and writing   *110*
6.3 Types of grammatical rules   *114*

Chapter seven: Pronunciation   *120*

7.1 Accents and norms of pronunciation   *120*
7.2 The functions of prosody   *122*
7.3. Studying learner prosody   *127*
7.4 Studying the learning of specific sounds   *129*
7.5 Explaining pronunciation errors   *135*

Chapter eight: Production, fluency and reception   139

8.1 Speech production   *139*
8.2 Fluency   *142*
8.3 Speech reception   *148*

Chapter nine: Communication strategies   *154*

9.1 Strategies in production   *154*
  9.1.1 Achievement strategies   *155*
  9.1.2 Sequences of achievement strategies   *159*
  9.1.3 Identifying achievement strategies   *160*
  9.1.4 Reduction strategies   *161*
9.2 Strategies in reception   *162*
9.3 Communication strategies and proficiency levels   *164*

Chapter ten: Communicative competence   *167*

10.1 The components of communicative competence   *167*
10.2 Exemplifying communicative competence   *172*
10.3 Dimensions of communicative competence   *174*
  10.3.1 Communicative competence in a foreign language
      as assessed by native speakers   *174*
  10.3.2 Context-reduced or context-embedded language   *177*
  10.3.3 Metacommunicative awareness   *178*

Part II: LANGUAGE LEARNING   *183*

Chapter eleven: Learning a foreign language   *185*

11.1 Input – intake   *186*
11.2 Processes in foreign language learning   *188*
11.3 Hypothesis formation   *190*
  11.3.1 The nature of hypotheses   *190*
  11.3.2 Where do learners' hypotheses come from?   *192*
  11.3.3 How do learners try out their hypotheses?   *194*
11.4 A model of foreign language learning   *200*
11.5 Types of knowledge, automatization and
      consciousness-raising   *201*
11.6 Foreign language learning related to classroom activities   *203*
  11.6.1 Teacher conducts translation exercise in the
      classroom   *204*

III

11.6.2 Teacher guides discussion of a literary text in class *204*

11.6.3 Pupils role-play in small groups, followed by general discussion in class of pupils' experiences in role-playing *205*

Chapter twelve: Individual variation *208*

12.1 Attitudes *208*

12.2 Age *210*

12.3 Aptitude *213*

12.4 Implications *215*

Part III: LANGUAGE TEACHING *219*

Chapter thirteen: Aims *221*

13.1 English in Denmark, second or foreign language? *221*

13.2 English as a school subject *222*

13.3 Specifying teaching aims – the Threshold Level approach *225*

13.4 A specification of aims – help or hindrance *228*

Chapter fourteen: From aims to teaching *231*

14.1 Principles of syllabus design *231*

14.2 Exemplifying teaching methods: "An Exercise Typology" *237*

14.3 Analysing the communicative and learning potential of classroom activities *240*

Chapter fifteen: Evaluation *244*

15.1 Achievement and proficiency testing *244*

15.2 Norm-referenced and criterion-referenced testing *245*

15.3 Formative and summative evaluation *245*

15.4 Validity and reliability *246*

15.5 Discrete point tests and integrative tests *247*

15.6 Towards a reform of school language examinations *249*

Chapter sixteen: Innovation *252*

16.1 Differentiation *252*

16.2 Consciousness *253*

16.2.1 Metacommunicative knowledge *254*

IV

16.2.2 Knowledge about learning *254*

16.2.3 Socio-cultural knowledge *255*

16.3 Negotiation of syllabus *256*

16.4 Inter-subject collaboration *257*

16.5 Project work *258*

16.6 Communicative foreign language teaching *259*

16.7 Language teacher education *262*

Part IV: PRINCIPLES AND METHODS OF INTERLANGUAGE STUDIES *267*

Chapter seventeen: Interlanguage *269*

17.1 Historical background to interlanguage studies *269*

17.2 Interlanguage: definition and characterisation *271*

17.2.1 Formal characteristics *272*

17.2.2 Functional characteristics *275*

Chapter eighteen: Some methods of analysis in IL studies *277*

18.1 Performance analysis *278*

18.1.1 Example 1: Description of IL vocabulary *279*

18.1.2 Example 2: Description of use of different types of noun phrase *280*

18.2 Error analysis *282*

18.2.1 Error identification *282*

18.2.2 Linguistic classification of errors *284*

18.2.3 Classification of errors on the basis of error causes *287*

18.3 Contrastive analysis *289*

18.3.1 Contrastive analysis of linguistic systems *290*

18.3.2 Contrastive performance analysis *291*

18.4 Tolerance testing *292*

18.5 Analysing interaction *294*

Chapter nineteen: Learner language data, collection and transcription *295*

19.1 The learner language corpus drawn on in this book *295*

19.2 Learner language data types *298*

19.3 Recording and transcribing learner language *301*

References *305*

Index *317*

V

Figures

Fig.   1   A learner language approach to foreign language pedagogy *11*
–   2   The framework of the book *17*
–   3   Speech act classification *50*
–   4   Speech act analysis of text 9 *51*
–   5   Speaker variation in use of speech acts *53*
–   6   Adjacency pairs *61*
–   7   Cohension analysis grid *65*
–   8   Four types of grammatical rules *115*
–   9   Example of interrule formulation *117*
–   10   Model of speech production *141*
–   11   L1 based strategies *156*
–   12   IL based strategies *157*
–   13   Components of communicative competence *169*
–   14   Input *187*
–   15   Foreign language learning seen as a process of hypothesis formation and testing *200*

Tables

Table 1   Type-token ratio for adjectives, 2 levels, 2 texts *82*
–   2   Adjectives in essays written by grade 8 learners *83*
–   3   Adjectives in essays written by university students *83*
–   4   Rank order of 9 meanings of breken, according to criteria of 'concreteness' and 'coreness' *92*
–   5   Text sample used for error analysis *104*
–   6   Errors, absolute figures *105*
–   7   Errors as percentages of total numer of words *105*
–   8   Frequent error types – "top 10 list" *106*
–   9   Errors/non-errors in inversion in three tasks *112*
–   10   Number of learners making inversion errors *112*
–   11   Obstruent error count, unprepared speech *131*
–   12   Dental fricative performance analysis *132*
–   13   Error percentages for /t/ and /dʒ/, performance analysis, reading aloud *134*

VI

Chapter one:
Introduction

1.1 "Learner English" as a variety of English

This is a book about English, though not in the way this is normally understood, and as implied by titles like "A Grammar of the English Language". It is not a book about the language spoken as a native language by a majority of the population of Great Britain, Canada, USA, and in a number of other places around the world. Nor does it focus, like many textbooks do, on the English spoken by well-educated native speakers of English in the southern parts of England. Indeed, the type of English this book is about is often not considered "English" at all, although what we are concerned with, English used as a means of communication by people for whom English is not a native language, is very widespread. One important aspect of this type of English, which we shall refer to as *learner English,* is that it is often primarily learnt inside a classroom, rather than in more normal communicative situations.

Learner English is by no means a homogeneous variety of English. It differs according to the linguistic background of the speakers (Swahili, Polish, Danish), the nature of the situation in which the language has been learnt (classroom teaching only, classroom teaching in addition to informal exposure) and to the competence level of the speaker. Furthermore, it differs from traditionally recognized varieties of English, like Australian or Indian English, in that it is not used as a means of communication among speakers from the same speech community, but typically between speakers from different speech communities who use different varieties of learner English (e.g. Danish-English and Dutch-English) or between a speaker using a variety of learner English (e.g. Danish-English) and a native speaker of English.

The book focusses on one particular subtype of learner English: the English used in a variety of communicative situations by Danes receiving instruction in the language either at school or at a university or college of education. It would have been interesting to include in the teaching of English for commercial or technical purposes. This book covers areas of foreign language pedagogy which are relevant for many types of foreign language education, an approach which is justifiable because it is the language learning element which is invariably present. A more practical motivation is the realization that higher education students need an education which is flexible and can prepare them for teaching in a variety of contexts.

Danish colleges of education have a long tradition of working with pedagogical issues as an integral part of the study of foreign languages. This is not the case at Danish universities, where the emphasis has been on educating students within traditionally established subjects, without considering how this knowledge was later to be used by the students. Students of English would acquire a thorough knowledge of the English language and of British (and possibly American) culture and society, but no theoretical or practical preparation for how this or other knowledge could be passed on to others. During the last decade the situation has changed somewhat. The new university centres have from the start integrated pedagogical elements into their study programmes, and students at the 'traditional' universities have been able to attend classes dealing with various aspects of foreign language learning and teaching.

As indicated, a fruitful way of incorporating didactic elements into the study of a foreign language at either university or college of education is to work with learner language. We shall present some arguments for this belief.

1. A learner language approach focusses on the learner and the situations in which the foreign language is learnt and used, and treats foreign language teaching as deriving from this. This is in line with current educational philosophy in being *learner centred*. Alternative didactic methods focus on teachers and on how they are supposed to act in the classroom, or on analyses of teaching objectives and the selection and grading of teaching content. These issues also form part of a learner language centred approach to foreign language pedagogy, but they are reached at a later stage, as illustrated by figure 1. The solid lines in the figure indicate the sequence of steps in a learner language approach to foreign language pedagogy. Analyses of learner language are the essential starting-point. They lead on to

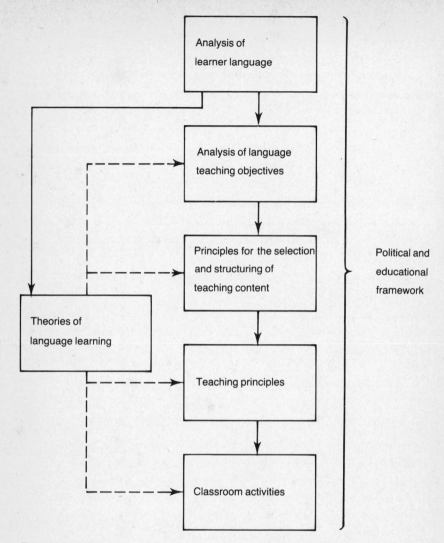

Fig. 1: A learner language approach to foreign language pedagogy

the analysis of language teaching objectives, and ultimately classroom activities. They also lead on to theories of language learning, and the dotted lines indicate that these may be relevant at each stage. All the boxed topics exist within an overall educational framework which is essentially political, some aspects of which are given expression in the educational aims sanctioned by parliament and given more detailed form in the official guidelines for individual subjects.

2. Higher education students usually have limited familiarity with foreign language teaching, based on what they remember of their own experience as learners of foreign languages. By being given the opportunity to observe classroom learning and to study samples of the written and spoken language of learners, students can *familiarise themselves with many of the professional problems* of language teachers. This means that the issues which are treated in foreign language pedagogy are not just of theoretical interest but firmly rooted in social reality.

3. By starting off with practical analyses of learner language rather than with reading and discussing articles by eminent linguists, psychologists or applied linguists, one can *avoid many of the frustrations* students often experience when they first start courses in foreign language pedagogy. They expect something directly related to the classroom, and instead they find the content theoretical and remote. A learner language approach can provide a foundation of actual experience of working with language on which study of a more theoretical nature can build.

4. A learner language approach can provide a stimulating way of supporting the students' training in how to *analyse and describe English*. Traditionally, this involves studying the grammar and phonetics of English, and students frequently experience these disciplines as having a greater utility and interest when directly linked with empirical learner language work. This can also help students to sort out the relative importance of different parts of the description of English.

5. A further link is with the *student's own proficiency in English*. Learner language studies can support this in an immediate way. For instance, analysis of the conversational ability of an intermediate learner necessitates an assessment of the relative contribution of such components as vocabulary, pronunciation, correctness and fluency to conversation in a particular context. It may be easier to get the issues into perspective when studying an intermediate learner than when analysing native speaker language or the student's own production. Informed work with such matters can lead

to an understanding of the issues which students can consciously apply in developing their own language proficiency.

6. As a final advantage of adopting a learner language approach, let us mention that it is particularly well suited for making students aware of the need for *interdisciplinary approaches* to analysing problems in foreign language teaching. It is not to be expected that any one discipline like linguistics or educational psychology can provide all the necessary solutions to such problems. Ideally, foreign language pedagogy uses an interdisciplinary approach. In practice, however, there are hurdles to overcome.

In the first place, different disciplines are typically organized according to their own internal logic, which means that an interdisciplinary approach is not automatically achieved by adding one discipline to another. Interdisciplinary studies not only involve the application of different disciplines to the solution of the same – complex – problem, but also the more difficult task of developing some common denominator for the relevant disciplines. For instance, the interdisciplinary field of psycholinguistics is not simply a conglomerate of psychology per se and linguistics per se, but in important respects a new discipline with its own identity and its own metalanguage. Foreign language pedagogy has to some extent developed such an identity, but there are important areas which are not sufficiently integrated as yet, eg the area of general didactics.

Second, the structure of Danish universities and colleges of education makes it difficult to integrate studies in various disciplines. At a college of education, students can attend courses in both psychology and didactics, but unfortunately these are frequently isolated from the study of the foreign language itself: students study English language and literature in the English department and psychology and didactics in the education department. They also get some teaching practice under the supervision of an experienced teacher. It is then left to the students themselves to make a synthesis out of the bits and pieces they have received at different points from different teachers.

Thirdly, even given the development of a new, interdisciplinary identity, there is a serious problem of resources. Adopting an interdisciplinary approach does not mean that special expertise in specific disciplines becomes redundant, but rather that specialists from different disciplines need to collaborate more. As foreign language pedagogy has mainly been developed by specialists with linguistic research interests, there is usually less participation by educationalists and psychologists. An unfortunate consequence of this could be that foreign language pedagogy concentrates on more linguistically oriented areas of study (learner language analysis), at the expense of other, and less clearly linguistic, areas: in the terms of figure 1, this would mean that foreign language pedagogy concentrates on the top-most box and does not spread out along the various arrows to the other boxes.

1.3 Learner language, foreign language pedagogy, and the teacher of English

Experienced teachers sometimes express scepticism about the applicability to teaching of theoretically oriented studies. One example of this was the reception of the "applied linguistics" approach, for instance Corder 1973, which took linguistic description as its starting-point, and then attempted to apply results.[3]

It is easy to understand this scepticism. Teachers have a first-hand knowledge of problems in foreign language education and inevitably assess theoretical studies on the basis of how well these can help to describe, explain and solve such problems. The present book contains a good deal of theorizing about learner language, foreign language learning and teaching, but by taking as its point of departure the learner's situation, the gap between theory and practice is hopefully reduced.

It should be possible for experienced teachers to follow the same route as students of foreign languages, namely working from analyses of learner language towards principles of language learning and teaching. But it is to be expected that some topics covered in the book will be relatively well-known to most teachers. However, as the book contains a description of methods for analysing language which have been evolved in recent years, as well as a presentation of recent research into principles of foreign language learning and teaching, we are confident that most teachers will find useful information in the book.

We hope that the book will inspire teachers to carry out analyses of learner language, an enterprise which is particularly well suited for small study groups. Such analyses may help teachers to see the learner language which they are very familiar with in a fresh light. If one spends five days a week in the classroom and marking written work, it is hardly surprising if the aspect of learner language which takes on almost obsessive proportions is errors. It can be something of an eye-opener to carry out analyses of learner language when learner texts are treated as texts in their own right, especially if these have been produced by learners in non-learning situations. The resultant "objectivization" of learner language is an important step towards a critical reassessment of one's previous (possibly restricted or even distorted) views on learner language.

One obvious question to ask is: "Will this book help me teach my class next Monday at 9 o'clock?". The answer is a definite "no – not directly". The book has no chapter called "10 ways of teaching communicative competence", nor a chapter called "How to mark written assignments faster and better". The primary function of the book is to *inform* about learner language communication and foreign language learning and teaching. The consequences this may have for the way individual teachers teach English are to be decided on and implemented by the teachers themselves. If the book can help further discussion and experimentation in the teaching of English in Denmark, we shall have reached an important goal.

1.4 The structure and content of the book

The book is divided into four parts:

I   *Learner language* (chapters 2–10)
II   *Language learning* (chapters 11–12)
III   *Language teaching* (chapters 13–16)
IV   *Principles and methods of interlanguage studies* (chapters 17–19)

Part I contains a systematic description of different aspects of communicative competence, which are covered at each of the traditional linguistic levels in turn (pragmatics, discourse, lexis, grammar, phonology) followed by chapters on production and reception processes, fluency, communication strategies, and finally communicative competence. There is a difference in character between chapters 2–5 and 8–10 on the one hand, and chapters 6–7 on the other. The chapters on communication, speech acts, discourse, vocabulary, production/reception/fluency, communication strategies, and communicative competence contain a general introduction to these areas, which are not covered by textbooks in current use in foreign language studies in this country. As regards the chapters on grammar and pronunciation, these areas are so well covered by existing textbooks that we have been able to devote more space to presenting methods and results in learner language studies.

Part II contains a description of basic aspects of foreign language learning, and thus provides a bridge between the learner language analyses of part I and foreign language teaching, discussed in part III. Chapter 11 outlines some central processes in foreign language learning, with a focus on language learning seen as the formation and testing of hypotheses. Chapter 12 discusses the impact of individual learner variables on foreign language learning.

Part III ties up learner language studies with areas traditionally covered within didactic courses: analysis of educational objectives, goal formulation, syllabus design, teaching methodology, and principles of language evaluation. Part III must be seen as a lead in to these areas, illustrating how the learner language approach naturally develops into other, and more general, areas of didactics.

Part IV contains a brief description of the theoretical background to learner language studies, information on data collection techniques, and a discussion of three methods of analysing learner language: performance analysis, error analysis, and contrastive analysis.

In part I, all chapters have *follow-ups,* which are largely of three types: suggestions for work with learner texts; exercises based directly on the chapter; and discussion points, whose main function is to probe various parts of the content in the preceding chapter.

Chapters 2–16 are followed by *references,* giving the sources on which the chapter is based as well as suggestions for further reading. At the back of the book there is a complete bibliography in-

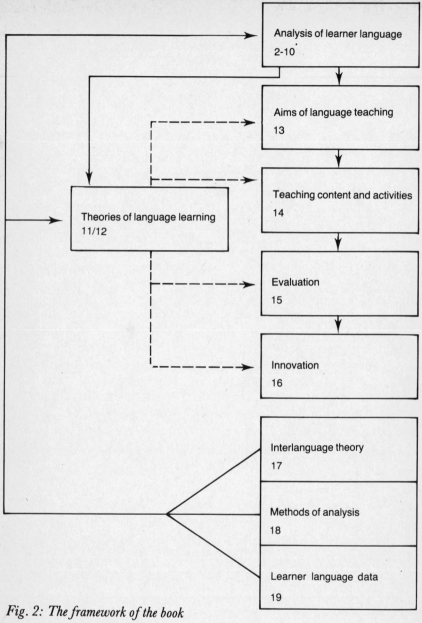

*Fig. 2: The framework of the book
(numbers refer to chapters)*

cluding all titles referred to in the 19 chapters. Finally, there is an index, which refers the reader to pages on which a particular term is used. Page numbers in bold type refer to the most comprehensive discussion of the concept in question (indicated in the text by capital letters).

Footnotes to chapter 1

1. Extract from a PIF-conversation with informant no. 97, a grade 6 pupil.
2. As it is impossible to find exact translation equivalents for the names of Danish schools, and as we are in any case referring to Danish institutions, we use the Danish names throughout the book. The Folkeskole comprises grades 1–9 (or 10), and the Gymnasium grades 10–12.
3. See the discussion in the introductory chapter to Glahn/Jakobsen/Larsen 1977.

Part I
Learner Language

Chapter 2 contains a selection of textual extracts illustrating different varieties of communication. It introduces and applies the concepts needed in order to analyse communication. The focus is primarily on the kind of communication that typically occurs in the foreign language classroom.

Chapter 3 deals with speech acts, the functions that can be performed by means of language. Two types of pragmatic analysis are presented, and the way politeness is expressed in language is explored. Chapter 4 deals with the structuring of language into texts, how coherence and cohesion are created, and ways of analysing this in learner texts. Also analysed is the way conversation is structured, turn-taking in speech, and how repairs are effected.

Chapter 5 (vocabulary) presents a number of methods for assessing the size and quality of learners' vocabulary, and considers how vocabulary in a foreign language may be structured and learned.

Chapter 6 (grammar) and chapter 7 (pronunciation) assume familiarity with a basic textbook on these topics and concentrate on methods for the analysis of these aspects of learner language.

Chapter 8 integrates the topics covered in isolation so far into a model of speech production and reception. Fluency is defined, and examples of fluent and non-fluent speech are given. Difficulties of communication may require the learner to resort to a communication strategy: these are analysed in relation to both speech production and speech reception in chapter 9.

Chapter 10 brings together all the components covered in the earlier chapters into a single model of communicative competence. Communicative competence is related to social and cognitive competence, and then expanded so as to include the reception of learner language, the role of context, and metacommunicative awareness.

Chapter two:
Varieties of communication

Our analysis of communication will primarily concentrate on VERBAL COMMUNICATION, ie on communication which is carried out by means of language. This excludes from attention such communicative activities as shaking hands, gesticulating, or kissing someone goodbye, in which the communication is exclusively *non-verbal*. What we are concerned with is the countless situations in which language is of major importance.

We need to distinguish between intentional and informative aspects of communication.[1] Communication which is INTENTIONAL is brought about by a person who *decides* to communicate. The INFORMATIVE side of communication relates to the situation when someone learns something not known beforehand from somebody else's verbal or non-verbal behaviour or appearance. Very often there is an overlap between intentional and informative aspects of communication, as for instance when somebody decides to break an important piece of news to friends. In certain cases communication is intentional without being informative, as when somebody tells a joke to the same person a second time without realising this. More common, perhaps, is communication which is informative without being intentional, as when somebody interprets a hoarse voice as indicating that the person has a cold or got to bed late the preceding night. In part 1 of the book we will be primarily concerned with communication which is intentional.

We have selected seven texts, exemplifying different varieties of communication, so as to highlight the variables which determine the form communication assumes in specific situations. Each variety will be illustrated by examples from either NATIVE SPEAKER COMMUNICATION, ie communication between individuals all of whom make use of their native language, or INTERLANGUAGE COMMUNICATION, communication between individuals at least one of whom is using a second or foreign language.

21

2.1 Basic concepts for the analysis of communication

We shall start our description of verbal communication by a sample of teacher-centred classroom interaction. There are three reasons for choosing this as our first variety of communication:

- in being institutionally circumscribed, classroom interaction in general and teacher-centred communication in particular exhibit the basic constituents of communication in a more lucid way than less formal varieties of communication
- classroom interaction is a distinctive variety of communication, warranting analysis in its own right
- to the extent that foreign language learning takes place in schools, classroom interaction is the variety of communication which exerts a particularly strong influence on the development of learners' interlanguage.

The following extract[2] is from a "traditional" classroom in which a group of Danish 16-year-olds are learning English. The class is discussing a short story which was read at home beforehand. At this point the learners are trying to draw conclusions about the main character's job, on the basis of their reading of the text so far.

Text 2
Teacher: now er let's er try to return to that question er of Mr
   Smith's job – er what do you think he is
(Anne raises hand)
Teacher: Anne
5 Anne: a detective (laughter)
Teacher: maybe maybe a detective
(Christine raises hand)
Teacher: Christine
Christine: I think he's working for the underground or something
10 Teacher: for the underground
Christine: he is a criminal
Teacher: er maybe – you mean a political underground movement
   – you don't mean
Christine: the mafia [meɪfɪə]

22

15 Teacher: the mafia [mæfɪə] yes – perhaps
Christine: it could be – hvad hedder hvid slavehandel
Teacher: white slavery – oh Christine this is a very romantic story you are making out of it
Christine: nej det er det ikke fordi det har man da set mange altså
20 Teacher: you know people who er
Christine: lokke
Teacher: they tempt people to come maybe – what would you say Karen
Karen: it could be organization which er which erm are erm – they
25 find out something about people
Teacher: yes
Karen: about their er politi
Teacher: their political
Karen: their political erm
30 Teacher: attitude
Karen: attitude
Teacher: yes
Karen: something like that

2.1.1 Communicative event

The text is an excerpt from an English lesson. This begins when the teacher says "Hello", "Good Morning", or "OK, let's get started", and ends when the bell rings or when the teacher states that the lesson is over.

The whole lesson constitutes a COMMUNICATIVE EVENT. A communicative event can be characterized as communicative interaction between at least two parties, beginning the moment the parties initiate intentional communication and ending the moment the communicative interaction comes to a stop.

Communicative events may have shorter communicative events embedded within them.[3] For instance, within the event of the English lesson, the pupils may work in groups for 20 minutes. Communication within each of these groups constitutes a communicative event in its own right, lasting from the moment the group members start communicating with each other until the group discussion stops and the lesson continues with the entire class assembled.

23

2.1.2 Setting

The English lesson takes place at a given time in a Danish Gymnasium, in a classroom that contains chairs and tables arranged in a certain way, a chalk-board, audio-visual equipment, etc. All of these constitute the PHYSICAL properties of the SETTING in which the communicative event takes place. Everybody familiar with education in schools would recognize that text 2 belongs to the specific INSTITUTIONAL SETTING of formal education. Other examples of institutional settings for communicative events are a church, the law courts, and Parliament.

The way people behave in particular settings depends on each individual's subjective perception of the setting, what we shall term the PSYCHOLOGICAL SETTING of a communicative event. This is determined by the participants' expectations, needs, interests, past experience, etc. In classrooms the actual communication that takes place is strongly influenced by the participants' perception of the purpose of the activity they are engaged in, of how the allotted time can be used, etc.

2.1.3 Participants – communicative roles

In the extract, the pupils and the teacher take turns in performing the communicative roles of ADDRESSER and ADDRESSEE(S). The roles are reversible[4] in the sense that any participant can take either role. The interaction consists essentially of a dialogue between the teacher and representatives of the class. There are differences however between the way the teacher functions as addresser and addressee and the way the learners do.

In the first 2 lines, the *teacher* addresses the whole class: all the learners are DIRECT ADDRESSEES. Later the teacher addresses individual learners, either nominating one to speak or responding to the reply given by an individual. At such points in the communicative event the pupil in question is the direct addressee, whereas the rest of the pupils are INDIRECT ADDRESSEES. They are expected to follow the dialogue between the teacher and each pupil, to nod rather than nod off. None of the dialogues are private.

When, in the classroom discussion from which text 2 is extracted, the *learner* functions as addresser, the direct addressee is invariably the teacher. This is so, even when a learner reacts to a contribution from another learner, as the following example shows. It comes from the same source as text 2, a few seconds later in the lesson.

Dorte: he must find out things
Teacher: yes
Torben: hvad sagde hun
Teacher: find out things

Torben is the indirect addressee of Dorte's remark, but when he asks for a repetition of what she said, he addresses his request not to Dorte but to the teacher.

2.1.4 Participants – social roles and status

The difference between the teacher and the learners in text 2 as regards the number of times they figure as addresser and direct addressee reflects the institutionally determined SOCIAL ROLES of teacher and pupil, as well as a difference in power between the two parties. The power of the teacher is associated with the teacher's responsibility for teaching, with her superior knowledge as well as with her right to sanction the behaviour of pupils, for instance by giving marks.[5] Analogous situations occur in many communicative events in which role relationships are socially determined, eg a doctor-patient consultation, or a service encounter in which the power relationship between customer and shop assistant is less predictable.

In addition to the social roles and the power implicit in these, the relationship between participants may also be affected by the social STATUS each participant assigns to the other(s). Status is related to power and social roles, though not directly dependent on these. The fact that the teacher performs a role which is inherently more powerful than the role of the pupils is likely to influence the status relationship in the classroom. But it is important to realise that whereas neither teacher nor pupils can change their respective roles in any significant way, the status they assign to each other is a matter for negotiation. And while one can hope that this will lead to a change in status, one cannot ignore the fact that in all negotiation an unequal distribution of power has certain consequences and the teacher may secure higher status than the learners.

Both social roles and status have to be seen relative to *specific* communicative events and to the participants in these. Whenever participants of equal status perform certain social roles which are equally powerful, the event is said to be SYMMETRIC. The alternative to this is ASYMMETRIC communication. Teacher-centred classroom interaction is a typical instance of asymmetric communication.

As a final relevant characteristic of the relationship between participants can be mentioned the degree of FAMILIARITY between these. Did the participants know each other before the event, and if so, how well? Familiarity may influence the symmetricality of communication, in that a high degree of familiarity may reduce the impact of differences in power and status.

2.1.5 Contact and channel

In face-to-face communication, whether in classroom, street or sitting-room, participants are in DIRECT CONTACT with each other, they share a spatio-temporal setting. This enables them to communicate by means of both the VISUAL CHANNEL (light waves received via the eye) and the AURAL CHANNEL (sound waves received via the ear). The aural channel will often be the dominant one, and the visual channel merely used for supporting communicative behaviour conveyed by facial expression or gesture.

A characteristic feature of most direct contact situations is the presence of IMMEDIATE FEEDBACK: the addresser is constantly provided by the addressees with visual and/or verbal feedback on the progress of the communication. In the classroom extract, it is highly likely that the teacher provides both sorts of feedback to the learners, although only the verbal feedback is conveyed by the tape-script.

Thanks to the telephone and some of the electronic media, direct contact communication can be achieved without participants being located in the same setting. In telephone communication, only the aural channel is available. This increases the need for verbal feedback: a long silence may be interpreted as meaning that the participants are no longer in contact.

Contact between participants is not always direct. Virtually all forms of written communication, or making a tape-recording and sending off a cassette, involve a delay in the contact. In these cases the *production* of language (eg writing a letter) takes place on a different occasion from its *reception* (eg the letter being read). A consequence of such NON-DIRECT CONTACT is that feedback is DELAYED, and occurs in a separate communicative event.

In communication in which there is no direct contact between participants, addressers need to express themselves more explicitly than otherwise: absence of direct contact, as well as irreversibility of the roles of addresser/addressee, deprives the addresser of immediate feedback.

2.1.6 Message

The term MESSAGE is used to cover what is said, the *form* in which a speaker's intentions are put across, and the *content* of what the speaker intends to say. A message can be as brief as one word, or a complete, lengthy text. Deciding on the number of messages in a text is a fairly arbitrary matter and will depend on the purpose of the analysis.

Our definition of message, covering as it does both content and form, can be readily applied in an analysis of foreign language learning. Text 2 is clear case of learners talking about something – Mr. Smith's job – and learning how to do so. Feedback from the teacher may relate to either content (eg a valid interpretation) or to form (eg correct pronunciation). The distinction between the two may at times be blurred. The teacher's echo question with rising intonation ("For the underground?" line 10) probably queries the content of Christine's statement a line earlier, but Christine's follow-up seems to indicate a concern with finding a new form ("criminal") for the same content.

2.1.7 Code

A CODE is a symbolic system, conventionalized as a means of giving form to messages. Codes can either be linguistic or non-linguistic.

In text 2, the LINGUISTIC CODE used is the special form of English which can be referred to as English INTERLANGUAGE. The pupils and the teacher speak varieties of this interlanguage, ie versions of an L2 which in some respects contain traces of an L1 (see chapter 17 for a discussion of interlanguage).

In addition to interlanguage English, one more code is employed in the extract, namely Danish used as a NATIVE LANGUAGE. In this particular excerpt it is the pupils only who resort to their native language, but the teacher also makes use of it at other points during the lesson, for instance when translating or explaining difficult words. It is significant that pupils resort to Danish in circumstances where they are under pressure or wish to communicate something urgently. This is the case in line 19, where Christine resists the teacher's (possibly sarcastic) rejection of her contribution to the discussion. Christine breaks into a whole utterance in her native language. Such a change from one code to another is referred to a CODE-SWITCHING.

Another code which is relevant in all face-to-face interaction is the NON-LINGUISTIC CODE of facial expressions, posture and gesture. Raising a hand is a conventional way of indicating a willingness to speak, and functions as such in the text (in lines 3 and 7). Here a non-linguistic sign has been used as an alternative to calling out, a convention young school children have to learn. Also communicative, but not part of any linguistic code, are laughs (eg line 5) and hesitation phenomena (eg line 24). Prosodic phenomena (intonation, loudness, tempo, pauses) accompany words, and are complexly related to the linguistic code (see chapter 7), with features of both linguistic and non-linguistic codes.[6]

2.2 Face-to-face communication

In this section excerpts from three texts will be presented. They are all interactional, involving either two or three people in face-to-face communication. Since the excerpts are, inevitably, very brief, only a few seconds or so, our discussion draws on our familiarity with the complete texts from which the excerpts come.

Text 3[7] is part of a conversation between 3 men who are close friends. The physical setting is a room in a private house. The three are cheerful and relaxed after a drink, the two guests quite unaware that the conversation is being recorded. The three have equal status, and because of the familiarity between them any differences in terms of social roles (eg host/guest) do not influence the interaction at this point.

Text 3

A	I mean cinema have b for a long time has been in trouble – – I mean that's
B	
C	

A	why well you got all these sex films – – it was a kind of a desperate attempt
B	sh it's a sure sign
C	

A	to	yeah	they're – they're trying to get them	(laugh)
B	of failure isn't it	once they resort to that really	(laugh)
C			what

A	
B	well it's – some people resort to beer (laugh) no but you know what I mean
C	once you resort to sex – you mean

A	yeah
B	i it to me it's always been a confession of failure you know tha the i it's
C	yeah

A	it's trying to get the crowds in
B	cheap isn't it a cheap way of – – – I er
C	

A	
B	
C	it's a confession

This transcript exemplifies many of the features of conversation between intimates from the same speech community. Speakers talk at the same time, complete each other's thoughts, the ongoing production process is revealed in hesitation and changes of sentence structure. The communication is symmetrical: all 3 seem to contribute on an equal footing, and have the same code at their disposal. This is by no means so in the following text[8], despite superficial similarities.

Text 4

NS	do you want to live in a collective or
L	no no I would like a flat for example I

NS	but they are hard to
L	wouldn't mind sharing a flat with a friend or some

NS	come by and and expensive (laugh) do you
L	yes very yes mostly they are very bad

NS	know what do most people here want to do when they finish or do they
L	(laugh)

NS	mostly want to teach em will they be
L	yes I think most of them want to teach

NS	able to find jobs what's the employment
L	some of them but not all of them

NS	situation like for teachers
L	very bad I think (laugh) no I think probably most

NS	is
L	people will be able to get jobs but of course it depends on what you study

NS	English a good a bet
L	it depends on what eh your other subject is

This extract is from a PIF conversation (cf chapter 18). The physical setting is a video-studio at the university. The two participants do not know each other, the native speaker of English having been called in for the express purpose of conversing with the PIF-informant, who is a university student of English. Both were encouraged beforehand to take an active part in the conversation, but the native speaker takes over responsibility for the progress of the conversation, virtually assuming the role of an interviewer: she puts all the questions, and changes topic (eg lines 3, 6, 8), while the learner merely answers questions. The learner thus resembles the learners in the classroom in text 2 more than the native speakers in conversation in text 3. The reason for this may be that the learner feels linguistically inferior, despite her good command of English. Also, the experimental situation may be intimidating, or the learner may be carrying over her classroom behaviour to the new situation.

The third interactional text[9] is also from a PIF conversation, but in this case with a much less proficient learner. The setting is the same as in text 4. The participants are discussing school work. At this point in the conversation they are manifestly having difficulties with the linguistic code.

Text 5

NS	but you like reading books about aha –
L	not about hist er this history – you

NS	
L	know – er er young histories – er not not with this old thing you know

NS	aha (laugh) in er in er for example – what
L	kings or – all that – but er (laugh)

NS	– 1930 – or so – do you mean – recent – in more recent years like that
L	yes er maybe

NS	– er I mean in years which aren't so far away – from us now –
L	er – a

NS	
L	book er – a a history is – maybe on a boy – girl and – er this er young

NS	oh you mean a story – maybe – just a story – about
L	people life and yer – yer

NS	people – yes not not necessarily not – in the past no – I see yes
L	yer – no

NS	– no now I understand you (laugh)
L	(laugh)

Almost the entire interaction focusses on code problems. The participants are somewhat laboriously trying to find out what content the word 'history' in the learner's interlanguage English actually refers to. As a result of their collaborative efforts, they finally succeed, as the native speaker's closing comment indicates. The participants have used the potential for immediate feedback inherent in face-to-face interaction in order to find out what the learner's initially intended message was.

The three texts presented in this section demonstrate three very different types of face-to-face communication, which we may loosely refer to as "conversation". The observable differences are attributable to variation in the setting, to differences in roles and the relative intimacy of the participants, and the mastery of the code.

2.3 One-way communication

In one-way communication, if there is any feedback at all, it will be *delayed*. This is true of virtually all uses of the written language. We shall now consider one variety of one-way, written communication, namely the written essay. This is a familiar genre in the education world, with the teacher generally functioning as the addressee, at least implicitly. Text 6[10] is part of an essay written for the PIF project, in other words for an unfamiliar addressee. The extract comes from near the end of an essay on violence, where the learner is summing up the points already made.

Text 6

It is difficult to say anything in general about the political prisoners, some of them are what I would call innocent, others perhaps guilty in various degrees.

I am by no means for violence, political or non-political, but I want to ask the question if the way violence is treated in the massmedia is fair. As I have tried to point out, some kinds of violence are more "fair" than others. But the mass-media do not always seem to notice this – at least one should not think so.

A written text has to be able to stand on its own. The message must be complete and unambiguous for it to function effectively, as there is no opportunity for immediate feedback. Although many native speakers would certainly formulate the text differently (eg using *whom* instead of *them* in the first sentence), there can be no doubt about what the learner's message is. She assists comprehension by explaining what she is doing (eg "I want to ask the question ..."); by making the structure of the text explicit ("As I have tried to point out, ..."); by using linguistic means to stress that the claims made are personal ("what I would call", inverted commas around "fair").

Whereas essay-writing is a familiar activity from school, producing an unprepared spoken narrative is not. In the PIF project we wished to contrast spoken and written language produced in the same setting. We therefore decided to elicit written and spoken narratives in a setting in which all the elements of the communicative event are constant except for channel. Learners watched a short film twice in the language laboratory, and then recorded a spoken description of the film, following this up with a written description. The film was about a man having difficulty waking up in the morning, and the instruction given was that the narratives were intended as summaries for fellow students who were absent at the presentation.

Texts 7 and 8 are from a university student, the same one as in text 6.

The main difference between the two texts is that the transcript of the spoken version reflects the language production process in a way that the written version does not. As an example of this, contrast lines 20–25 in the 2 texts. In the spoken version (text 7) the learner makes a generalisation, which is that the makers of the film satirise the roaring lion of MGM. The learner then realizes she must be more explicit, and information is added bit by bit. This reflects the sequence of her thoughts. In the written version (text 8) the facts necessary for understanding the satire are neatly presented, and the reader is left to infer what was comic.

Secondly, there is evidence of difficulty in simultaneously *planning and speaking*. There are a number of symptoms of hesitation, such as pauses (2, 16, 24), slips of the tongue (8), and fillers to gain time (*sort of*, 16).

Thirdly, in many ways the written text is more *precise and explicit* than the spoken one. This can be seen if lines 1–2, 7–9 or 17–19 are contrasted. The greater precision of the written version can be seen at many levels:

Text 7: Spoken text	Text 8: Written text
1a and a little time after we heard the 2a – phone calling	1b When he had got out of bed, 2b the phone suddenly rang,
3a and he was (coughs) talking to a woman	3b and we saw a woman talking to the man.
4a – who was crying	4b At the end she started crying,
5a 6a	5b and the man looked pretty sorry (and 6b still very sleepy).
7a – (5 seconds) – and er after having talked to her 8a he found out that he'd better mate make 9a some coffee	7b After having talked to the woman the man 8b decided to make some coffee, which 9b he obviously needed badly!
10a – – and er obviously it was pretty difficult 11a for him because he was still very sleepy 12a 13a	10b It was as if he couldn't quite 11b control his movements, but in the 12b end he actually succeeded in making 13b some coffee.
14a when he had made the coffee (coughs) 15a he saw that he suddenly er mm really woke 16a and – sort of s started living again	14b 15b Then he had some of the coffee, 16b and suddenly be became "normal" again.
17a 18a this film was a – experimental film 19a	17b As for the form of this film, I've 18b already mentioned that it was an 19b experimental film.
20a – and er – at times they were mocking 21a – other films as far as I remember it's 22a er (coughs) Metro-Goldwyn-Mayer who 23a has a lion roaring in the beginning of 24a this film – and in this film we saw 25a a man – er – instead of a lion	20b Metro-Goldwyn-Mayer have 21b a lion roaring at the beginning of 22b their films. Fiasco-films who 23b produced this film, had the man 24b yawning. 25b

- while the spoken text consists of rather bald statements (eg line 18a), the written has points explicitly linked together and their relevance to the narrative as a whole is stressed (eg line 17a, "As for the form of the film ...")
- lexical choice is more appropriate (compare *rang* and *calling* in line 2)
- a time adverbial is given in writing but not in speech (line 4)
- in the coffee episode, reference is made to actually drinking it in

the writing, whereas in speech this information has to be inferred (lines 14–16)
- there is backpointing reference ("I've already mentioned ..." line 17b)
- the listener has to guess who *they* refers to in lines 20/21a, whereas in writing the makers of the film are named.

Our coverage of three examples of one-way communication has highlighted the fact that since there is no immediate feedback, addressers need to express themselves clearly and explicitly. This is more likely to be achieved in writing than in one-way spontaneous speech.

2.4 Characteristics of educational communication

Whereas text 2 ("teacher-controlled communication") is specific to communication within an educational setting, texts 3–8 exemplify communication as it may occur in a variety of situations outside school. This does not imply that educational communication is necessarily teacher-controlled in the way text 2 is. Educational communication in itself covers a range of varieties of communication, some of which come close to non-educational communication. Indeed, an important innovation in the last decade has been the attempt to introduce varieties of communication into the foreign language classroom which are less strictly teacher-controlled and therefore less like traditional classroom communication.

This might lead one to assume that the distinction between educational and non-educational communication is becoming blurred, that there is a continuum of varieties of communication, with a borderline area in the middle where educational and non-educational varieties merge. But although this assumption is intuitively appealing, it ignores the fact that communication in educational settings, particularly in the foreign language classroom, necessarily differs from communication in non-educational settings in a number of important respects. The fact that communication takes place within an institutional setting implies that communication is supposed to aim at specific goals. Some of these are explicitly formulated, both in the official guidelines for specific subjects and in statements of general educational objectives. Others derive from the function of education in society, one role of schools being to channel pupils into future occupational roles. Changes of communication in schools may be brought about in so far as they do not conflict with these institutionally determined constraints. This means that some of the components listed in 2.1 are invariable, as seen from the teachers' and the learners' point of view, some are variable within limits, and a few are truly variable. A clear understanding of which components are variable and which are not is an essential prerequisite for deciding in what ways communiation in the classroom can be changed if one wishes to make it closer to communication outside schools.

One invariant factor in schools is the amount of time allocated to each subject. Provided this remains unaffected, there is a certain freedom to organize communicative events in other ways than in lessons of 45 minutes each. One alternative to lesson-based events is project-oriented teaching conducted on an inter-subject basis where the communicative event may, in principle at least, occupy a full school day. Readjusting communicative events like this may have a significant impact on the psychological setting, ie the learners' and teacher's conception of the physical setting in which communication takes place. On a different level, but also significant, is the possibility of altering the physical setting, for instance by arranging the classroom so as to encourage the learners to communicate amongst themselves, as an alternative to communicating exclusively with the teacher.

An important constant in educational communication is the role configuration into learners and teachers. No matter how learner-centred the teaching is, there are still participants who are 'learners' (who are present in order to learn, in the broadest sense of the term) and participants who are teachers (who are responsible to the learners, parents, educational authorities, and to society at large, for what goes on in the classroom). What teachers can change is not the roles but the status associated with these roles. Learners can acknowledge the teacher's role as teacher, and the responsibilities associated with this, without at the same time investing themselves with a "low" status relative to the teacher.

One aspect of the teacher's role is the obligation to provide feedback. This is another invariable aspect of educational communica-

36

tion. What the teacher *may* vary, however, is the way feedback is provided. In teacher-controlled communication, the direct contact between teachers and learners means that feedback can be provided immediately, as seen in text 2. Other types of communication in the classroom (eg group work) may not provide for direct contact between teacher and learners, but for the teacher to be able to provide feedback there has to be contact between groups of learners and the teacher. Feedback is then delayed, for instance with the groups providing a summary of results to be discussed with the teacher or in a plenary session.

Finally, reference should be made to one further constant in educational communication, namely the fact that in much foreign language classroom communication the participants share a language which most of the time is not being used as the medium of instruction. In other words, whenever communication takes place in the foreign language, the learners and the teacher use a code which, from a purely communicative point of view, is not the most efficient one at their command. This means that one of the objects of the communication, foreign language learning, has a direct impact on the communication itself: communication contains an element of pretence. This "fictitious" nature of foreign language classroom communication may also affect the content of the communication in that in certain cases communication is performed for its own sake and not primarily to give the learners a chance to express views, to infer meaning, or to act by means of language. Although teachers and learners may try to change this situation to make possible more "genuine" exchanges of information, it remains one of the constituent features of foreign language educational communication that communication has certain fictitious characteristics, both in terms of codes and – especially at the initial stages – in terms of content.

Footnotes to chapter 2

1. This well-established distinction is discussed in several studies. See eg Corder 1973:32f, Lyons 1977: 1/32ff.
2. This extract comes from a recording made as part of their English studies by 2 RUC students, Monica Hassel and Cim Meyer.
3. This is not to be confused with the division of discourse into discourse phases, cf chapter 4.
4. In certain types of communicative event, there is no reversibility of communicative roles: one participant is invariably the addresser, the other(s) the addressee(s). Such irreversibility of roles is characteristic of mass communication.
5. The English language is male-dominated, in that traditionally *he, his, chairman,* etc. are regarded as unmarked forms. We have avoided the fundamental sexism of the language by a) using *he* or *she* according to the sex of the speaker, when this information is known to us, b) in all other contexts, rather than opting for the rather clumsy egalitarian *s/he* and *her/his,* using *she* and *her* as ummarked forms (ie our learners and teachers may be male or female).
6. Facial expression and gesture belong to the area commonly referred to as "paralinguistic communication". Abercrombie (1972) draws a primary distinction within paralinguistic communication between "non-vocalized" and "vocalized" communication. The former refers to communicative behaviour not expressed by means of the speech organs, eg eye contact, gesture and facial expression (using the visual channel). Vocalized communication contains two main categories: elements which are *independent* of the code in that they can occur on their own such as *tut tut, ugh, haha,* and features that are dependent on and co-occur with the linguistic code such as loudness, tempo, pitch and rhythm. Here paralinguistic means of communication merge with prosody.
7. Extract from conversation no. 13 in Crystal/Davy 1975:78.
8. Extract from PIF-conversation with informant no. 150, a university student.
9. Extract from PIF-conversation with informant no. 73, a 10th grade student.
10. Extract from PIF-essay written by informant no. 150, a university student.

Chapter 2. Follow-ups

1. While observing an English lesson, note all instances of code-switching. When and why do these occur? Does the teacher use code-switching in a different way from the learners, and if so, why?
2. Record a learner or a native speaker delivering a two-minute talk. Make a transcript of this, including pauses, hesitation etc. (see chapter 19). Rewrite this text in the form of a reader's letter to a newspaper, retaining the content of the spoken version. Contrast the two texts, and identify characteristic features of each. Do these correspond to those identified for texts 7 and 8?
3. Decide on a communication game, for example A instructing B on how to build an object using Lego bricks. Carry out the task a) with the participants in visual

contact; b) with two other participants without visual contact (for instance by putting up a screen between them). In what ways does the difference in contact affect the interaction? (An audio-recording may prove useful for going back over the interaction.)

4. Consider a *range of communicative events* from non-educational situations (eg a news programme on TV, an advertisement, a discussion with the bank manager) and note in what way each of these can be characterised in terms of the components of communication introduced in chapter 2.

5. Find examples of communication which are difficult to relate to the definition of a communicative event. How useful is this concept? Could it be defined differently?

6. Consider the following quotation from the text: "... whereas neither teacher nor pupils can change their respective roles in any significant way, the status they assign to each other is a matter for negotiation." What do you envisage this negotiation comprising?

Chapter 2. Sources and further reading

The description of the components of communicative situations is based on work in the "ethnography of communication", see Hymes 1972 b. Introductory descriptions are Coulthard 1977 chapter 3 and Criper/Widdowson 1975. Three excellent anthologies containing studies within the field are Giglioli 1972; Laver/Hutcheson 1972; and Pride/Holmes 1972, especially parts 3–4. Van Dijk 1977 offers a lucid discussion of the relationship between aspects of the communicative situation and communication. Much work in stylistics is also relevant for the topics dealt with in chapter 2, see for instance Crystal/Davy 1969.

Chafe 1982 is a useful survey of differences between spoken and written language. Brown 1977 discusses characteristic features of spoken language, and in Davies/Widdowson 1974, the focus is on written language.

For educational communication see Sinclair/Brazil 1982, Wagner/Petersen 1983.

Chapter three:
Pragmatics

How do the various components of the communicative situation influence the nature of the communication that takes place? This question can be clarified by considering the functions language serves and the way utterances combine into spoken or written texts. Describing what can be done by means of language is the concern of *pragmatics*, and is discussed in chapter three. The description of language as "texts" is dealt with in *discourse analysis*, the topic of chapter four. Despite the fact that pragmatics and discourse are intimately related, we have been obliged to separate out utterances from their textual context in chapter three, in order to simplify our presentation.

The chapter presents two ways of characterising how language is put to use, "language functions" and "speech acts". The chapter finishes with a discussion of "speech act modality", the way the realisation of speech acts is influenced by speakers' attitudes towards their addressee(s), including their perception of status relations.

3.1 Language functions

Utterances serve a wide variety of functions. One way of characterising these, proposed by Jakobson (1960), is to relate the functions of utterances to the components of the communicative event and to distinguish between different functions when different components are in focus. Although other models of language functions have been proposed and successfully applied to the description of communication[1], the Jakobsonian model is still influential and the most relevant one for our purposes.

The following is a list of language functions and the components of communication which each focuses on.

Function	Focus on
Expressive	Addresser
Directive	Addressee
Referential	Setting
Metalinguistic	Code
Phatic	Contact
Poetic	Message form

We shall exemplify these functions in relation to text 9. This is also from a classroom in which Danes are learning English; the learners are the same age and at the same level as in text 2. There are three participants in a group discussion producing a joint written summary of part of a novel they have read.

Text 9
Peter: erm how long have you reached
Susanne: (reading) one of his workmates comes comes and tells Joe that Alice is dead
Peter: yes first reaction is that he first doesn't really take any
5   reaction at all – but later on he finds out that he has to to to feel sorry for her
Susanne: but first say it again
Peter: er he doesn't really feel pain for her and doesn't express any any sorrow but then he finds out that he has to
10 Susanne: but when he realizes that she er hasn't
Peter: that she is dead
Susanne: nej hvad hedder det hasn't dead death nej
Peter: died
Susanne: died at at one second
15 Peter: oh yes
Susanne: when she realizes that she has
Peter: a long painful dead death
Susanne: (writing) I will write first he doesn't really feel pain for her er
20 Hanne: but then he
Susanne: but but tries to follow her what she has done after he has
Hanne: is it called pain to

41

Peter: for
Susanne: he tries
25 Hanne: he does – he does
Susanne: he does hvad (writing) he tries to follow her way after he
has gone –
Hanne: after he has left her
Susanne: is it necessary to write all that
30 Peter: it's very important
Hanne: no you can imagine his feelings
Peter: don't you think it's important
Susanne: no I don't think so
Peter: oh I think so
35 Hanne: what do you write then
Susanne: he tries to follow her way after he has left her (writing) she
has er – she has gone into a pub where they used to go – or what
do you want
Peter: I just want to er to describe all the places where Joe and Alice
40 erm had been together
Susanne: then go on –
Peter: what
Susanne: say what you want
Peter: it's not what I want

With the EXPRESSIVE function, focus is on the addresser. The utterances in 1. 30 ("it's very important") and 1. 44 ("it's not what I want") are expressive because they convey the speaker's attitude, opinion or feeling. Interjections such as "oh no!" or "too bad!" are likewise expressive utterances.

When focus is on the addressee, when someone is being asked or told to do something, the utterance is DIRECTIVE. Directive functions are illustrated in 1. 1 ("how long have you reached") and 1. 7 ("but first say it again").

With the REFERENTIAL function, focus is on the setting, in the broadest sense of the word, meaning that part of the context which is being talked about or referred to. In text 9, most utterances refer to the novel which the group are discussing and to the written summary which the group secretary (Susanne) is writing down, and are therefore referential.

42

When focus is on the code, the function of the utterance is METALIN-GUISTIC. In text 9, the utterances in which the learners discuss the language of their English summary ("hvad hedder det – hasn't dead death", 1. 12) are metalinguistic. Although this function is par-ticularly important in interlanguage communication (especially in classroom communication), it is also important in native language communication, for instance when clarifying what a word means. Such "repair work" is discussed in chapter four.

The PHATIC function focuses on contact between participants. It serves to establish, maintain or discontinue communication. When Susanne tells Peter to go on (1.41) her directive utterance also has the function of ensuring that the discussion continues, that contact is maintained. A clear example of the significance of the phatic function comes from telephone conversations. A fixed set of "routine for-mulae" exist for establishing contact (*hello, how are you* ...) as well as for discontinuing it (*bye, see you,* ...). During the main body of a tele-phone conversation, confirmation is needed to ensure that there is still contact between the participants. If A is talking, and B does not mutter the occasional word or just "mhm", A will be worried.

A rather special case of the phatic function is the situation in which it is important to maintain contact even though participants may have nothing particular to say to each other and silence would be im-polite. People typically chat about the weather or news of some kind in such situations. In text 9 there are no instances of this type of purely phatic utterances, but in section 3.2 we shall consider an ana-logy between phatic language and classroom communication.

The POETIC function covers all uses of language in which message *form* is of primary importance, for instance aesthetic effects in poetry, alliteration in advertising, or children's rhymes. Because of the nature of text 9, it is not surprising that there are no utterances which have primarily poetic focus.

A closer analysis of the language functions reveals a number of im-portant facts about descriptions of communication in terms of these functions. Firstly, different language functions can co-occur in one and the same utterance. The utterance "but first say it again" (1.7) is directive in that the addresser (Susanne) focusses on the addressee (Peter) and directs him to repeat what he just said. The utterance is also referential in that Susanne refers to the immediately preceding text. Finally, the utterance is phatic as Susanne ensures that the interaction continues, giving Peter responsibility for its development. Had Susanne said "But first repeat the brilliant thing you just said" the utterance would also have been expressive.

Secondly, because of the "multifunctional" character of speech, any classification of utterances into speech functions is in fact based on assessing which one of several functions dominates in a given case. As an example consider this extract from the teacher-directed classroom interaction (text 2):

Teacher: now er let's er try to return to that question er of Mr Smith's job – er what do you think he is?
(Anne raises a hand)
Teacher: Anne
Anne: a detective? (laughter)
Teacher: maybe maybe a detective
(Christine raises a hand)

"Maybe maybe a detective" serves a referential, an expressive and a directive function. That the students (or at least Christine) interpret it as directive, ie as a request, is clear from Christine's action, raising a hand. It is a characteristic feature of educational discourse that until explicit acceptance or confirmation has been offered, teacher utterances will be interpreted as directives. Outside the classroom the same utterance would probably be interpreted as predominantly expressive.

Thirdly, classifying communication into one of six functions is a crude operation. For instance, utterances which are all categorized as directive may in fact have very different communicative purposes. "How long have you reached?" can be classified as a request for information, "say it again" as a reqest for verbal action, "give it to me" as a request for non-verbal action, "if you don't give it to me I'll tell your sister" as a threat, and "yes, you can" as granting someone permission to do something.

These points indicate that although a functional description may give a general impression of the type of communication which goes on in a specific event, it is too undifferentiated a tool for a more complete analysis of how people act by means of language. For this purpose we have to adopt a different starting point from

44

the components of the communicative event, and focus on the individual participants and their communicative intentions instead.

3.2 Acting by means of language – speech acts

When the teacher in text 2 says "now er let's er try to return to that question er of Mr Smith's job" (lines 1–2) she is steering the conversation in a certain direction. The way she does so is by producing an utterance which the pupils interpret as a *request* for them to focus their attention on a specific aspect of the text which they are discussing. But the form of the teacher's utterance is such that in a different situation, it could be interpreted as a *suggestion,* like "Let's go to the movie tonight".

Requests and suggestions are examples of different types of acts performed by using language. Such acts are referred to as SPEECH ACTS, a term mainly associated with the philosopher J. L. Austin.[2] Both requests and suggestions can be characterized as FORWARD-POINTING, because they aim at a future action, and DIRECTING, because the addressee is expected to carry out the action. The two types of speech act differ in so far as a request typically involves the addressee in an action the result of which is desired by the addresser exclusively, whereas the future action implied by a suggestion is assumed by the speaker to have some positive consequences for the hearer. Also a suggestion often involves the speaker herself in the future action ("let's go to bed now").

The difference between the two types of act is brought out by the following examples:

(1)[3] Anne is complaining about a noisy party with loud music in the flat next to hers

Anne: I just wanna get this work done and it's very important do you really – I mean do you think you could turn it down

John: well yeah – w – well good

[Role-play data from two native speakers of English]

(2) Joan is telling Susan why she may have to cancel her exams next week

Joan: and then I opened the door and there was Peter's Mummy carrying an enormous suitcase and she says she's not gonna leave

till Peter's Dad has quit the flat and er –
Susan: but don't you think you could ask her to go and stay with her
    sister instead
[contrived example]

In (1), Anne *requests* John to turn down the music, in (2) Susan *suggests* how Joan can get rid of Peter's mother. Requests and suggestions also differ with respect to how much they commit the hearer to perform the future action: it is easier to turn down a suggestion than to reject a request without offending the speaker. In performing a request, the speaker assumes the right to direct the hearer, and if the hearer rejects the request this is easily seen as evidence that the hearer does not accept the speaker's right to direct. With a suggestion, the speaker's prestige is not at stake to the same extent, and the hearer can disagree with the content of the suggestion without at the same time questioning the speaker's right to suggest. This is no doubt the reason why requests are often *formulated* as suggestions, an issue we return to in our discussion of politeness.

The classroom transcript (text 2, chapter 2) contains other directing speech acts, most of which are performed by the teacher: "what do you think he is" (1.2), "you mean a political underground movement you don't mean" (11. 12–13). Such *questions*, as we would refer to them in everyday language, constitute a special type of request, namely requests for information. A striking feature of the classroom transcript is that when the pupils ask questions, these are either metalinguistic ("hvad hedder hvid slavehandel", l. 16), or they are replies to questions put by the teacher (" a detective?", 1.5, in reply to the teacher's "what do you think he is"), where the rising intonation indicates that the pupil wants the teacher to confirm that the answer is right.

As a last type of directing speech act, also seen in the classroom transcript, we can mention *granting permission*. This usually follows on from someone applying for permission, which is exactly what happens in the classroom all the time: the pupils apply or bid for the right to speak by putting up a hand, and the teacher grants permission by nominating one pupil as the next speaker.

The types of directing speech acts we have discussed are the following:

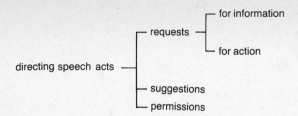

After identifying all the directing speech acts in the classroom text, we are still left with a considerable number of acts to identify. In many cases, the acts have the function of *informing*. The pupils inform the teacher how they interpret the text: "I think he's working for the underground or something" (l. 9). The teacher provides factual information, often of a metalinguistic kind ("white slavery", 1.17; ['mæfɪə], 1. 15), but also frequently expresses an opinion of what the pupils say (11.5–6):

Anne: a detective?
Teacher: maybe maybe a detective

INFORMATIVE SPEECH ACTS are used to convey factual information (or rather, what the addresser considers factual information) and to express personal opinions, beliefs and feelings. Typically, a condition for using informative speech acts is that the addresser considers the information conveyed as new and relevant for the addressee, but there are two important exceptions to this. First of all, as discussed above, there are situations in which it is more important that something is said than what is being said, because the purpose is phatic. In such cases, eg talking about the weather or the news headlines, it is not required that the apparently informative acts actually convey new information to the hearer. The foreign language classroom bears some resemblance to this in so far as one aim is that the pupils learn and practise the foreign language. For this reason there may be situations, in particular with learners at the elementary levels, in which the fictitious situation makes it more important for the pupils to say *something* rather than to say something really informative.

Secondly, informative speech acts are used in exam-type situations in which the overall purpose of the communication is to check whether the pupils know something which the teacher also knows.

47

Because of the uneven distribution of knowledge between pupils and teacher, pupils cannot inform the teacher in the true sense of the word if the topic of the communication is restricted to what the teacher already knows. As long as it is the teacher who controls the topics, the classroom situation easily develops into an exam-type situation in which the pupil's "informative" speech acts come to look more like guesses or even questions. Both can be illustrated from the teacher-centred classroom example: "I think he's working for the underground ..." (l. 9), which is a guess, and "a detective?" (1.5), in which, as already indicated, the rising intonation marks both uncertainty and an appeal to the teacher for confirmation.

The speech acts we have looked at so far have been characterized as either "directing" or "informative". This implies a principled classification of speech acts.[4]

Speech acts can be divided into three major types of act: *attitudinal* (eg "I don't like this"), *informative* (eg "This is the way to the station") and *ritual* (eg "Good-bye").

For ATTITUDINAL SPEECH ACTS, the following principles can be used as a means of subclassifying the acts:

(1) Does the event take place in the future, or not?
(2) Is the speaker involved in this event as an agent, or is the hearer?
(3) Is the event considered desirable, or undesirable?
(4) Does this positive or negative evaluation affect the speaker or the hearer?

(revised from Edmondson/House 1981:49).

Adopting the first criterion means that we obtain two types of attitudinal acts: back-pointing and forward-pointing. All in all we now have four types of act:

(1) *Back-pointing acts,* ie attitudinal acts referring to past events (or states of affairs)
(2) *Forward-pointing acts,* ie attitudinal acts referring to future events (or states of affairs)
(3) *Informative acts*
(4) *Ritual acts*

48

What we have referred to as "directing" speech acts above belong to (2): forward-pointing acts. Directing speech acts involve the *hearer* in the future event (Edmondson/House's principle 2). Forward-pointing acts which involve the *speaker* in the future event are "committing" (eg offering, promising and intending).

For back-pointing acts, the distinction between speaker and hearer responsibility for the implied event results in a division similar to the division into directing and committing forward-pointing acts. Speaker responsibility is found in back-pointing acts like apologizing and justifying, hearer responsibility in acts like thanking, complaining and congratulating.

The last two major classes of speech acts, informative and ritual acts, cannot be subclassified by means of the four principles listed above. INFORMATIVE ACTS are best subclassified on the basis of what type of information is communicated (eg factual or emotive). RITUAL ACTS can be subclassified on the basis of how they relate to the opening and closing of a communicative event ("greeting" and "taking leave").

The classification system we have now outlined is summarised in figure 3, which contains examples of different types of speech act.

To illustrate how a communicative event could be analysed into speech acts, we return to text 9 (group-work within an English lesson). The first step in a pragmatic analysis is to divide the text into acts. Here we immediately run into a difficulty. Do we say that one TURN at speech, ie what one person says from getting the floor till somebody else takes the floor, corresponds to one act? Or do we allow for more than one act within a turn? The simplest solution would be to adopt the 'one turn – one act' approach, but it is easy to find examples which show that there can be several acts in one turn:

John: Then why didn't you call me
Anne: I'm sorry – I should have done so – – I promise I'll try and remember another time
John: OK – that's all right
[Contrived example]

Attitudinal	Back-pointing	Speaker responsible	apologize excuse	
		Hearer responsible	accept/reject agree/disagree thank congratulate	complain forgive
	Forward-pointing	Speaker responsible ("commit")	intend offer promise	
		Hearer responsible ("direct")	request suggest permit	
Informative			state factual information express opinion express emotional attitudes explain	
Ritual			greet take leave	

Fig. 3: Speech act classification

Anne's turn both points backwards ("I'm sorry") and forwards ("I promise"), and to describe the acts on the basis of the classification just established, we are forced to identify two acts in Anne's turn.

In our speech act analysis of text 9 we use the acts listed in figure 3. The double slash // indicates a division point within a turn between two acts. We have not classified Susanne's written acts, in order to simplify the analysis. These would have to be incorporated into a more comprehensive pragmatic description. We have decided to treat Hanne's "no you can imagine his feelings" as two acts (disagree + explain), but Susanne's "no I don't think so" as one act (disagree). This illustrates the amount of interpretation needed in such analyses: we interpret "you can imagine his feelings" as an independent act, explaining the disagree, whereas "I don't think so" adds nothing to the "no".

A classification of the acts contained in the text could be as follows (the numbers refer to acts in figure 4):

Act number	Speaker	Text	Type of act
1	Susanne	I will write First he doesn't really feel pain for her er (writing)	intend
2	Hanne	But then he	suggest
3	Susanne	But but tries to follow her what she has done after he has	intend
4	Hanne	Is it called pain to?	request
5	Peter	For	state
6	Susanne	He tries	intend
7	Hanne	He does – he does	reject
⌈8⌉	Susanne	He does hvad? / / He tries to	request
⌊9⌋		follow her way after he has gone (writing)	intend
10	Hanne	After he has left her	reject[5]
11	Susanne	Is it necessary to write all that?	request
12	Peter	It's very important	express opinion
⌈13⌉	Hanne	No / / you can imagine his	disagree
⌊14⌋		feelings	explain
15	Peter	Don't you think it's important?	request
16	Susanne	No I don't think so	disagree
17	Peter	Oh I think so	disagree
18	Hanne	What do you write then?	request
⌈19⌉	Susanne	He tries to follow her way after he has left her (writing) she has er – she has gone into a pub where they used to go – / / or what do you	intend
⌊20⌋		want?	request
21	Peter	I just want to er to describe all the places where Joe and Alice erm had been together	explain
22	Susanne	Then go on – –	request
23	Peter	What?	request
24	Susanne	*Say* what you want	request
25	Peter	It's not what I want	disagree

Fig. 4: Speech act analysis of text 9.

Back-pointing acts:
7, 10 (reject)
13, 16, 17, 25 (disagree)
Forward-pointing acts:
4, 8, 11, 15, 18, 20, 22, 23, 24 (request)
1, 3, 6, 9, 19 (intend)
2 (suggest)
Informative acts:
5 (state)
12 (express opinion)
14, 21 (explain)

The *back-pointing acts* either function as corrections of the preceding ("rejects": 7: *he does* ..., correcting *he tries*, see also 10), or they express direct disagreement as in 13, 16, 17 and 25.

Of the *forward-pointing acts,* requests (directing acts) are by far the most frequent type of act in this extract. The requests subclassify into "requests for information" (4, 8, 11, 15, 18, 20, 23) and "requests for action" (22, 24). Of the requests for information, one is metalinguistic (4: *is it called pain to*), two are questions for clarification (8: *he does hvad*, 23: *what*), and the rest ask for the other participants' opinion (11, 15), wishes (20) or activity (18). The function of the requests for (verbal) action could be termed "metacommunicative": they relate to what is going on within the communicative event. The acts in 1, 3, 6, 9 and 19 are classified as intends, as Susanne announces what she intends to write. But because of her function as secretary for the group, what she writes is not her own responsibility exclusively, and the 'intend' therefore comes very close to a 'suggest', like Hanne's act (2). That there are 5 intend-acts is based on the assumption that a new act is necessarily initiated whenever there is a change of turn. This rules out the possibility of speakers being interrupted while performing a speech act and continuing performing the act after the interruption has been dealt with. If, on the other hand, we accept this possibility, we would have to say that 1, 3, 6 and 7 represent *one* intend act which gets interrupted three times by Hanne.

Of the *informative acts,* one is metalinguistic (5), and three convey the opinions of Hanne and Peter or express their reasons for disagreeing with Susanne.

If we try to arrange the speech acts according to *who* performs which acts, we obtain the following picture:

Speaker	Type of act	Frequency
Susanne	disagree	1
	request for information	3
	request for action	2
	intend	5
Hanne	reject	2
	disagree	1
	request for information	2
	suggest	1
	explain	1
Peter	disagree	2
	request for information	2
	state	1
	express opinion	1
	explain	1

Fig. 5: Speaker variation in use of speech acts

This analysis sheds some light on the different roles which the participants have in the communicative event. Susanne is the person who takes the initiative, 7 of her 8 acts are forward-pointing. Hanne reacts to what the other two participants say: 3 of her 7 acts are explicitly back-pointing, her two requests for information both relate to the preceding turn, and her 'explain' follows up her own rejects. Peter is slightly more passive, though both cooperative and constructive: he provides information which he considers relevant to the interaction between Susanne and Hanne (5 and 12), and his last two acts are reactions to Susanne's directing acts.

How does the group discussion compare with the teacher-controlled conversation (text 2, chapter two) in terms of speech acts? A quick look at the teacher-pupil interaction reveals that if we lump together the teacher's and the pupils' acts, there is no apparent difference in the total range of speech acts used in the two communication

53

events. But if we compare the pupils' own productive use of English in the two extracts, the differences are quite marked. When talking with the teacher, the pupils almost exclusively make use of informative acts of various sorts. Back-pointing and forward-pointing acts (eg accepting and requesting) are carried out in English by the teacher only. In the group discussion, the pupils take over some of the acts typically performed by the teacher and get practice in using them. But anybody familiar with group-work in the foreign language classroom will know that there are at least two additional factors to consider, along with this fairly positive characterization of group work. The pupils may carry over from teacher-centred classroom work their tendency to switch codes and use Danish for non-informative acts. Or one pupil may be more than ready to take over the teacher's directing functions, hereby restricting the other pupils to using speech acts that they would normally use when talking to the teacher.

3.3 Questions of politeness – speech act modality

In the preceding section, we pointed out how the teacher in text 2 makes use of what looks like a suggestion, in order to perform what is really a request ("now er let's er try to return to that question er of Mr Smith's job"). What lies behind this observation is that speech acts often have specific linguistic forms (words and structures) associated with them, so that one directly associates the form with a certain speech act:

speech act	linguistic structure
suggestion	let's + infinitive
request for information	interrogative
request for action	imperative

Whenever there is a clear match between linguistic form and speech act, one talks about DIRECT SPEECH ACTS. The following are examples of a direct suggestion, a direct request for information and a direct request for (non-verbal) action:

let's go to the movie tonight
how far is it to the station
close your books now and listen to me

Very often, however, the forms used do not directly convey what speech act is being performed, so the hearer has to "interpret" what the speaker's intended speech act was. To return to text 2, the pupils had to guess that in spite of the teacher using the form *let's* (directly marking a suggestion), the act he intended to perform was in fact a request – for which reason it would have been inappropriate for the pupils to reject the teacher's "suggestion".

Speech acts expressed by forms which do not directly convey the intended function of the act are referred to as INDIRECT SPEECH ACTS. In everyday conversation, we are reminded of their existence whenever we have problems in identifying the speech act behind an utterance ("I heard what you said, but why did you say so?"). Indirect speech acts also lie behind wilful or facetious misunderstandings of the following type:

Peter: Can you pass the butter, please
John: Yes I can
[and then John doesn't pass the butter]

Indirect speech acts can be found within all the main groups of speech acts mentioned above; a well-known example is the "rhetorical question", which is an indirect informative act. But indirect speech acts are particularly frequent within the group of directing speech acts, their primary function being to make demands look less peremptory than they in fact are, and therefore more polite. This is in accordance with the general principle of conversational behaviour that participants typically perform acts in a way that minimally threatens the social identity of both themselves as speakers and other participants as hearers. The term "face" is usually employed with reference to this social identity (cf Goffman 1972), and the term "face-saving" as referring to the endeavour to perform acts in such a way that participants do not lose face. We can therefore reformulate what we just said about the primary function of indirect speech acts. Such speech acts primarily serve to save the other

55

person's face. The hearer *appears* to have considerable freedom to react, but is likely to threaten the speaker's face if she reacts accordingly, for instance by questioning the speaker's authority. But it is worth remembering that although much conversation seems to follow a maxim of mutual face-saving, this does not imply that the power relationship between participants is not perfectly clear generally. One could hypothesize that it is exactly because of social differences that the concept of face is so important. Indirect speech acts often obscure inequality, as when the teacher says "let's return to page 25" or the nurse to the patient "let's swallow that little pill now and go to sleep".

So far we have only talked about direct and indirect speech acts as if politeness was a question of choosing between these two types of act. The situation is really much more complicated. SPEECH ACT MODALITY has been suggested as a general term used to express all the features of social relationship, politeness, intimacy, status, etc. (House/Kasper 1981). To express these interpersonal features, it may be appropriate to select a modal verb, an adverb, a certain intonation, or a particular term of address. As a demonstration of the range of possibilities, consider the following ways of expressing a request:

> the money
> the money, please
> I'd like the money
> do you have the money
> could you give me the money please
> John, could you give me the money please
> do you think you could give me the money, please
> Mr. Smith, could you possibly give me the money, do you think.

On the face of it there appears to be a progression in these acts from least polite to most polite. However it is possible to envisage situations in which each of the utterances is ideally suitable and expresses an appropriate degree of politeness. The last two, for instance, are scarcely likely when cashing a cheque in the bank, unless the addresser is being sarcastic! Essentially speech act modality involves choosing the right degree of politeness, and the necessary language

56

forms to express this, in a given communicative situation.

The risk for foreign users of a language is that they may use forms which are either too polite or not polite enough. Danes have been known to err in both directions. Thus a Danish learner doing the same role-play as the native speaker Anne in example 1 (p. 45) might have said "turn it down, please" instead of "do you think you could turn it down", expressing a speech act modality which she might not consider appropriate in the given situation and which she would probably not have used if she had been talking in her native language. The reason for this might be that the learner did not feel confident in using the modal verb *could*, in connection with *do you think*, used as a 'downtoning' structure. Authentic examples heard in England of learners not being polite enough are "my room is bloody cold" said by a 16-year-old pupil to a hotel receptionist and "this is my seat man", uttered by a student in a theatre. But errors in speech act modality, ie errors caused by learners not knowing which words and structures to use in order to perform a specific speech act appropriately may also be of another type: the learner may make use of structures which are too complex in a given situation. This is particularly the case with advanced learners. An example of this is making a request in a pub, where many advanced Danish learners of English would use "I would like a pint of lager, please" instead of the more appropriate "(a) pint of lager, please". The psycholinguistic explanation for these realisations of a request is probably transfer from Danish, where the functional equivalent to the postposed *please* is often a preposed *jeg vil gerne have* (= 'I would like').

In considering the issue of appropriacy relative to the way speech acts are performed it is necessary to touch upon the question of social norms and the individual's different degrees of compliance with such norms. As we mentioned above, different situations call for different types of speech act modality as the most appropriate way of expressing speech acts, and when individuals follow such conventions they may be said to perform speech acts in a way which is *unmarked* with respect to politeness. Maybe it needs emphasizing that the objective of teaching learners about speech act modality is not to socialize them into always performing speech acts in an unmarked way in the foreign language, but to enable them to choose how marked they want to express themselves in a given communicative situation with respect to politeness, so that they do not create *unintended* effects by using marked forms in situations in which they aim at using an unmarked form.

Footnotes to chapter 3:

1. Especially Halliday 1973, which was developed for the study of child language acquisition.
2. Speech acts have been extensively discussed since Austin's book with the telling title *How to do things with words* (1955). Austin's work and the ensuing studies within the tradition of "the philosophy of language", notably by Searle, constitute the theoretical background to our description of speech acts. Some introductory works in this area are listed at the end of this chapter.
3. This data is taken from a project at Ruhr-Universität Bochum on communicative competence and foreign language teaching. See Edmondson/House/Kasper/Stemmer 1982.
4. One such set of principles has been suggested by Searle (1976) and elaborated by various linguists. An alternative set of principles, resulting in a different classification, has been formulated in Edmondson (1981). The text draws on Edmondson/House 1981:48 ff.
5. Hanne's turn could also be interpreted as functioning as a suggest, particularly if a rising intonation is used.

Chapter 3. Follow-ups

1. Analyse an extract of classroom communication in transcription. Note which language functions occur and which do not. How does the pattern of language functions used reflect the type of interaction which learners and teacher engage in?
2. Study the teacher's books accompanying a couple of recent, intermediate level coursebooks. Do the authors make use of the concept "language function"? If yes, are the functions the same as Jakobson's, or is a different classification system used?
3. Tape record a group discussion situation. Transcribe a brief extract from it, and classify the utterances using the terminology of figure 3 to identify the types of speech act used (as in figure 4). For each speaker, group the acts according to whether they are back- or forward-pointing, informative or ritual (as on page 52), preparing a profile as in figure 5.
4. A group of intermediate learners are recorded doing a role play in English based on a situation in which the speech act *request* is obligatory. This is followed

by different learners carrying out the same role play in Danish. The recordings are analysed and compared with respect to speech act modality.

5. Austin identified speech acts by means of the "performative verbs" conventionally associated with speech acts (eg *to object, to claim, to refuse*) and typically used in reported speech ("Peter objected that ..."). Discuss the pros and cons of this approach.

6. Contrast the classification of speech acts used in chapter 3 with that introduced in Fraser 1983. What are the salient differences? Find instances of speech acts contained in one taxonomy which are difficult to accommodate in the other.

7. Discuss ways in which learners can be given the opportunity to develop mastery of a wide range of speech acts, and become sensitised to speech act modality.

Chapter 3. Sources and further reading

Several contributions to Richards/Schmidt 1983 cover the same ground as chapter 3 in a more detailed way. Of particular interest are Fraser 1983 dealing with speech act analysis; Wolfson 1983 which addresses the broader topic of rules of speaking, including the notion of "communicative interference"; and Scollon/Scollon 1983 which discusses the concept of "face" and the politeness dimension to speech act realization. Leech 1983 contains a very stimulating and comprehensive discussion of principles of pragmatics.

A good overview of Halliday's model af speech functions is Halliday 1973, further extended in Halliday 1978. Austin's seminal description of speech acts (1955) is still very readable, and provides a useful historical dimension to more recent work in pragmatics. The same holds for Searle's analyses of speech acts, for instance the paper "What is a Speech Act?" (1972).

The problem of speech act classification has been tackled differently in Searle 1976 and Leech 1980, which provide radically different principles for classification from the one adopted above. See Fraser 1983 for a classification following Searle's approach.

Speech act realization, including considerations of politeness, is discussed in Brown/Levinson 1978 and Leech 1980, both of which offer a principled basis for the description of politeness (or 'tact'). Studies of speech act realization in different languages (and across languages) are House/Kasper 1981 and Kasper 1981 (German, English, German learners of English); Blum-Kulka 1982 (Hebrew, Hebrew learners of English). Instances of pragmatic failure are lucidly discussed in Thomas 1983.

Chapter four:
Discourse

Our description of speech acts so far suffers from the limitation that the individual acts have been characterized atomistically, as if they could be performed in isolation from each other. This is seldom the case. In actual communicative events, choice of a speech act at a specific point in time is conditioned by whatever acts have been previously performed, and the act itself conditions subsequent acts. Sequences of acts performed in a communicative event constitute a structured *text* rather than a haphazard jumble of unrelated utterances. The sequential characteristics of speech acts are usually referred to as *coherence*. The description of coherence is part of DIS-COURSE ANALYSIS, the analysis of the structuring principles, other than grammatical ones, which speakers follow when producing a text within a certain communicative event.

4.1 Coherence: initiating and responding acts

Probably the most important structural unit within discourse analysis is the ADJACENCY PAIR: two speech acts, typically following each other, with each act pointing to the other. The best-known example of this is the pair 'question' – 'answer'. The following exchange between a learner and a native speaker[1] contains four such pairs:

NS	do you like to go into the country		you do		what did you do last
L			oh yes	yes	

NS	summer			mm	
L		eeer I I was in Holland – for fourteen days		with a group	

NS	what were you doing there	
L		er I was er enjoying a group ...

The utterances can be grouped more clearly into pairs as follows:

Adjacency pair no.	I	II
1	NS: do you like to go into the country	L: oh yes
2	NS: you do	L: yes
3	NS: what did you do last summer	L: eeer I I was in Holland – for fourteen days [NS: mm] with a group
4	NS: what were you doing there	L: er I was er enjoying a group

Fig. 6: Adjacency pairs

Each of the turns listed in column I marks the initiation of a new adjacency pair. The turns in column II are responses to the initiating acts and mark the completion of the adjacency pair.

It is apparent that it is the learner who performs all the responding acts in the extract. As there is considerably less freedom when responding than when initiating, it is evident that in this particular extract the native speaker is in the more dominant position: the native speaker can control what type of act the learner is to perform through selecting initiating acts. Furthermore the native speaker can decide whether to adhere to the same topic as in the preceding adjacency pair or to change topics.

In our speech act analysis in chapter 3 we did not use the terms 'question' and 'answer', but referred to 'request for information' and to 'informative acts'. The main reason for this decision was that the terms 'request' and 'inform' emphasize the actional aspect and largely ignore the sequential aspect of communication. It is possible to maintain a systematic distinction between a (context-free) pragmatic analysis of speech acts and a discourse-related analysis of the same, for instance distinguishing between 'request for information'/ 'informative act' (pragmatic categories) and 'question'/'answer' (discourse categories). Rather than do this, we maintain the basic principles of the classification established in chapter 3, adding to each of the four classes of acts a characterization of the discourse function(s) of acts belonging to the class:

forward-pointing acts are typically *initiating acts* in adjacency pairs (eg 'request for information'); they may also point forward to future events located outside the communicative event (eg 'promise')

back-pointing acts, in a similar fashion, are typically *responding acts* in adjacency pairs (eg 'accept' following an 'offer'), but the event implied by the act may also be located outside the communicative event at some earlier point in time (eg 'thank' following the receipt of a letter)

informative acts can function as both *initiating acts* (eg 'express opinion', followed by eg 'agree' or 'disagree') and as *responding acts*, following a request for information. This versatility is an important reason why acts which have the form of informatives are often used as indirect realization of both forward-pointing and back-pointing acts:

A. I'm getting hungry
B. It's your turn, dear

ritual acts constitute a special case of acts, seen from a discourse point of view, in that they are frequently reflexive: a ritual act performed as an initiating act typically elicits the same type of act as a responding act (eg greet – greet).

4.2 Coherence, cohesion and variation

As we have just shown, one way in which COHERENCE is established in texts is when a speech act conditions another speech act and/or is conditioned by previous speech acts ("speech act coherence"). For instance there is a "tie" of coherence between an initiating and a responding speech act. Another type of coherence is established through ties between the content or propositions expressed by different acts ("semantic coherence"). In the example just analysed, the four turns contained in the last two adjacency pairs all refer to "last year's holidays". This means that in addition to the learner's "I was

62

in Holland" being a reply to a question put by the native speaker, it is also related to the topic "last year's holidays". Had the learner been talking about what she did, say, four years earlier during the autumn holidays, the semantic coherence between her turn and the learner's preceding turn would have been violated.

Coherence is one way in which structure is created in texts without making use of special formal means for expressing ties between turns (or, in written texts, sentences). A different way is to establish COHESION, which can be defined as the creation of ties between sentences by lexical and grammatical means.

A clear example of cohesion is the use of pronouns referring back in the text (anaphoric reference):

A: where's Mary
B: *she*'s working late today

In order to understand who *she* refers to it is necessary to know that it is used as a substitute ("pro") form for Mary, or, put differently, in comprehending *she* we acknowledge the existence of a tie between the second and the first sentence.

A different means for creating cohesion is the use of elliptical constructions like in the following example:

A: where did Peter go?
B: to the baker's

Again, in order to comprehend B's turn we have to take into account the complete sentence which has been reduced to the adverbial phrase "to the baker's". We do this by filling in subject and verb from A's sentence ("Peter went –").

A third, very important means for creating cohesion, especially in written texts, is the use of conjunctions, adverbials and adverbial phrases: *and, but, however, on the other hand*. That these express ties between sentences is self-evident.

An additional and very simple way of creating cohesion is by repeating a word or a phrase verbatim from a previous sentence:

The teacher left school and went home. *The teacher* went to bed and read a book. *The teacher* fell asleep and slept soundly till 10 o'clock.

The risk with this type of cohesion, if used too repetitively, is monotony. This can be avoided if different lexical (including pronominal) means are used. The teacher can be referred to as "the exhausted old man", "Mr Blackwell", "he" or equivalent forms of lexical variation. What we want to demonstrate by this example is that cohesion and variation in texts are two sides of the same coin, and that a very simple type of cohesion may be achieved at the expense of variation.

We shall now briefly describe one way in which it is possible to obtain a clear picture of cohesion.[2] The principle behind the analysis is that a text is divided into semantic and functional units, and that all manifestations of each unit are added together. A practical way of doing so is to draw a number of vertical columns on a sheet of paper and use one column for each of the units. The horizontal lines divide the text up into sentences (see figure 7).

As a demonstration, consider the following extract from a learner text[3]:

The film starts when a man is yawning very loudly. Then he sleep and dreams ... Then in the morning his watch are ringing. He put his finger on the watch to stop it, but he can't get his finger off the watch. Then he is fighting with the watch ...

If we divide this up into semantic units we might get something like the following: 'film', 'begin', conjunction, 'man', 'act', 'time', 'watch', 'finger', modal. Some of these are repeated more often than others, and we decide to analyse conjunction, 'man', 'act' and 'watch' because they occur several times. When the grid has been filled in, the analysis is as below.

What appears from this analysis is that the text has an extremely simple though effective cohesive structure, achieved through repetition of *he* and *watch*. The inventory of conjunctions is very limited and emphasizes the simple structure of the text. The only area where variation is found is within the 'act' unit, which is to be expected as the various acts provide the new information in each sentence.

64

Text:	Unit Sentence no.	conjunction	'man'	'act'	'watch'
The film starts	1				
when a man is yawning very loudly	2	when	a man	yawn	
Then he sleep and dreams ...	3	then	he	sleep dream	
Then in the morning his watch are ringing.	4	then	his	ring	watch
He put his finger on the watch to stop it,	5		he his	put stop	the watch it
but he can't get his finger off the watch	6	but	he his		the watch
Then he is fighting with the watch ...	7	then	he	fight	the watch

Fig. 7: Cohesion analysis grid

The following extract[4] exemplifies problematic cohesion:

> Allright, the violence scenes at television is not good, but then you can ask yourself: shall we protest against 'em? Then we can't see violence anywhere? Wouldn't it be to fool ourselves? The violence is going on everywhere, that's a fact. So if we didn't know anything about it, we couldn't do anything against it. It would be rather terribly too. So I would like to suggest, that DR had two programs and only sendt films a.s.o. with violence scenes at one of the programs. It could be a possibility, a solution. But it is a problem, I think and something have to be done.

A primary reason for the problems is the learner's use of *it* with varying anaphoric reference (to 'violence scenes', 'violence in general' and to the learner's proposed solution).

4.3 Discourse phases

Coherence and cohesion represent important ways in which structure is created in texts. What other structural properties do texts exhibit? Consider the following imagined telephone conversation between Fred and Alice:

Text 10
[phone rings in Fred's office]
- (1) F: Fred Johnson speaking
- (2) A: hi Fred – this is Alice
- (3) F: oh – good morning Alice
- (4) A: morning Fred – I am calling you because I want to know whether you've – remembered about [F: mm] I mean about tonight
- (5) F: you mean – oh yes Alice – of course I remember – I'll be there round seven
- (6) A: that's fine Fred – that was all I wanted to know – er – I'm afraid I have to dash now
- (7) F: oh – all right
- (8) A: so I'll expect you round seven
- (9) F: yes – that's fine
- (10) A: good – see you later then
- (11) F: see you Alice – good-bye
- (12) A: bye Fred

[contrived example]

What we have here is a complete communicative event, consisting of 12 turns equally divided between Fred and Alice. The event consists of three phases, each of which has a specific function relative to the interaction between the two participants: an OPENING PHASE (turns 1–4, up to *morning Fred*), a CORE PHASE (turns 4–6, up to *to know*), and a CLOSING PHASE (6–12). If we look at the speech acts performed within each of the three phases we notice a difference between on the one hand, the opening and closing phases and, on the other hand, the core phase. The acts of both the opening and the closing phases are ritual (greeting and leave-taking), the primary function of which is to open and close the communicative event. The acts performed in the middle phase, the core phase, are forward/backpointing and informative, it is these acts that determine what the interaction is really about.

Each of the three phases has an internal structure of its own.

(a) In the *opening phase* in the telephone conversation, we find a speaker identification phase and a greeting phase. Sometimes the opening phase is initiated by an attention-getting subphase, followed by another subphase in which the person who is initiating the conversation apologizes for disturbing the other participant: "Professor Johnson" – "Yes" – "Sorry to disturb you but this is terribly urgent" – "Hm" – "My name is ...". In the telephone conversation, the attention-getting subphase is carried out by Alice calling Fred's office.

(b) Very often, the *core phase* contains a series of 'preparatory' subphases before the initiator gets to the heart of the matter, the business part of the core phase. Preparatory subphases are particularly common if the core phase contains speech acts which involve cost to the hearer and benefit to the speaker, typically, asking a favour of somebody. Such preparatory subphases are often phatic, like asking about the other person's health or plans, or talking about the weather, the political situation, etc. Coming before the actual business phase, they enable the initiator of the communicative event to support the other person's face by treating him as somebody he wants to interact with, not just a person to do business with. As the need for such "face work" obviously differs in various situations (cf also the discussion of modality markers in chapter 3), there are situations in which preparatory phases are not required, for example in service encounters like buying a ticket.

(c) The *closing phase* typically contains a preclosing subphase in which the reasons are given for bringing the communicative event to an end ("I'm afraid I have to dash now" in the telephone conversation) and a summary of the core phase ("so I'll expect you round seven"). These are then followed by the actual closing which, like the opening, is performed by means of ritual speech acts ("leave-taking").

One might perhaps feel that what we have just described is part of our common-sense knowledge of the world, or that these issues are irrelevant in learner language communication because we are dealing with social, rather than with verbal competence. Or that when learners communicate in their English interlanguage, they can simply rely on what they would do in a native language situation. It is generally the case that Danish and British or American cultures are very similar with respect to how communicative events are structured into smaller phases. However, learners quite often do not transfer from their native language in situations in which there is similarity between native and target language norms. An example of this is the learner who says "hi you've taken my seat" to someone in the university library who has occupied her seat, instead of saying something closer to what a native speaker did in the same situation.[5]

x oh
y (looks up)
x er (clears throat)
y yes
x excuse me I I don't know you do I
y I don't think so no
x well er – (embarrassed laugh) I'm terribly sorry but er –
   I'm afraid you're in my seat – ...

Although there are probably very similar norms for a situation like this in Danish and English, learners are often found to reduce on the more phatic elements in speech. There may be two important reasons for this:

(1) Learners are not quite sure *what* to say. Phatic speech is often expressed by means of ritual acts, which are typically expressed by routine formulae, and one has to have a good knowledge of *when* to say *what* to *whom* in order to use these appropriately.

(2) If learners generally feel uncomfortable when communicating with native speakers, it is not surprising that they concentrate on saying what is perceived as being minimally necessary, ie getting the message across. But if the message is to get somebody else to do something, it is not a bad idea to support one's directing speech acts in the core phase by more phatic elements in the opening and closing

phases. Learners rarely have a sufficient metacommunicative awareness of how they communicate in their *native* language, nor a precise knowledge of the effect of different types of reduction on the hearer, for example reduction of phatic speech.

4.4 Turn-taking

Conversation implies that more than one person is active as a speaker, ie that the text can be divided into turns. Language provides fairly strict conventions for how the change from one speaker to another, turn-taking, operates. We shall consider two aspects of this issue: (1) the question *when* turn-taking is possible for another participant without interrupting the speaker; (2) if there are more than two participants, the question *who* gets the next turn.

Turn-taking is possible (and at times necessary) in one of the following situations:

(1) The present speaker completes an initiating speech act, which elicits a responding act from another participant.

(2) The present speaker indicates a wish to no longer keep the floor but give the turn to somebody else. This can be done by means of speaker-nomination ("so that's what we're going to do, right John"), by means of a "gambit" of appeal (see below) like a tag-question, or by means of gaze and head movement (by looking steadily at the listener *before* finishing speaking).

(3) The present speaker comes to a possible completion point in a turn. This is determined by a combination of phonological, syntactic and semantic criteria and typically occurs when these converge after a main clause or, as in two of the examples below, after a main clause followed by its subordinate clauses. In the sixth turn in the telephone conversation there are three possible completion points:

that's fine Fred// – that was all I wanted to know// – er – I'm afraid I have to dash now//

Fred *could* have taken a turn at either of the first two points without interrupting Alice.

SPEAKER SELECTION is either the responsibility of the present speaker or is achieved by the other participants independently of the speaker. If the present speaker nominates a next speaker, a third party cannot claim the floor without interrupting, except for brief comments:

Anne: let's hear your opinion John
Michael: yes that's a good idea
John: well – I don't know ...
[contrived example]

Certain communicative events are structured in the way that speaker selection is preceded by a verbal or non-verbal bid from another participant, followed by a speaker nomination either by the present speaker or by a chair-person. This is the case in formal meetings and in classroom conversation, where the teacher often has the function of nominating the next speaker (not necessarily following a bid from a pupil). In classrooms in which all speaker nomination is controlled by the teacher, there will automatically be an equal split between the pupils' number of turns and the teacher's. If the teacher then, in addition, takes longer turns than the pupils, it is easy to understand why analyses of teacher-centred classrooms have shown that teachers talk two thirds of the time.

There are rather compelling reasons for the teacher to control speaker nomination: she can provide feedback and check on the preceding turn before nominating the next speaker, and she can make sure that everybody in the class gets a chance to speak. But it is possible to envisage other ways of selecting speakers which activate the pupils more, and give them the possibility to practise turn-taking without having to rely on the teacher as an intermediary. One way of doing this is to let the pupil responsible for a turn nominate another pupil to take a new turn, with or without a previous bid from those interested to participate as next speaker.

4.5 Gambits

When learners talk to native speakers, they often have difficulty in getting the floor, and once they have won the right to speak they easily lose it again when they come to the first possible completion point in their turn. Learners, much more than native speakers, not only have to plan what to say but also how to say it. It is therefore useful to know how native speakers claim and maintain the right to speak, even when they do not know exactly what to say next.

One particularly useful way of both taking and keeping a turn at speech is by using one of a whole range of words and expressions the primary function of which is to signal that the person wants to get or keep the floor. Such items are often referred to as GAMBITS, which can be defined as words and expressions that help regulate conversation. In the telephone conversation, Fred makes use of a *turn-taking gambit* (*oh*) at the beginning of turn 3, apparently in order to make up his mind about how to handle the situation. Other turn-taking gambits are *well, now, oh yes but,* or a repetition of part of the preceding turn ("it was awfully nice" – "*awfully nice* – well I don't know"), often followed by a filled pause (*er*).

Some of the turn-taking gambits can also be used in the middle of a turn, at a possible completion point, signalling to the other participant(s) that the present speaker intends to continue. Other *turn-keeping* gambits comprise expressions like *I mean, you know, what I wanted to say.* Related to this use of turn-keeping gambits is the use of a conjunction, uttered immediately after a possible completion point. There is no possible completion point following a conjunction, except in very special cases (*but* or *and,* both followed by *er,* pronounced weakly and with the voice pitched low, which may mark turn-abandonment).

As gambits have the function of regulating conversation, it is not surprising that they occur less frequently the more fixed the organization of turn-taking. Whenever teachers regulate turn-taking, there is little or no need for either pupils or teacher to claim or mark turn-keeping, and gambits are rare. In direct pupil-to-pupil interaction there is more scope for practising some of the discourse functions realised by means of gambits. Such training may be useful to the pupils in less regulated types of conversation outside school.

71

4.6 Repair work

Feedback from a native speaker in the form of gambits like *aha, mm, yeah* (see for instance text 5, chapter 2) signals UPTAKING, ie it encourages the learner to go on. A range of words and expressions can be used with this discourse function: *yes, no, oh, hm, you don't say so.* Uptaking is also signalled non-linguistically by gaze and head movement, which either accompany or alternate with gambits.

In conversation between a learner and a native speaker, there is a constant risk of misunderstanding because of the mismatch in linguistic resources. Signalling understanding is therefore particularly important in this type of communication. Related to this is the need, whenever speaker and listener do not understand each other, for REPAIR WORK.

By repair work is meant that either the speaker or the listener "repairs" something the speaker has said, and which appears to be a problem. A listener can request the speaker to repair what she just said, in which case we refer to OTHER-INITIATED REPAIR. The speaker herself may realise that a repair is needed and use a SELF-INITIATED REPAIR. A further distinction in repair work is between INTERACTIONAL and NON-INTERACTIONAL REPAIRS. If either speaker or hearer both initiates and completes the repair, we have a non-interactional type. If there is a shift from speaker to hearer or from hearer to speaker, the repair is interactional. This gives four basic types of repairs in all[6]:

(1) the speaker both initiates and completes a repair (self-initiated, non-interactional repair) ("She wants to study archaeology – anthropology")
(2) the speaker initiates a repair by requesting the hearer to repair (self-initiated, interactional repair)
    A. She wants to study archaeology or was it anthropology
    B. Anthropology I think
(3) the hearer initiates a repair by requesting the speaker to repair (other-initiated, interactional repair)
    A. She wants to study archaeology
    B. Archaeology (rising intonation)
    A. Nonsense anthropology

(4) the hearer both initiates and completes a repair (other-initiated, non-interactional repair)
   A. She wants to study archaeology
   B. Anthropology you mean

We have singled out two of these for more detailed discussion: other-initiated, interactional repair and self-initiated, non-interactional repair.

Other-initiated, interactional repair
A listener may signal lack of understanding indirectly by withholding uptaking gambits at appropriate points. Or she may express lack of understanding directly by explicitly requesting the speaker to repair. These are illustrated in the following two examples:[7]

(1) NS: what do you think about the unemployment (learner shows no sign of understanding) that people have no jobs in Denmark
(2) NS: how did you come here [L:er] how was it arranged
   L: (sigh) I don't know what –
   NS: er did somebody come and ask you – – if you wanted er if you wanted to join in
   L: yes

There are various ways in which the repair can be completed: substituting for an open *wh*-question a closed *yes/no* question or an alternative question, using a more general word or a paraphrase. The first of these is illustrated in the following example:

(3) NS: well how do you take your papers round – – do you cycle or walk

In the classroom, both the teacher and pupils constantly assess their contribution to the ongoing conversation in the light of how the other participants react. But whereas the pupil can rely on the reaction of the teacher when responding to a teacher-initiated act, the teacher faces the more difficult task of addressing a group of perhaps 25 at the same time, a group which normally represent a wide range of

73

proficiency levels. Some teachers elicit non-verbal feedback from the pupils by fixing their gaze on one pupil at a time, but the selected addressee may not be supposed to express repair requests in the middle of the teacher's turn. The need for repair work may instead be signalled indirectly, through lack of (non-verbal) uptaking.

Self-initiated, non-interactional repair

If the teacher decides that there are reasons to believe that the class have not understood an utterance she may repair by reformulating it. Such self-repairs may be swift and convenient shortcuts:

... he could be a kind of a security officer sikkerhedspolitibetjent

The disadvantage of the teacher self-repairing is that the pupils are not given the possibility to infer the meaning of the word. A too extensive use of self-repair, though it may ensure comprehension, impedes the pupils' inferencing abilities in the long run (for inferencing see chapters 5 and 8).

Consider another example of teacher talk:[8]

Teacher: is there any new er – no look at the way the two fathers behave to their children – Mr Robinson to Elaine and Mr Bradley to er Benjamin (clears throat) is there any er er do the different ways of behaving have anything in common do you understand my question – do you see some parallels between the way the two fathers treat their children here – Jette

This transcript shows the teacher self-repairing in order to clarify the communication of an idea that initially was formulated ambiguously. There is a succession of false starts and reformulations, the teacher attempting to bring the same point in focus, before the final question is put.

Other self-repairs by teachers are even more problematic when seen from the learner's point of view:

what information do we get about his – his job – what is part of his job – I mean what what is what must he *do* in that job
(from the same lesson as text 2, chapter 2)

74

Whether the teacher self-repairs because the pupils do not show any sign of reacting to her first question, whether she repairs in order to ask her question in different ways for the benefit of different learners, or whether she simply self-repairs because she has not quite made up her mind what question to ask, the result is that she makes it more difficult for the pupils to respond because each of the three questions calls for a different responding act.

The topics covered in this chapter and the two previous ones have all in various ways demonstrated how different factors in a communicative event influence the specific type of discourse that occurs. This is not the place for a discussion of teaching methods, but we should like to stress one rather obvious point in conclusion. If learners are to be equipped to use the pragmatic and discourse functions of non-educational varieties of communication, this goal cannot be achieved by paying attention to the content of teaching only. To practise pragmatic and discourse functions which go beyond those which pupils perform in teacher-centred communication, it is necessary to vary the types of interaction so that other varieties of communication occur. This can be facilitated by learners working in groups or pairs, and by the teacher interacting informally with learners in smaller groups.

Footnotes to chapter 4

1. Extract from PIF conversation with informant number 17.
2. This type of analysis was first developed by Winburne 1962, and has been used in various analyses of English essays written by Swedish learners, see Linnarud 1978.
3. Extract from PIF written film description, informant number 93, 10th grade.
4. Extract from PIF essay, informant number 27, 1g.
5. Both examples are role-play data from the Bochum corpus.
6. This is true of *symmetric* communicative situations. In asymmetric situations it is necessary to distinguish between different speakers and listeners, which increases the number of repair types. In classroom communication, for instance type 1 (self-initiated, non-interactional repair) may relate to either the teacher or the pupil.
7. The extracts in examples 1, 2 and 3 all come from PIF conversations.
8. This comes from a lesson in a Gymnasium recorded by students attached to PIF.

Chapter 4. Follow-ups

1. Carry out a *cohesion* analysis of the text on page 65, using the grid system of figure 7. Draw conclusions about the pattern of lexical variation, and consider how a teacher might follow this up, in the way of feedback and remedial activities.

2. Take text 10, or an equivalent text, and print each turn on separate pieces of paper. Fit the turns together so as to create as many *adjacency pairs* as possible. By juggling with the turns, is it possible to re-create the dialogue with a different pattern of *opening, core* and *closing phases*, or a different sequence of turns in these?

3. In spoken English texts (drama, transcripts, etc) that you are studying, or in television programmes you watch, make a note of *turn-taking* and *turn-keeping gambits*. Do you make use of them in your spoken English?

4. Let a group of students discuss a highly specialised topic which one of the group is particularly interested in. Note down the use of repairs and classify them according to the categories used in this chapter.

5. Observe a teacher-centred discussion and note down instances of teachers' self-repair. What is the effect of them? Are the worries voiced in the text justifiable?

Chapter 4. Sources and further reading

Much of the pioneering work in describing discourse principles, especially in conversation, was done by American researchers associated with "ethnomethodology". See for instance Schegloff's paper in Laver/Hutcheson 1972. A good, comprehensive introduction to discourse analysis is Coulthard 1977, whereas Sinclair/Brazil 1982 is more restricted in scope. Edmondson 1981 presents a model for discourse analysis which integrates pragmatic and discourse functions.

Particular emphasis on classroom discourse is found in Sinclair/Coulthard 1975, which presents a model for the analysis of teacher-controlled classroom interaction. Kramsch 1981 contains useful information on discourse analysis, as well as interesting discussion of the implications for foreign language teaching. A stimulating discussion of teacher-controlled interaction is contained in Harms Larsen 1977.

Within more specific areas of discourse analysis, mention should be made of Halliday/Hassan 1976, which is a comprehensive treatment of cohesion in English; Edmondson/House 1981, which discusses discourse phases (especially chapter 5); Færch/Kasper 1983a which establishes a framework for the description of gambits and analyses gambits in Danish and German. A clarification of the basic principles in repair work is contained in Schegloff/Jefferson/Sachs 1977, whereas Færch/Kasper 1982 presents an analysis of repair work in learner-native speaker interaction.

Chapter five:
Vocabulary

Inexperienced learners tend to think that learning a foreign language primarily means learning new words for old concepts. A Danish child wanting to know the English for "så kan hun jo engelsk" might ask how to say 'så', 'kan', 'hun', 'jo', 'engelsk', one word at a time, a procedure which completely obscures the structural differences between Danish and English sentences. It is no surprise that children pay special attention to vocabulary in foreign language learning: even quite young children are capable of dividing up their L1 speech into units which by and large correspond to what are considered words by literate native speakers. And although learners soon realize that there is more to learning a foreign language than learning words, vocabulary remains of central concern.

This chapter presents some ways in which learner vocabulary can be described, quantitatively and qualitatively, and suggests criteria for vocabulary selection in teaching materials. In the second half of the chapter we discuss possible ways in which interlanguage vocabulary may be organized in the learner's mind.

5.1 What is a word?

The simplest definition of a word, based on written language, is the following: "a word is any sequence of letters which is bounded on either side by space". According to this definition, the following example would contain six words:

my aunt Mary is my favourite

We refer to words identified in this way as WORD TOKENS.

The definition of word tokens obviously does not capture the assumption underlying a statement that a learner's active vocabulary should amount to 2000–3000 words. What is meant here is that the learner's vocabulary should contain 2000–3000 *different* words

6*

or WORD TYPES. We therefore need another definition: "a word type is a sequence of letters bounded on either side by space (ie a word token), and which (1) has a meaning that differs from other word tokens, and/or (2) has a form, orthographic or phonological, different from other word tokens". Word types correspond roughly to entries in dictionaries.

Anybody trying to apply the definition of word types to a text will run into a number of difficulties. Thus many words do not have fixed and restricted meanings. They have POTENTIAL FOR MEANING, and only specific meaning in specific contexts. In the three examples *a horse race, a race against time,* and *a race to catch the train,* the three word tokens for *race* are related, though far from identical, in meaning. Similarly, in *race relations* and *discrimination on grounds of race* the two word tokens share approximately the same meaning. If one now looks at the entire batch of the five examples, it is impossible to conceive of the five meanings as contextually determined variants of one and the same meaning potential. Rather, it is reasonable to group them into two word types, each of which has a meaning potential centred around a core meaning.

In the examples in question this would be:

race (1) contest or competition in speed, eg in running or swimming or to see who can finish a piece of work, or get to a certain place, first,
race (2) of several subdivisions of mankind sharing certain physical characteristics, especially colour of skin etc; used for people having a common culture.[1]

This is the kind of information and classification found in dictionaries. Those forms that are treated as different entries in the dictionary can be considered different word types, and those that are listed as variant meanings of one entry are taken to be one "word".

At times we need to establish separate word types for tokens which have almost the same meaning if the tokens have different forms: "they are in the sitting-room/living-room". This is the area of synonyms. But there are also many cases of tokens having different forms but similar meanings where we would definitely not posit different types. "I *like* red wine" – "I *liked* red wine". This is a case of *systema-*

78

tic differences between word tokens, reflecting verb inflection. Rather than say that a learner knows two word types *like* and *liked*, we would say that the learner knows the word type *like* and a rule for past-formation. Similarly, with cases of word derivation like *bake/baker*, and of compounding (eg *blood-thirsty*) we might treat the product in terms of the constituent elements and a rule for derivation or word-compounding. On the other hand, there may be a case, particularly with beginning learners, for not assuming that the learner knows such a rule and for classifying each of the tokens as a separate word type.

Irregular declensional forms like *go – went* represent a further problem. A description of the native language would normally treat such forms in a parallel way to regular pairs (ie as tokens of the same type), whereas it might be sensible in learner language studies to treat the tokens as two types, because they comprise two learning problems.

Idioms and prefabricated patterns present special problems for the description of vocabulary, because they contain more than one word but form a single unit of meaning. The meaning of an IDIOM is quite different from the sum of the meanings of each word, eg *kick the bucket*. A learner may know the idiom *of course*, but familiarity with the idiom does not imply knowledge of the meaning of the constituents, eg the word *course*. PREFABRICATED PATTERNS, like *excuse me, how do you do*, which are typically used in ritual speech acts (cf chapter 3), are invariant units, and are learned as such. In analyses of learner language vocabulary, they should therefore, in the same way as idioms, be treated as single word types.

Measures of the size and quality of vocabulary will produce drastically different results, depending on how one decides to define a word. A learner's vocabulary at a specific point in time may perhaps be 1700 words if one adopts a very restricted definition of "word types", and 2500 words if "word types" is taken to mean something closer to word tokens. Without precise definition it is impossible to determine whether a given learner's vocabulary corresponds to what is stated in official guidelines, for instance those for the Folkeskole.

5.2 How to analyse richness of vocabulary in learner language

Even if there is agreement on defining a 'word', there remains the crucial problem of how to assess the "richness" of a learner's vocabulary. To do so, one either has to resort to tests which specifically tap learners' vocabulary knowledge, or to describe vocabulary on the basis of learner texts.[2]

We shall concentrate on the analysis of vocabulary in texts. Such analyses present two separate problems:

(1) what texts should be used? how many? how different?
(2) given a collection of texts, how does one analyse the vocabulary in the text?

The first question raises the issue of representativity, which is particularly tricky within the area of vocabulary. In pronunciation, the learner's complete inventory of sounds is likely to be activated even within fairly short texts. With vocabulary this is not so, which means that descriptions of vocabulary will inevitably have to be related to identified topics, for instance, ecology, air traffic control, or smoking. Our comments on frequency studies later in this chapter will make this point clearer.

As for the second problem, in addition to simply calculating the number of word types ('size of vocabulary'), the following are possible methods of vocabulary analysis in learner texts:

(1) the ratio between number of types and the number of tokens ('lexical variation')
(2) the ratio between the number of content words and the total number of word tokens ('lexical density').

5.2.1 Lexical variation

The degree of variation in a learner's vocabulary (as used in a text) can be expressed as the ratio between word types and word tokens. This can either be done for a whole text or for selected elements within the text, for instance particular word classes.

A *type-token ratio* for a text is a measure of how frequently the learner makes use of one and the same word type. The ratio is calculated by dividing the number of word types by the number of word tokens:

$$\frac{\text{number of word types}}{\text{number of word tokens}}$$

As an illustration, consider the following learner text (written film description, grade 8):

The film starts when a man is yawning very loudly. Then he sleep and dreams a lot of funny things ... Then in the morning his watch are ringing. He put his finger on the watch to stop it, but he can't get his finger off the watch.

The text contains 47 word tokens and 35 word types. The type-token ratio for the text is $\frac{35}{47} = 0.74$. If we consider the first sentence only in the text, we obtain a ratio of 1.0 ($= \frac{10 \text{ types}}{10 \text{ tokens}}$). If we take the first and the second, the ratio is 0.95 ($= \frac{19 \text{ types}}{20 \text{ tokens}}$). Had we calculated a ratio for a longer stretch of text than the 47 tokens included here, the figure would have been below 0.7. What this illustrates is that the ratio of lexical variation is influenced by the length of a text. The first sentence of a text necessarily contains more new words than the last sentence. In comparing ratios for lexical variation between texts, it is therefore necessary to be aware of any differences in length there may be. And to ensure that the texts are not too short, as all texts approximate to a ratio of 1.0 for lexical variation the shorter they are.

The following results exemplify a type-token analysis for one word class, the adjectives used by grade 8 learners and by university students in the two written PIF texts (cf chapter 19).

Although there are differences between each set of texts as regards the sum total of adjective tokens (the equivalent of text length in this investigation), it is possible to use the figures to make some important points about type/token ratios.

Table 1: Type-token ratio for adjectives, 2 levels, 2 texts

Level	Text	Sum total of adjective tokens in corpus	Sum total of adjective types in corpus	Type/token ratio
Grade 8	film-descriptions	72	35	.49
	essay	222	84	.38
University	film-descriptions	244	124	.51
	essay	568	273	.48

As is to be expected, the larger number of adjectives in the essays as compared to the film descriptions correlates with a drop in the type-token ratio: the larger the number of tokens, the lower the type-token ratio. But the drop is much greater between the two sets of grade 8 texts than between the two sets of university texts. The main reason for this is that the relationship between text length and type-token ratio is not linear. The longer the text, the less the type-token ratio is affected by increases in text length. This means that provided texts are long enough, one may in fact compare type-token ratios from texts of differing lengths.

Because the sets of university texts satisfy the length requirement, we can treat them as directly comparable. The university ratios are as high as the ratio for the small grade 8 corpus and considerably higher than the ratio for the grade 8 essays. It is therefore safe to conclude that the university students use a much more varied inventory of adjectives than do the learners from grade 8.

To investigate further how the two groups differ, the relative frequency of individual adjectives was calculated. Tables 2 and 3 list the 13–14 most frequent adjectives in the essays written by the two groups of learners.

Table 2: Adjectives in essays written by grade 8 learners				Table 3: Adjectives in essays written by university students		
	%	% cumulative			%	% cumulative
big	5.9	5.9		political	4.6	4.6
old	5.0	10.9		violent	3.2	7.8
little	3.2	14.1		mental	2.1	9.9
bad	2.3	⎫		German	1.2	⎫
Danish	2.3	⎬ 21.0		physical	1.2	⎬ 13.5
different	2.3	⎭		young	1.2	⎭
good	1.8	⎫ 24.6		guilty	1.1	⎫ 15.7
red	1.8	⎭		innocent	1.1	⎭
hard	1.4	⎫		aggressive	0.9	⎫
poor	1.4	⎪		difficult	0.9	⎪
sure	1.4	⎬ 31.6		real	0.9	⎬ 21.1
thin	1.4	⎪		peaceful	0.9	⎪
wrong	1.4	⎭		recent	0.9	⎪
				whole	0.9	⎭

In addition to providing information of a quantitive kind about variation, the lists interestingly illuminate the content expressed by means of adjectives by learners from the two groups.

Type-token ratios for lexical variation should be used with caution when analysing learner language. In the first place, the ratio obtained is sensitive to the development of the content in the text. If one learner writes on five different topics within 200 words and another learner concentrates on one topic, the first learner will need more word-types – which does not prove that her vocabulary is more varied.

Secondly, learners may decide to make use of a restricted set of words in a certain communicative event, either because they avoid running the risk of using "difficult" words or because they do not experience the need to vary the vocabulary they use. This point becomes clear if one applies the type-token method to individual semantic units in a text. As an example, consider the unit "man" from the text discussed in chapter four p. 64. After one use of the noun phrase *a man,* the learner pronominalizes and uses the pronoun *he* all through the remainder of the text. This is operating at a minimal level of lexical variation, and one can expect this to reflect the low proficiency level of the learner (grade 8). In a comparable communicative event, a university student used the following: *the "anta-gonist", he, him, him, this man, his, the man, the man, the man, "our" man (not in Havana)*. This shows more variation, not so much because the learner uses *many* types but rather because the types are used in a varied way. A type-token analysis of the words used in referring to "man" in the two texts would reveal a slight difference, but the primary means of creating variation by *alternating* between various ways of referring would not be captured by the method.

5.2.2 Lexical density

A measure of the lexical density of a text can be obtained by calculating the ratio between the CONTENT WORDS, comprising the open word classes, and the FUNCTION WORDS, comprising the closed word classes. Nouns, verbs, adverbs and adjectives make up the classes which are "open" in the sense that the number of words in the class is not limited and can be extended. By contrast the "closed" word classes, determiners, pronouns, conjunctions, prepositions, etc typically contain a smaller, fixed number of words in each class.[3] The ratio between the open and closed words is an indication of how "dense" the text is. The underlying assumption is that as it is the content words which primarily convey information, a text is dense if it contains many content words relative to the number of function words. Let us return to the text analysed for lexical variation in 5.2.1 and illustrate the method of analysis.

The text contains 21 content words out of the total of 47 tokens. The lexical density of the text is calculated on the basis of the formula:

$$\text{lexical density} = \frac{\text{number of content words}}{\text{total number of word tokens}}$$

This gives us a ratio for the text of $\frac{21}{47} = 0.45$. Unlike the measure of lexical variation, this measure is not *systematically* dependent on the length of the text. It is therefore possible to compare ratios for lexical density for texts of different lengths. However it needs emphasizing that the shorter the text, the less reliable the figure obtained. By extending our analysis to 100 words of the same text we obtain a ratio of 0.38, which indicates that the 47 word long extract is not representative of the whole text with respect to lexical density.

The following is an excerpt from an essay written by an English 16-year-old pupil:

> Anyway, I went to the toilet and then went to go to wash my hands. Then suddenly I saw something being thrown from one cubicle over the division, into the next. After this came a shout. The next thing that happened was that a well built black man came running ...

The text is 50 words long and contains 24 content words, which gives a lexical density of 0.48. The figure for the whole essay is 0.49, so the excerpt is representative of the essay with respect to lexical density.

The native English text gives us some examples of what it is that creates high lexical density: adjectival modification of nouns (*a well built black man*), adverbial modification (*suddenly*), and omission of pronouns (*and then went ...*). Choice of sentence pattern also affects lexical density. There is one more closed class item in *I saw that something was thrown* than in the syntactic structure actually used in the text, *I saw something being thrown*. It can therefore be argued that the figure for lexical density measures the syntactic complexity of a text in addition to measuring richness of vocabulary.

5.3 Some principles for the selection of vocabulary

Our discussion so far has paid little attention to *which* words the learner knows. The main issues have been difference, captured in the notion of "word types", quantification and comparison. But supposing that a learner knows a fixed number of words, are there ways in which we can assess how *useful* these words are for the learner? The question is of central importance in the selection of vocabulary for teaching materials, especially at beginning and intermediate levels. We shall therefore present briefly three approaches to vocabulary selection which have been influential in deciding what should be taught to learners.

5.3.1 Frequency

The principle of frequency, often alluded to by publishers, rests on the assumption that the most frequent words are the most useful ones for learners. In fact this assumption only holds true for a very limited part of the vocabulary. But before we document this claim, there is a fundamental problem to discuss, namely that of "sampling". Frequency counts are based on samples of texts. How are these texts selected in the first place?

All available frequency lists for English (as well as for Danish) are based on written texts.[4] These lists are obviously only relevant for the spoken language to the extent that there is overlap between words used in spoken and written texts, and with the same frequency in the two types of texts. Certain words which are frequent in specific types of spoken language (eg gambits in conversation, cf chapter 4) only occur if the written texts contain genres which represent spoken language, like dramatic texts. But even in drama, gambits are of low frequency.

The sampling question is not just a problem of spoken versus written language. Within the wide field of written language, what sort of texts make up the corpus? For instance a frequency list for American English press reportage (Zettersten 1978) lists the following words among its 120 most frequent: *government, national, university, bill, states, program*. It is unlikely that these words would occur with the same high frequency in a sample of, say, literary texts.

Let us now turn to the frequency figures themselves and see what can be learned from these. In a recent analysis of a 250,000 word corpus of Danish fiction texts (Maegaard/Ruus 1981), it was found that only 15 words account for 25 % of the total number of words in the texts. Not surprisingly, these are all function words.[5] 50 % of all word tokens are covered by 76 word types, and 75 % of the words in the texts by 800 different words. Beyond this figure there is a drastic drop in the frequency of individual word types: to reach 88 % of all tokens requires 4128 types, the last of which only occur 4 times each in the whole of the corpus.

Results like these clearly indicate how limited the usefulness of frequency counts is for the selection of vocabulary. One can reasonably expect the 100–200 most frequent words to occur in most types of texts, ie they belong to a "common core" of vocabulary (but cf the example of *government, national,* etc. above, and the warning about differences between speech and writing). These words are therefore likely to be indispensable for the learner. The further we get beyond this very restricted set of words, the greater the dependency on the texts contained in the corpus, until we reach a point where the presence or absence of a word becomes very much a question of chance. This point is reached well below the level of 2000 words specificed in the official guidelines for English in the Folkeskole (Undervisnings-ministeriet 1976).

5.3.2 Availability

Availability studies are concerned with identifying which words are used in particular situations. One way to pinpoint availability is to give native speakers a topic or situation and ask them to write down the words which first come to mind. Possible topics might be "visiting a pub" or "parts of the body". Words mentioned by a high proportion of the informants are then considered the most available words, and these are assumed to be useful for a learner of that language.

Availability studies have the advantage of being able to throw up idioms and prefabricated patterns, whereas these are lost in frequency studies which operate with single words. A second advantage is that availability studies, to a greater extent than frequency studies, manifestly depend on the prior selection of topics and situations. This selection can be made on the basis of learners' interests and communication needs.

5.3.3 Coverage

High coverage words are words of such general meaning that they can be used in many situations. Typical examples are words like *get, go* and *put.* These enable learners to achieve a certain level of communicative competence fairly rapidly. They can be particularly useful when paraphrasing (cf the discussion of communication strategies in chapter 9), for instance referring to a 'puppy' or a 'kitten' as a "young" dog or cat, or when using *get* as an imprecise substitute

87

for *receive* or *become*.

However, a word of caution is needed about the usefulness of high coverage words. First, high coverage words are useful for production, but less so for reception. A native speaker would typically say *puppy* or *kitten*, rather than use a paraphrase. Second, high coverage words often become highly automatized, so that they tend to be overused. Accordingly, learners may produce texts with low lexical variation, as illustrated by the following excerpt from a PIF film description, written by a learner in grade 8:[6]

> Then he got angry, and he got his finger into the phone and he coulden't get it out. He ran out to the kitchen and want to make coffee but he got the water over him, evry thing was going rong until he got his coffee.

Although native speakers also occasionally overuse high coverage words, the learner who wrote this text could well be expected to improve it by incorporating some of the following lexical items: *become, get stuck, remove, spill, drink*.

We have presented three principles for the selection of vocabulary which are sometimes referred to in descriptions of teaching materials. Of these, 'availability' seems better suited than the two others to select vocabulary relative to learners' communicative needs, specified in terms of what topics the learners would like to talk about productively and/or understand receptively within specific types of communicative events. We return to this issue in our discussion of the "threshold level" approach to specifying teaching objectives (chapter 13).

5.4 The structure of learner vocabulary

We now go on to consider what structure the learner's interlanguage vocabulary may be supposed to have. We assume that the structure of the vocabulary is to some extent conditioned by the way the learner has been taught, and that the structure of the vocabulary has some conditioning effect on the way new words are learnt.

We want to consider three structuring principles: (1) the learner relates L2 words directly to what they refer to in the world around her; (2) the learner relates L2 words to Ll words; and (3) the learner relates new L2 words to already learned L2 words. Other principles, for instance phonological or orthographic, have also been suggested but will not be considered below.

5.4.1 Relating L2 words directly to their referents

The "direct method" in foreign language teaching implies that the learner learns the foreign language by relating this directly to objects, situations, concepts, actions, etc. One could refer to this as referential learning and say that those parts of a learner's vocabulary which are established according to this principle are *referentially organized*.

Using a direct approach in the teaching of beginners, the teacher relies heavily on objects, visual representations, and actions. Learners are encouraged to make a direct connection between an object and the word referring to this in the foreign language. The world outside the classroom is brought in by means of wallcharts, slides, sound and video tapes. The underlying assumption is that foreign language learners have already established relevant concepts in their primary socialization in the native language, and that the learning task is one of learning new "names" for familiar "objects".

One problem with this approach is the assumption that concepts are neutral with respect to both the native and the foreign language. Even with closely related cultures there are many areas in which this is not tenable.

Another problem is that there is no compelling reason to assume that because the teacher introduces a new word referentially, eg by showing the learners a blue ball and saying *ball*, the resulting representation of the word *ball* in the learner's IL vocabulary is purely referential in character. The learner has to *interpret* the meaning of the word *ball* and decide that it means 'ball' and not 'round' or 'blue'. This interpretation is a result of a process of guessing, in which the learner activates various types of knowledge: knowledge of the world, situation-specific knowledge, knowledge of the native language and of the L2. It is therefore most improbable that the net result of this should be a representation of the word which has no connection whatsoever to these other types of knowledge.

Finally, even if we assume that the result of the learning process could be a referential type of representation of the word's meaning – an assumption which would be more realistic in connection with L1 than with L2 vocabulary – it is very unlikely that this would be a sufficiently economic way of organizing the whole of the vocabulary, as the structure of both the L1 and the IL vocabularies would reflect the structure of the world as perceived by the learner. We shall come shortly to the structure of L2 vocabulary, but first consider the relationship between L1 and IL vocabulary.

5.4.2 L1 – IL vocabulary

In considering the structure of a learner's IL vocabulary, an essential question is how this is influenced by the structure of the learner's L1. We shall approach this question by first reporting a series of experiments carried out with Dutch learners of English (Kellerman 1978).

The assumption underlying the experiments is that a potentially important factor in the development of learners' IL vocabulary is "transfer" from their L1 (for the notion of transfer, see chapter 11). Learners establish translation links between words in the two vocabularies and transfer at least part of the meaning potential from the word in the L1 to the corresponding IL word. Readiness to transfer is thought to be particularly strong in the case of COGNATE forms in the two languages,. ie words which are formally similar, like Danish–English *drømme–dream, gå–go, ja–yes*. The purpose of the Dutch experiments was to find out whether in such cases learners were more prone to transfer certain types of meaning than others.

The experiment was conducted in two steps. The purpose of the first part was to investigate whether a group af 50 Dutch native speakers would agree which of 17 different meanings of the Dutch verb *breken* ('break') were most central to the meaning potential of the word. This was tested by presenting the informants with 17 cards. On each of them was a sentence in which *breken* was used with a specific meaning. Some idea of the range of meanings can be obtained from the following list:

de golven braken op de rotsen
(the waves broke against the rocks)

zijn stem brak toen hij 13 was
(his voice broke when he was 13)

't kopje brak
(the cup broke)

zijn val werd door 'n boom gebroken
(his fall was broken by a tree)

hij brak zijn woord
(he broke his word)

na 't ongeluk is hij 'n gebroken man geworden
(after the accident he has become a broken man)

hij brak zijn been
(he broke his leg)

zij brak 't wereldrecord
(she broke the world record)

zij brak zijn hart
(she broke his heart)

The informants were asked to sort the cards into piles according to "similarity of meaning". A computer analysis of the results indicated that the informants had based their classification of the 17 *breken* examples on two criteria: (1) *concreteness,* which placed *the cup broke* and *he broke his word* at opposite ends of a continuum; (2) *coreness* (what people consider the most central meaning of a word), placing *he broke his leg* and *a broken man* at the core-end and *she broke the world record* and *his voice broke* at the non-core end of the continuum.

The results are summarised in the following table.

Table 4: Rank order of 9 meanings of breken, according to criteria of 'concreteness' and 'coreness'

Concreteness	rank order	Coreness	rank order
cup	1	leg	1
leg	2	cup	2
fall ⎤		man	3
waves ⎦	3/4	heart	4
voice	5	waves	5
record	6	word	6
man	7	record	7
heart	8	fall	8
word	9	voice	9

In the second task, the 9 Dutch sentences listed above were presented to 210 Dutch students and schoolchildren, all of whom were learning English. The informants were asked to decide whether *breken* in each sentence could be translated by *break*. In point of fact, in all the 9 sentences *break* is perfectly possible in English. The result of this transferability experiment was the following rating:

leg – heart – cup – man – word – record – waves – fall – voice

where "break a leg" was considered most transferable and "his voice broke" least transferable. Comparing this list with the results listed in table 4, it is easy to see that there is a high correlation between the ratings for coreness and the transferability judgements, and a fairly high correlation between the concreteness ratings and the transferability judgements. This indicates that learners base their assumptions about word meaning in the L2 on the way word meaning is organized in the L1, with features such as coreness and concreteness potentially relevant for transferability judgements. A corollary of this is that learners are reluctant to translate literally in sentences with more metaphorical use of language.

These findings hold for one isolated part of the lexicon of Dutch and English, but they corroborate anecdotal evidence about Danish and English learners of each other's language. Such findings are of course more likely to apply between languages which are as closely related as Dutch, Danish and English, and less so between one of these and a non-Germanic language.

The *breken/break* example illustrates a situation in which there is exact semantic and formal equivalence between two languages, at least with respect to the 9 meanings of *breken* investigated. Even so, learners hesitate to transfer in certain cases. The reverse situation is found when there are cognate word forms in L1 and L2 but different meanings, words usually referred to as "false friends" (eg Danish/English: *aktuel/actual, eventuelt/eventually*). Here the learner may be led astray by a false friend into transferring word meanings from L1 which are inapplicable in L2 (eg using "an actual event" for "a current event").

The Dutch learners who participated in the transferability experiment knew that the form *break* exists in English. Sometimes learners, especially at the elementary level, who do not know the L2 word, will invent words by applying "conversion rules" of a morphological and orthographic or phonological kind. Consider the following examples of this:

we make ['pɛɪpskɛ:vz] ("we produce waste paper baskets")
it's ['ståɪŋ] in Danish ("it's written in Danish")

In the first example, the learner apparently knows the English word *paper*. He stablishes a compound based on the Danish word *papirkurv*, converting [kuɔ] phonologically into [kɛ:v]. In addition, he adds the English plural morpheme (Danish would have *-e*). The *s* in [pɛɪps] can either be another plural marker or – a more interesting possibility – the Danish segment used for compounding (though not in fact used in combination with Danish *papir*). In the second example, there is no phonological conversion but conversion at the morphological level (Danish *stå+ing*).

The examples in this section so far have been of concepts for which there are equivalents in other languages. It is however easy to find concepts which are difficult if not impossible to convert. What would be an exact equivalent in English of Danish *hygge, gider ikke,* or even *morgenbrød* or *parcelhus?* Both the exact referential meaning and all the connotations which form part of the terms for Danish native speakers are virtually impossible to render in any foreign language. Such concepts are most likely to be learnt in a context of use, whether in direct experience, or in Danish texts which make their meaning clear.

5.4.3 Relating L2 words to familiar L2 words

For advanced learners, who have a fairly large vocabulary, it seems plausible that they try to fit new L2 words into an existing L2 structure. In other words, we assume that advanced learners of an L2 function in much the same way as native speakers of that language. It is probable that there are structuring principles which underlie the vocabulary of *any* language and which enable language users to place words in relation to other words so as to form semantic networks. We shall briefly discuss some of these principles in relation to English.

Consider the following mixed bag of lexical items:

child   old   flower   lend   young   sell
cat   hyacinth   parent   buy   animal   borrow.

Anyone familiar with English would, if asked to group the words according to a principle of relatedness of meaning, produce pairs as follows:

parent/child   old/young   buy/sell
borrow/lend   flower/hyacinth   cat/animal.

The principles guiding such a choice include three types of relationship:

- hyponymy (or inclusion), eg *cat* is a hyponym of *animal* and *hyacinth* of *flower*,
- antonymy (or oppositeness), eg *old* and *young*,
- converseness, eg *parent* and *child*, *buy* and *sell*, *borrow* and *lend*.

For an account of this complex topic, it is necessary to consult textbooks on semantics. For present purposes it is sufficient to stress that the organizing principle of lexis we are concerned with here is the relations between words which make up a lexical set.[7] The meaning of a word is determined by its relationship to other words with which is contrasts, for instance by a relationship of conversenees or hyponymy. Examples of such lexical fields on which detailed analysis has been done are kinship and colour terms, in which the structuring principles are relatively easily identifiable.

It must be admitted that few lexical fields are so neatly structured that it is possible to make systematic use of relations between words when introducing these to learners. Still, an awareness of such relations can be of considerable help to intermediate and advanced learners. Experienced teachers frequently make relationships within the L2 vocabulary clear and explicit when they introduce new words.

A special type of structuring principle within vocabulary has to do with the links between a lexical item and the words it keeps company or COLLOCATES with. *Tea* can be *strong,* but not *heavy,* whereas a person can be a *heavy drinker* but not a *strong drinker.* There are many restrictions on which words collocate with which. Adjectives like *nice* and *good* collocate with a large number of nouns, animate and inanimate, *handsome* has a more restricted range of application (*man/present/...*), while *rancid* collocates almost exclusively with *butter.*

When a new lexical item is introduced to learners it may be a good idea also to introduce the most common collocations into which the word enters. For instance, beginners will learn that *kettle* collocates with *put on* and *boil* (even if it is more logical to think of the water rather than the kettle boiling). When learners commit collocational errors, the teacher may not be able to explain the error but only state that word x is not used together with word y. This is understandable since there is often no logic behind the collocational restrictions on a word (cf the *strong/heavy* example).

Having a word in one's vocabulary includes knowing the most frequent collocations of that word. CLOZE-procedure is a test or exercise which, among other things, tests the student's mastery of collocations. In a cloze test, a text has had every n'th (eg 7th or 9th) word removed from it, and the learner has to fill in the missing words, one word for each blank. The appropriate word is listed on the right in the following example:

Gus had ..... the office against all   held
opposition for the ..... ten or fifteen   past
years, and from the ..... things looked,   way
he would continue being assessor.

It is assumed that the more collocations the learner knows, the better she is able to foresee, for each blank in the text, which words are the most probable ones to occur (eg "*holding* office" and "the *past* ten years").

5.5 Lexical inferencing

We have discussed the nature of IL vocabulary by considering the learning of L2 words in relation to their referents, links between the L1 and IL vocabulary, and L2–L2 links. We shall conclude this section by reporting a small-scale empirical investigation which was designed to show what sources groups of learners draw on when making qualified guesses about the meaning of unknown lexical items, a procedure we refer to as LEXICAL INFERENCING.

Small groups of intermediate learners were presented with unseen written texts about smoking and related health problems. In each text 20 lexical items were underlined and the groups were asked to discuss the meaning of these. The discussion, or "thinking-aloud session", was recorded. Examples below are drawn from the transcripts of the recorded group discussions.

Three types of cues to meaning can be identified: contextual, interlingual, and intralingual (Carton 1971). When using CONTEXTUAL CUES learners draw on their "knowledge of the world", especially in relation to the topic in question, as well as on the immediate linguistic context of the lexical item. For example, when confronted with the word *vapour*, students come up with *pollution* and *tar*, reasonable guesses at substances related to the dangers of smoking.

INTERLINGUAL CUES draw on learners' L1 and knowledge of other foreign languages. Our data contain examples both of learners benefiting from interlingual similarities and of learners being misled: *to increase* is interpreted as *at indkredse* (to delimit) and *physician* as *fysiker* (physicist). Examples of helpful interlingual cues are loan words common to the two languages, eg *nicotine* (from French), *stimulant* (from Latin) and *psychological* (from Greek).

INTRALINGUAL CUES are supplied by the target language, which presupposes a reasonable knowledge of the L2 for them to be used. Exploiting cues of a morphological kind, learners infer the meaning of *a narrowing* from the adjective *narrow*, *deadly* from *dead*, and *anxiety* from *anxious*. Likewise, learners make use of their knowledge that the notion of agency is expressed by the suffixes *-or* or *-er* (eg *operator* or *baker*) and that *-ive* indicates "having the property of" in eg *suggestive* or *addictive*.

The text below[8] is an extract from three learners' discussion of the term *addictive*. The sentence the word occurs in reads:

"You can regard it (the withdrawal symptom) as a mild syndrome, but it is a withdrawal syndrome and nicotine is an *addictive* drug."

Text 11
B det er nok noget med
A afhængig eller vanedannende eller sådan noget
C addictive addictive ja hvad helvede kan det betyde i den her for-
    bindelse – – – addictive stuff – eller addictive – – det kan
5   både være et farligt stof
A vanedannende
C kan vi ikke finde frem til et eller andet der minder om addictive –
    er der ikke noget fra latin
B åh nej
10 C addere – hvad betyder addere på dansk
A addere
B addere
C ovenikommende – sådan kan det da – kender vi ikke et eller an-
    det ord addictive drug –
15 B jeg har hørt det der i en sang eller sådan noget det der "I'm an
    addict"
C kan du huske sådan et par linier omkring det
B sådan noget med "you're an addict"
C hvad betyder det
20 B det ved jeg ikke
C addictive og nicotine er et

97

B det der drug hvad var det nu det betød

C drug – et stof – det kan også betyde noget andet er der ikke noget der hedder a drugstore eller sådan noget lignende

25 A en drugstore det er jo bare et værtshus eller sådan noget

C ja drug – drug store nej – addictive det var det vi kom fra –
der er uendelig mange muligheder altså synes jeg selv om vi har

B ja det kan – et eller andet stof ja

A det er garanteret vanedannende

30 C ja – der står – man kan se det som et mildt symptom – men det
er abstinens symptom og nikotin er altså et eller andet vanedannende – skal vi skrive det

A ja

B ja

The text illustrates how several hypotheses about word meaning compete with one another. A suggests "vanedannende" (correctly) in line 2, but C has a hunch that *addictive* is related to *adding* (line 10). Contextual cues are drawn on with the references to a song (lines 15–16); the fact that *addictive* collocates with *drug* is explored (1. 22), and again we have contextual inferencing in *drugstore* (lines 24–26). C finally gives in and accepts A's initial hypothesis, repeated in line 29. As we know the identity of the participants, we can add that what is at work here is a boy (C) who finds it difficult to give in, and a girl (A) who is too reticent to press her point.

We have rounded off this section on learner vocabulary with an account of lexical inferencing procedures. Our assumption is that learner inferencing indicates ways in which learners' vocabulary is structured. In other words, the fact that three types of cues (contextual, interlingual, intralingual) are followed up supports the hypothesis that there are three ways of storing lexical items, referentially, in relation to L1 words, and in relation to L2 words.

5.6 What does it mean to know a word?

By way of summary, we can state that the following conditions must hold for a learner to fully "know" a word:

- the learner must know the full meaning potential of the word, not just one specific meaning
- the learner must know what the appropriate situations are for using the word
- the learner must know in what ways the word can combine with other words (eg collocational restrictions)
- the learner must know the relations between the word and other words within a lexical set (relations of hyponymy, antonymy etc).

There is one issue which we have so far completely avoided, namely the familiar distinction between 'active' and 'passive' vocabulary. Not only are these concepts terminologically misleading – in no sense are reading or listening "passive" activities. More importantly, even though it seems intuitively probable that learners can understand far more than they can express, a binary distinction between active and passive lexical knowledge is too crude.

The inferencing examples showed that learners may be able to understand words they do not know already. This is often possible with closely related languages. To quote a particularly clear instance of this, Danes reading or listening to Swedish will be able to understand a fair number of words, primarily by utilizing interlingual cues from Danish. In this situation we would probably not want to say that Danes have a receptive *vocabulary* in Swedish: There is no reason to believe that somewhere in their brains Danes have a number of words stored, marked as being Swedish, and which can only be activated receptively. Rather, we would say that Danes have the ability to use inferencing procedures by means of which they can reconstruct the meaning of the Swedish words that they do not "know", in the sense of having the words stored in the brain as words belonging to Swedish.

Even when dealing with languages which are not as closely related as Danish and Swedish, we can distinguish between learners being able to *make sense* of a word and learners *knowing* a word. The latter is obviously a precondition for being able to use a word for productive purposes. But even when we would say that a learner knows a word as a word belonging to a foreign language, knowing it is a matter of degree rather than a question of either/or. There are words which learners know in the sense of knowing what the words mean whenever they come across them, but which it is impossible to activate for productive purposes. There are words which it is possible to retrieve only with considerable effort. Some words are momentarily inaccessible (the tip-of-the-tongue phenomenon). And finally there are words which become activated almost automatically when a speaker forms a particular communicative intention. Rather than make the simplistic opposition between "active" and "passive" vocabulary, we should think of vocabulary knowledge as a continuum between ability to make sense of a word and ability to activate the word automatically for productive purposes.

Footnotes to chapter 5

1. These core meanings are based on the *Advanced Learner's Dictionary*, 1980 edition.
2. Vocabulary tests for global proficiency are inherently problematical because vocabulary is so closely linked to topic areas. A particular vocabulary test will consequently have content validity (see chapter 15) for very specific purposes only. In addition, vocabulary tests frequently suffer from the limitation that they test vocabulary out of context, ie isolated words.
3. There are difficulties of classification, for instance with adverbs some of which fit into the open and others into the closed classes. For a discussion see Quirk/Greenbaum/Leech/Svartvik 1972, pp 44–47.
4. A corpus of spoken English, namely the Lund/London corpus, has recently been made available on computer tape, with a description in book form (Svartvik/Eeg-Olofsson/Forsheden/Oreström/Thavenius 1982). The book includes a table of the 100 most frequent words in this spoken corpus, contrasted with those in two corpora of written English.
5. The ten most frequent words are *og, det, i, at, han, var, jeg, en, ikke, til*, which correspond to *and, the/this/that, in, that/to* (particle), *he, was/were, I, a(n)/one, not, to*.
6. PIF-learner no. 91.
7. Due to the brevity of the discussion of some basic semantic concepts we have not observed the distinction between sense and meaning. Section 5.4.3 discusses the sense of words exclusively and not their full meaning. We have also avoided using technical terms such as 'sense relations'. For a detailed discussion of the distinction between 'sense' and 'meaning', see Lyons 1977.
8. PIF-data, level 1 gs, collected by Målfrid Berg-Sørensen and Finn Haastrup. Translated into English the text reads: it is something like/ dependent on or habit-forming or something like that/ addictive addictive, what the hell do you think it means in this context, addictive stuff or addictive – it may be a dangerous drug as well as/ habit-forming/ can't we find something which sounds like addictive – isn't there something in Latin/ oh no/ addere what does addere mean in Danish/

addere/ addere/ added to – like that – don't we know some word or other/ addictive drug/ I have heard it in a song or something like that this expression "I'm
an addict"/ can you recall a few phrases before and after it/ something like
"you're an addict"/ what does it mean/ I don't know/ addictive and nicotine is a/
what did you say drug meant/ drug – dope – it may have a different meaning –
isn't there something called a drugstore or the like/ a drugstore – that is just a
pub or something like that/ that's it – drug – drug store no – addictive this was
where we left off – there seem to be lots of possibilities I think even if we have/ yes
it may be – dope of some kind/ I bet it is habit-forming/ well – it says – you may
regard it as a mild symptom – it *is* withdrawal symptom and nicotine is well
something which is habit-forming – shall we write that/ yes/ yes/.

Chapter 5. Follow-ups

1. Compare the principles adopted for vocabulary selection in two or more textbooks for beginners or intermediate learners. Base your analysis on the
   teacher's guide as well as on the texts themselves.
2. Contrast a page of a novel such as *Oliver Twist* with the equivalent pages in a
   simplified edition of the novel, working out the lexical density for both. In what
   other ways has the original text been modified?
3. Arrange an availability study with a group of native speakers. Everybody writes
   down the words that first come to mind when hearing a concept such as 'job',
   'unemployment' or 'race'. Compare results and discuss the degree of overlap.
   Could the results be used in planning what to teach learners of the language?
4. Translate a text from Danish into English. Identify cognates and false friends.
   Are there problems due to differences in collocational restrictions?
5. Arrange an inferencing exercise as in 5.5. Are there examples of the three types
   of cues discussed in the chapter? examples of combinations of cues? examples of
   contradictory cues? Is there a causal link between the types of inferencing the
   learners resort to and the teaching to which they have been exposed?
6. Are the concepts "active" and "passive" vocabulary as potentially misleading as
   the text suggests?

Chapter 5. Sources and further reading

Pioneering work within vocabulary analysis of learner texts has been done by Linnarud (1975) and (1976), particularly on lexical density and lexical variation. For
an annotated bibliography of research within vocabulary in second language learning see Meara 1983.

Our description of the selection of vocabulary in teaching materials is inspired by
Howatt 1974. For a discussion of simplified reading texts see Davies/Widdowson
1974. For processes of lexical simplification see Blum-Kulka/Levenston 1983.

For an up-to-date summary of Kellerman's work on transfer see Kellerman (in press). Our discussion of semantic issues is based on Lyons 1977, which is a demanding standard work. For a more popular introduction to semantics see Palmer 1976. On semantics and language teaching see van Buren 1975. For Danish learning problems see Davidsen-Nielsen/Færch/Harder 1982. Lexical inferencing is based on Carton 1971 and Færch 1983a.

Chapter six:
Grammar

Grammar comprises syntax and morphology. Syntax has received considerable attention in recent decades, whereas morphology has been relegated to a less prominent position. The main reason for this is that linguists have been concerned to discover the nature of linguistic creativity, the human ability to comprehend and produce an infinite number of sentences not yet encountered, and this has been assumed to be intimately related to the productivity of syntactic rules.

True though this undoubtedly is, holding up syntax as the most productive area of language should not be taken to imply that syntax is in any sense more important for communicative purposes than, say, morphology or vocabulary. The importance of syntax is of a different sort.

Both Danish and English are highly ANALYTIC languages. Word order helps express specific types of meaning, for instance agentivity (compare "the child scolded the teacher" with "the teacher scolded the child"). This means that Danish learners of English are used to word order being strictly fixed. Learners with L1s which are more SYNTHETIC, ie languages which like Latin express many types of meaning by means of affixes or declension, and which have a freer word order, have difficulty in learning an analytic language because they are not accustomed to paying sufficient attention to word order. The reverse situation, speaking an analytic language and learning a synthetic one, is equally difficult, as when Danes attempt in vain to identify subjects and objects in a Latin text by means of word order only.

Inexperienced learners are probably much less conscious of word order characteristics than of vocabulary. This implies that they may be more inclined to transfer L1 syntactic patterns to L2 than to transfer vocabulary. The fact that the similarities between Danish and English syntactic structures outnumber whatever differences there are between the two languages makes it possible for Danish

103

learners to make extensive use of L1 structures in IL speech, and to gradually modify L1 structures as learning progresses.

This book is not the place for a systematic contrastive description of Danish and English grammatical structures.[1] What we shall do is to present results from various analyses of learner language which serve the dual purpose of exemplifying interlanguage grammar analysis and of describing a number of characteristic aspects of the learning of English grammatical structures by Danish learners. Finally we shall consider the nature of grammatical rules.

6.1 Analysis of errors in written texts

In this section we present some results from the PIF analysis of errors in essays and film descriptions written by learners at different levels. The main focus will be on grammatical errors made by Gymnasium learners, but in order to put these in a wider perspective, we also consider texts written by learners from grade 8, as well as errors in orthography, punctuation and vocabulary. Table 5 provides details of the three sets af data.

Table 5: Text sample used for error analysis

Grade	8	1gs	3gs
Numbers of informants	12	12	11
Total number of words	4846	7859	8892
Average length of individual essays in words	404	655	808

An analysis of all errors identified in the texts (for the procedure of error identification, see the description in chapter 19) resulted in the following figures, divided into four broad categories.

On the basis of these figures alone, it would be possible to answer questions such as "are lexical errors more frequent than grammatical errors in texts written by learners at grade 3g?". However, the

In order to interpret these figures, it is necessary to scrutinise closely the error types which actually occur. We shall discuss each of these.

(a) Concord. These are errors in subject-verb concord, following either a pronominal or a non-pronominal subject. Concord errors at the Gymnasium levels do not usually occur when the subject is a countable noun and the verb follows immediately. They primarily occur in the following situations:

1. the sentence is initiated with *there* ("There *are* violence as well in the school")
2. the subject is not a countable noun with singular and plural form ("... the police *has* never found his mordereres")
3. the subject is an indefinite pronoun ("Some *maintains* that ...")
4. the verb is divided from the head noun in the subject ("The fights in Ireland *is* not because of political problems ...")

(b) Determiners. Most of these errors involve using *the* instead of no determiner in noun phrases which would contain a determiner in Danish, typically when marking generic reference:

"*The* violence has been developed ..."/ "*The* schools are also a place where violence ..."

or with reference to institutions, following a preposition:

"... in *the* school you do not call it violence but mobing".

Overuse of determiners when marking generic reference is by far the most frequent type of determiner error at 3g level; whereas the "in the school" type is common at level 1gs but hardly ever occurs in 3g.

(c) Predicate. These errors are a very heterogeneous group. Approximately half the errors are borderline cases between grammar and use of idioms, as illustrated by the following example:

"... it's of course also good to see movies about people who *have it worse* than you".

Such errors are often caused by transfer from Danish. A less frequent group of predicate errors are due to wrong verbal complementation, eg:

"... when you walk in New-York in the night you can *risk to be dagged*".

(d) Verb phrase. Errors of tense, aspect, auxiliary and modal verbs, and concord have been analysed separately. This category covers all other verb phrase errors. Most frequent are morphological errors ("... the man ran after the woman he loved and *beated* her"), whereas errors in the use of *do* as a prop word are extremely rare at these levels.

(e) Tense. These errors, which are much more frequent in 1gs than in 3gs, mostly involve a shift to the present tense in a context which requires past reference:

"It wasn't that kind of violence we have now, but *it's* surely a start to it".

Interestingly, there is only one occurrence of a learner using a perfect tense instead of a past tense form ("The picture which I've seen some minutes ago") and very few examples of wrong reference to the future ("They say that if their demand is not being followed they *are going to* kill the people ...").

(f) Noun phrase. This category does not contain errors of number or determiner usage, but typically errors of nominalization of adjectives or numerals:

"You also see some reel pictures like *two* shaking hands",

wrong compounding:

"To get to a quite other *violence-problem* it is the terrorism in Germany"

or lack of pronominalization:

"It's very confused to see the film the first time but after having seen it two or three times you begin to understand a bit of *the film*".

108

(g) Word order. By far the most frequent type of word order error is adverbial placement, both in 1g and 3g texts:

"All kind of violence *dayly* take place in all kinds of ways at all kinds of places"
"Violence is *today* a very big problem...".

Wrong inversion does not seem to present many problems at these levels (see below for the situation at grade 8).

(h) Adverbial phrase. These errors are all caused by the learner choosing a wrong structure for expressing an adverbial phrase:

"For some weeks ago, I read ..."
"... they were looking all over *for to find guns".*

(i) Aspect. This type of error is less frequent in the PIF data than we had expected. When the number of aspect errors is related to the number of finite verbs in the corpus (1133 in the 1gs texts and 1179 in the 3g texts), it is found that only 2 % of the verb phrases at 1g level and 1.5 % at 3g level are wrongly marked for aspect. It is more usual for learners, especially at the lower level, to overuse the progressive aspect where none is required than vice versa: At level 1g, the ratio between these two types of aspect error is 10:1, at level 3g it is 3:1. The relatively low figures for aspect errors must in part be due to the nature of the two writing tasks.

(j) Number. A few of these errors are due to learners not marking for 'distributive plural': "...they [people] are blaming them [the terrorists] that innocent people become the victims of *their act* [ie acts]".
    Other errors, especially at level 1gs, are of the type *"informations"*, *"peoples"* (for *people*).

These results suggest that when learners leave the Gymnasium, they generally know how to handle English morphology; that some aspects of English syntax (determiner usage and adverbial placement) remain a problem; that certain error types which occur at the Folkeskole level are very infrequent at the Gymnasium level (use of *do;* inversion; aspect); and finally that *many* errors, broadly categorized as 'predicate', 'noun phrase' or 'adverbial phrase', are borderline errors between grammar and idiom usage, and seem to be modelled on Danish.

Certain categories of function words, like prepositions and conjunctions, have not been covered so far in the analysis of grammatical errors. Like idioms they belong to the border area between grammar and vocabulary. We shall complete our description of grammar errors in written texts at the 1gs and 3gs levels by considering the most frequent type of errors in the selection of function words, namely errors in prepositions. At both 1gs and 3gs levels, 7.3 % of all prepositions used are erroneous. One might speculate that the reason for this apparent lack of progress is a greater inventory of prepositions at grade 3gs. However, both levels have exactly the same type/token ratio (0.47). If we assume that this PIF result also holds for other Danish learners, we might conclude that Gymnasium learners do not seem to improve their knowledge of when to use which prepositions. This is an area which needs much more systematic treatment in teaching – which presupposes the availability of both good descriptions of prepositional usage in English[3] and contrastive descriptions of prepositions in Danish and English.

6.2 Analysis of errors in speech and writing

The results presented above give a very simplified picture of grammatical errors in learner language. Among the most obvious limitations are that:

– within each group of learners (cf table 5), individual variation has been levelled out,
– the analyses focussed on errors exclusively and did not consider to what extent learners knew how to use grammatical structures correctly,
– the analyses were based on written language texts only, and variation in the individual learner's spoken and written interlanguage was not considered.

The following example (based on Færch 1983c) illustrates how each of these considerations can be tackled in learner language analyses.

110

To do so it is necessary to narrow the focus to specific types of grammatical error.

The area investigated was subject-verb inversion following an initial adverbial element. This is obligatory in Danish in all cases, but restricted in English to certain types of adverbial phrases (cf Quirk/Greenbaum/Leech/Svartvik 1972, chapter 8, Davidsen-Nielsen/Færch/Haarder 1982:44ff.):

Danish "I går *mødte jeg* en flot ung fyr"
English "Yesterday *I met* a handsome young guy".

The analysis was based on PIF texts produced by 12 grade 8 learners: an oral film description, a written film description, and an essay (cf chapter 18). In each text, clauses were identified which would have inverted word order in Danish because of an initial adverbial element. The result of this phase of the analysis is presented in table 9, line A. The next phase involved calculating how many of these English clauses actually did contain inverted word order, and whether inversion was correct or erroneous. These results are listed in lines B–D, table 9. As can be seen, the essays contained the largest number of inversion errors (16.7 %), followed by the written film descriptions (9.2 %). It is striking that the oral film descriptions contain no inversion errors whatsoever, and that none of the initial adverbial elements was such that inversion was required in English (cf line C).

Table 9 takes up two of the three problems mentioned above (errors – non-errors and speech – writing), but it still levels out individual variation. In order to investigate this, a calculation was made, see table 10, of how many learners made inversion errors

– consistently, line x,
– variably, line y,
– or not at all, line z.

The results show that in the essays, more than half the learners make inversion errors (one consistently, the rest variably). In the film descriptions, only one third of the learners make inversion

Table 9: Errors/non-errors in inversion in three tasks

		Oral film description	Written film descr.	Essays
(A)	Number of clauses in which inversion would be obligatory in Danish	34	65	84
(B)	Number of clauses with inversion, erroneous in English	0	6 = 9.2 %	14 = 16.7 %
(C)	Number of clauses with inversion, correct in English	0	0	0
(D)	Number of clauses with non-inverted syntactically de-termined word order	34 = 100 %	59 = 90.8 %	70 = 83.3 %

Table 10: Number of learners making inversion errors

(x)	Number of students who use inversion only	0	0	1
(y)	Number of students who use inversion and non-inversion variably	0	4	6
(z)	Number of students who use non-inversion exclusively	12	8	5

errors (variably). And as could be seen in table 9, no learner makes inversion errors in the oral film descriptions.

At first sight, the inversion results in the three tasks look surprising. One might reason that with more time available, the better the learner's chances of finding the correct rule. As compared with writing away quietly, speaking in the language laboratory with a cassette recorder switched on might be expected to increase, rather than reduce, the transfer of L1 grammatical structures. Why then

112

do the learners produce correct English sentences in the most demanding situation, and make consistently more errors the more time they have at their disposal to 'monitor' speech (cf chapter 8)? The answer is probably that the learners at this level have practised English structures containing non-inversion to such a degree that, as long as they perform without thinking too much about it, they can perform correctly. Their less monitored performance is highly 'automatized' (cf chapter 11). In situations which allow them to be more conscious about their language, some of the learners become uncertain about the rule and at times end up writing what they would *not* say spontaneously.

This uncertainty is in fact directly attested in one of the essays. The learner's handwritten text reads:

"... if you run with the ball ~~the defender~~ would the defender kick you".

The result of the learner monitoring his language is in this case a self-correction, leading to an error.

The 'de-automatization' effect of self-monitoring can be compared to the well-known situation of opening a bicycle combination lock. We can perform the operation of pressing and pulling the right buttons a thousand times, without thinking about it. But when lending the bicycle to a friend, we may have difficulty explaining which buttons to pull and which to press, and if we then try to demonstrate it at the same time, we fail. One might say that we switch from a 'skill-based' type of performance to a more cognitively based performance, and that we run into difficulty if we do not have a cognitive representation which matches our skills. To return to the grade 8 learners, it is a fair guess that the written texts would have contained fewer inversion errors if the learners had cognitively *known* the correct rules for inversion/non-inversion in Danish and English.

6.3 Types of grammatical rules

We demonstrated above that there was variation in the inversion rules followed by some of the learners at grade 8 in three different tasks. In doing so, we conflated two distinctly different ways of talking about rules:

(1) LINGUISTIC RULES: rules etablished in order to account for language data, formulated in linguistic terminology and belonging to a specific model af language description.
(2) PSYCHOLINGUISTIC RULES: rules as psychological entities, activated by individuals when they produce language.

In 6.2 we took as our starting point linguistic rules, established on the basis of learner language data, and 'projected' them onto the learners' skill-based or cognitively-based representation of language. This is defensible as long as we make it clear that in referring to learners' rules as psychological entities, we do not imply that the rules are *psychologically* represented in a way which necessarily looks like the *linguistic* formulation of the rules. Linguistic models provide convenient and, hopefully, adequate ways of talking *about* language. The extent to which they can be assumed to have psycholinguistic validity is a very debatable issue (see for instance Gregersen/Hermann 1978 and chapter 11 for a discussion of this).

Another distinction needs to be observed between

(3) NATIVE RULES: used by native speakers or rules which aim at being descriptively adequate for the performance of native speakers
(4) INTERRULES: rules used by learners of a foreign language or formulated for the benefit of foreign language learners.

The four types of rules are brought together in figure 8.

We need to be more specific about the differences between linguistic rules of type C and D. Ideally, native speaker linguistic rules (C) exhaustively describe the language performance of native speakers. By means of C-rules, one can 'generate' all grammatical structures

114

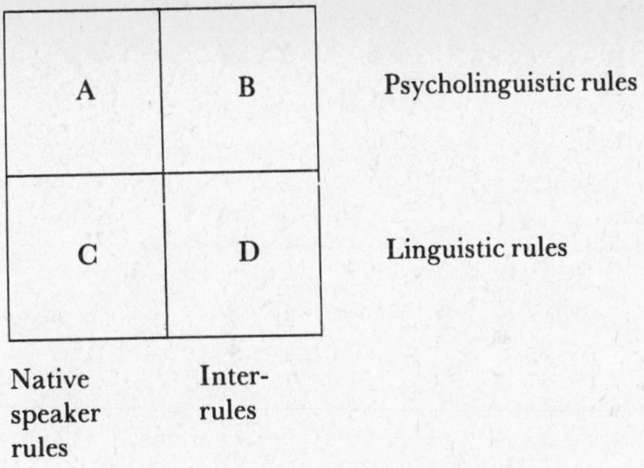

A	B	Psycholinguistic rules
C	D	Linguistic rules

Native   Inter-
speaker   rules
rules

Fig. 8: Four types of grammatical rules

accepted by native speakers as belonging to the language (cf Lyons 1981). Interrules (D), on the other hand, can be one of two types:

(5) rules describing the performance of IL users (ie the exact IL parallel to C-rules)
(6) PEDAGOGICAL INTERRULES constituting af (simplified) subset of native speaker rules (C) and established for didactic purposes.

Learner language studies, of the kind demonstrated in 6.1 and 6.2, are concerned with type (5) rules. We shall now go on to consider pedagogical interrules (6). Use is chiefly made of these in grammar books and teaching materials produced for foreign language learners. Various criteria are relevant when considering the nature of pedagogic grammars, among others the following:

(1) The relationship between a pedagogic grammar and a descriptively adequate native grammer. Differences may reflect *selection principles* (are there rules which have been left out in the pedagogic grammar?) or *degree of detail* (how precisely has a rule been formulated?).
(2) The linguistic theory on the basis of which the pedagogic grammar is written (word-class based? syntax based? eclectic approach?).

(3) Whether the pedagogic grammar is written for learners with a particular mother tongue. Such grammars may select areas in the L2 which are specially problematical because of the contrastive relationship between the two languages. They may also explicitly mention native language structures wherever these can clarify specific problems.

(4) The extent to which the pedagogic grammar incorporates considerations of language learning, for instance by discussing typical cases of learners' grammatical errors.

(5) Whether the pedagogic grammar is intended as primarily a reference grammar or a 'teaching' grammar.

The follow-ups make suggestions for applying these criteria in the analysis of a number of pedagogic grammars currently used in Denmark.

A different use of pedagogical interrules occurs in the classroom, when teachers formulate grammatical rules. Sometimes these are identical with rules found in grammar books. But in addition there appears to be a tradition of using 'rules of thumb', ie rules which are easy to remember and which work in some, but not necessarily all cases. The study of such rules may provide us with valuable information about the types of grammatical knowledge that learners develop.

In the first example the class are translating sentences from Danish into English. For homework they had been asked to prepare the past tense forms of *bend* and *break*. For this reason the teacher has difficulty accepting the learner's plea of ignorance.

Text 12 [3]

T	now
L	naturally he didn't − − jeg ved ikke rigtig hvad det hedder at bøje −

T	− wait a minute − are you seeking for the past tense − remember − now
L	

T	you said − he didn't − and what then − yes you
L	det ved jeg ikke (giggle)

116

T	know – when you use do and did – which form of the verb is that we use
L	

T	then I know you know – OK er – Thomas –
L	nej det ved jeg ikke – –

T	"naturligvis bøjede han den ikke" she said naturally he didn't – –
L	how –

T	BEND it – because you use the infinitive Susanne – don't you know
L	bend it

T	– yes –
L	

We can extract points from the text as below, identifying the activity types carried out by teacher and learner and the way the rule becomes formulated. In the middle column are key words from the extract:

Activity type	Keywords from performance	Interrule
Problem formulation	past tense? (T)	
Induction	he didn't – and what then? (T)	
		when you use *do* and *did* ... (T)
	he didn't? (T)	
Solution	bend it (L) BEND it (T)	
		you use the infinitive (T)

Fig. 9: Example of interrule formulation

It is the teacher who formulates the problem. She tries to elicit the correct response from the learner, partly in terms of performance ("he didn't – and what then?") partly by shifting to the linguistic rule level and giving the first half of a rule which she apparently expects the learner to know. She then elicits the correct completion to the sentence from a different learner, repeats this and then gives

117

the second half of the rule ("you use the infinitive"). Immediately after this, the teacher goes on to the next sentence and never returns to the *do* + infinitive rule.

We end this chapter by quoting another example of the teacher correcting a learner and formulating a grammatical rule. In this instance the rule finally formulated by the teacher is of rather dubious validity, or at the very least an overgeneralisation.

Text 13 [4]

T	i stedet for instead of
L	everyone could see that it would break – instead of

T	what – yes – if you say instead
L	instead of bending – – (laughter in class)

T	of bending – then it is correct – can't you hear it sounds strange – to say
L	

T	that you will do something instead of – – you never end it – Søren
L	every-

T	instead yes – you can't end a
L	one could see that it would break instead

T	sentence with a preposition like that – either you have to add some-
L	nå –

T	thing or you leave out the the – er for instance here the of – you just say
L	

T	instead – yes er –
L	

Footnotes to chapter 6

1. For a description of some areas of grammar, see Davidsen-Nielsen/Færch/Harder 1982.
2. The error categories in table 8 have been conflated from many more error categories in the original analysis. See the discussion of error analysis in chapter 18.
3. See chapter 4, footnote 8.
4. Same as text 12.

Chapter 6. Follow-ups

1. Identify grammatical errors in a set of free compositions (for the procedure of error analysis see chapter 18). Compare results with the "top10 list" in table 8.
2. Identify all instances of the simple and the progressive present tense forms in a set of learner texts. Calculate the proportion of errors relative to the total number of occurrences of each category. Which of the two tense forms seems to be most troublesome to the learners? Check in a number of pedagogical grammars whether the pedagogical interrules formulated for the simple/progressive tenses adequately explain the use of these. Could learners have avoided their errors by correctly following the interrules?
3. Compare the description of a certain grammatical phenomenon in (a) Quirk/Greenbaum/Leech/Svartvik 1972 (b) a number of pedagogic grammars of English, using the criteria listed on p. 115. Are there other relevant criteria?
4. Ask fellow students/teachers to note down examples of "rules of thumb". Find criteria which can be used to characterise them. Discuss the pedagogic value of such rules.

Chapter 6. Sources and further reading

Hatch 1978a describes different approaches to the analysis of grammar in IL data. Further studies of a more theoretical nature are listed in chapter 17 and 18.

The concept of linguistic rule is covered in most introductory textbooks on linguistics. See for instance Lyons 1981, chapter 2. Pedagogical interrules are discussed in Bausch 1979, which is a comprehensive collection of articles on pedagogic grammar. For a brief introduction to pedagogic grammar, see Færch 1977. "Rules of thumb" and other teacher-formulated rules are discussed in Færch 1983d.

The relationship between explicitly formulated grammatical rules and language teaching is discussed in various places in Krashen 1982. For different views, see Seliger 1979, Sharwood Smith 1982, Bialystok 1982.

Chapter seven:
Pronunciation

The first half of the chapter is concerned with prosody, which comprises intonation, stress and rhythm, and considers some of the functions performed by prosody in relation to Danish learners' difficulties with this aspect of English pronunciation. The second half presents some results from a study of the learning of selected consonants, and shows how performance analysis and contrastive analysis can elucidate learning problems. The chapter begins by considering accents and norms of pronunciation.

7.1 Accents and norms of pronunciation

All speakers of English have a pronunciation that says something about their geographical and social origins. Such ACCENTS are created partly by differences in the way individual sounds are realized, partly by differences in intonation, in the amount and direction of pitch movement. What remains much more constant across different accents is rhythm, the patterning created by stressed and unstressed syllables.

Danish learners of English are exposed to a wide variety of types of spoken English, both in the media and when interacting with foreigners. They encounter English in various North American forms (Texan, Californian, Toronto, etc.) and British forms (middle class London, working class Liverpool, etc.), as well as English used as a lingua franca by Japanese tourists, Vietnamese refugees, EEC spokesmen, etc. It is therefore a reasonable teaching objective for listening *comprehension* that Danish learners should be able to understand a wide range of varieties of English, spoken by native speakers as well as by other interlanguage users.

When it comes to the teaching goals for learners' speech *production*, it is more difficult to specify what the pronunciation norm should be. A widely accepted norm throughout the world for learners aiming at British English pronunciation is Received Pronunciation, RP for short.[1] RP is a class accent, used by educated native speakers of English wherever they live, and does not reveal the geographical origin of the speakers (although RP is usually associated with the southern parts of Britain).

To decide whether RP is a reasonable teaching objective for Danish learners' speech production, three criteria might be considered: *communicative efficiency* (is the type of pronunciation generally easy to understand?), *easy of learning* (are certain accents conceivably easier for learners than others?), *attitude* (what reactions does this type of pronunciation evoke?).

So far as *communicative efficiency* is concerned, it is hardly surprising that those accents which are most commonly encountered in the media are generally felt to be more comprehensible than regional accents. Because of the close link between RP and the BBC, it is a reasonable assumption that native speakers will find it easier to understand a foreigner who tries to speak RP rather than any other dialect of English.

The second criterion for selecting a norm for foreign language learners to aim at is *ease* of learning. It has been argued (Abercrombie 1956) that the Edinburgh accent is linguistically simpler than RP. Similarly, Danish learners of English are sometimes heard to claim that they find American pronunciation easier to imitate than RP. Such impressions may reflect similarities between the learner's L1 and accents of the target language, or the fact that learners find those accents easy which they either encounter frequently or have a positive attitude towards. Irrespective of these reasons, there remains the significant fact that RP is the best described of the accents of English, with a great deal of published teaching materials available.

As regards ATTITUDE, we are extremely sensitive to pronunciation when we interact with native speakers of our mother tongue. Pronunciation is a powerful indicator of group membership, and touches deep emotional roots. A considerable amount of work in social psychology has gone into probing people's reactions to accents, and has confirmed that these are used as a means of stereotyping people, and as a source for judgements about people's competence (eg intelligence or industriousness), personal integrity (eg trustworthiness) and social attractiveness (eg friendliness). RP is a

121

prestige accent, regional accents rather less so, and urban accents tend to be stigmatised.[2]

Unfortunately very little work has been done to clarify native speaker attitudes to the speech of foreigners. Foreigners, at least those on short visits (immigrants tend to be assessed differently), are not members of the social network of a speech community, and will not be judged as such. In what ways the role of "foreigner" affects native speaker attitudes, formed on the basis of accents, is a topic which has scarcely been investigated. However it is perfectly possible that Danes speak English in a way which conflicts with native speaker norms and which creates unintended impressions. We shall be exploring this issue in 7.2.

By accepting that RP is the most eligible model for the teaching of pronunciation in Denmark, we do not wish to imply that no other accent can have the same status, or that RP should be treated in a restricted, purist sense. Teachers or learners who, for whatever reason, have a good command of a different accent (whether New Zealand, New York, or York) have an asset compared with other learners who are still trying to break away from a Zealand or Jutland accent in their English. In any case the overlap between different accents of English is far greater than the differences.[3] This means that for most learners keeping exclusively to one accent is an ideal goal which is difficult to attain. There is nothing reprehensible about sounding "mid-Atlantic", whereas it is unfortunate to get stuck on Dogger Bank.

7.2 The functions of prosody

PROSODY is an extremely complex and controversial topic, and we can therefore do no more than single out some of the consequences that may ensue if a learner has incomplete mastery of English prosody. We devote so much space to prosody, despite the difficulties of carrying out interlanguage studies in the area, because we suspect that teachers tend to spend a good deal of time on the individual sounds of English and hope that rhythm and intonation will look after themselves. It is arguable that this is a false sense of priorities, and that it is the prosodic aspects of the learner's mother tongue that are the hardest to shake off. In order to classify what is involved, we

122

shall begin by stating some of the functions performed by prosody.

In the examples that follow, syllables which are stressed (ie said with greater prominence than other syllables) are s p a c e d, while pitch movement or intonation will be marked by the position of syllables in the vertical axis.

INTONATION has three main functions in English. It contributes to the way the speaker's attitude is conveyed, to the marking of the grammatical structure of utterances, and to the purpose of these in the ongoing discourse. It is difficult to come with hard and fast rules for intonation, because there is no one-to-one correspondence between *prosodic* features (such as a rise or a fall) and either *grammatical* categories (such as clause or imperative) or *discourse* concepts (such as turn). There are however tendencies of co-occurrence.

In the *unmarked* form of intonation in RP, the pitch descends gradually from fairly high in the voice and ends with a fall to fairly low.[4] This phonetic contour or tune is used in conjunction with many grammatical categories, and textbooks on both intonation and grammar list examples of the co-occurence of various patterns. We shall relate intonation contours to the framework of the pragmatics and discourse chapters, because we are interested in the communicative function of utterances, and intonation and grammar are determined by choices at the levels of speech act and discourse.

The unmarked form of intonation contour can be used with informative acts:

1) J o h n is out d r i n king

and initiating acts in the form of a question with an interrogative pronoun:

2) W h e r e are you g o ing

The intonation of utterances 1) and 2) is identical.

What would the significance be of using a *marked* form, an intonation contour which differs from the unmarked form? We can consider two types of divergence. If, in the first utterance, the emphasis is placed earlier in the utterance:

    3)   i
                 s
        J o h n   out drinking

the likely context is the speaker contradicting an earlier statement by someone else ("John is not out drinking"). In discourse terms, the items *John, out, drinking* are "given", they have all been mentioned in the preceding utterance. The "new" element is the speaker's counterclaim, which is why the word *is* is highlighted. Putting the main fall on this item, as opposed to *drinking* in the unmarked form, alters the shape of the intonation contour and produces a marked form.

In *pragmatic* terms, utterance 3) is a rejection of an assertion. If, by contrast, the speaker wishes to query the assertion, rather than contradicting it, the pitch movement on *is* would rise from low instead of falling:

    4) J o h n   drink^ing.
                    out
             i^s

This is an "echo question", which exactly repeats the words of the previous speaker (whose statement would probably be in the form of utterance 1)), and queries their truth value, often with an element of surprise on the part of the speaker. Echo questions invariably have the marked form of a rising contour.

The second type of departure from the basic unmarked form is a marking for *speech act modality*. This is so when the pitch direction is reversed finally:

    5) W h e r e
                  are you
                          .ing.
                       g o

124

This is marked for politeness, whereas utterance 2) is not. The same applies when a command is uttered with a rising intonation, as opposed to the unmarked fall, this making the order appear less peremptory. These remarks do not imply that utterance 2) is necessarily impolite. The meaning of an utterance, including such general notions as "politeness", is carried by the lexis, the syntax, the tone of voice of the speaker, as well as the prosody. The important point here is that intonation in RP has an unmarked form, and that reasons for the use of a marked form must be looked for at the level of pragmatics and discourse.

Foreign learners of English need to recognize and produce the appropriate unmarked form of English prosody, and to know when and how the relevant marked forms are used. To exemplify Danish learners' difficulties, we shall now single out 3 characteristic features of Danish accent. The first two are directly attributable to transfer of mother tongue intonation patterns, the third may be, though it is possible that the prosody is due to insecurity in speaking a foreign language and resultant hesitancy or tentativeness.

1. A tendency to pitch the unstressed syllables higher than the preceding stressed ones (the normal pattern in Copenhagen Danish), creating a weaving or lilting impression.

2. Instead of full glides (falls, rises, fall-rises), flattening them out (as is the case in Danish) and consequently making them less clearly marked.

3. Using a narrow range of pitch rather than the full range from top to bottom of the voice, the tendency being to remain in or just below the middle range.

These three aspects of Danish accent can be seen in the following example:

6) W h e r e ^{are you} g o ing ^{to} b e ^{to} n i g h t

Pronouncing the unstressed syllables higher than the stressed ones upsets the contour and gives more prominence to the grammatical words (eg *you, to*) than the lexical items. The effect of having no clear glide up or down finally may be that it is unclear whether the question is marked for politeness or not. Before we can do justice to the question of the narrowness of the pitch range used, we shall have to consider the relationship between prosody and the communication of attitudes.

Attitude is a very general term, covering emotional involvement, interest, mood, and much else. Prosodic features such as relative loudness and tempo and the amount of pitch movement of the voice reflect the relative animation or interest of the speaker. Greater interest, enthusiasm or excitement are often expressed by more frequent or extensive rises and falls in the pitch of the voice.[5]

The following example is highly marked for emotional involvement, possibly indicating amazement or exasperation:

7)
$$\text{W}_\text{h}{}_\text{e}{}_\text{r}{}_\text{e}\ \text{are}\ \text{y}^\text{o}{}^\text{u}{}^\text{g}{}^\text{o}\text{ing}$$

There is a risk of Danish speakers of English, because of either pitch movement fluctuating too much (eg the "weaving" intonation) or moving too little (eg narrow pitch range or absence of glides) conveying attitudes that are unintended and triggering off reactions inadvertently.

For instance, if a Dane says "Do come tomorrow" without a considerable fall in pitch on the word *do,* from the upper range of the voice to low, this could be interpreted as indicating a lack of enthusiasm. There is anecdotal evidence that Danes sound "flat and sombre", "apathetic" and "hesitant".[6] These subjective, impressionistic judgements are probably attributable to impressions made by prosody. They have been pronounced by professional linguists, rather than people without technical insight into the issues, and should be taken with a pinch of salt, until supported by empirical evidence.

Our brief coverage of the functions of prosody needs to be completed by pursuing further the relationship between intonation and *discourse*. Unfortunately it is impossible to state categorically that particular intonation contours signify a speaker's intention to continue a turn, and others a wish to give someone else a turn. What we have stated so far about WH-questions indicates that both a final fall (unmarked) and a final rise (marked) can complete a speaker's turn. The fact that a speaker intends to give a turn to someone else is marked lexically (eg *Where*) and/or syntactically (eg word order inversion) as well as in the intonation. If on the other hand a declarative statement is to function as an eliciting act, a marked form of intonation should be used, ie a final rise. However, in some contexts, for instance a lawyer addressing an accused person in a court of law, or a teacher in front of a class of pupils, there may be a clear understanding that whatever the lawyer or the teacher says should be interpreted as an initiating act, irrespective of whether the intonation rises or falls finally. Intonation needs to be studied in context.

The risk for Danish speakers is that departure from native speaker prosody norms, for instance flattening out a final fall or rise, could mean that there is no unambiguous marking for turn completion or turn continuation. The distinction between a marked and an unmarked form may be blurred. If we return to the marked forms of examples 3) and 4), Danish foreign accent in producing such utterances could mean that it is unclear whether the Dane is querying the preceding statement or contradicting it. The risk of being understood as producing a quite different speech act is probably at least as serious as either not marking turn boundaries clearly or of unintended attitudes being conveyed.

7.3 Studying learner prosody

There have been very few studies of Danish problems in learning or using appropriate English prosody (cf Chatman 1966, Hartoft 1980). One explanation for this state of affairs is that the multi-functional nature of intonation, when compared with lexis, grammar or the phonemes of English, makes it a difficult object of study. There are problems in establishing norms, and error analysis is not possible in the same way as for the other levels of language. Correct or incorrect prosody is far more a question of degree than of being right or wrong. Shortcomings are likely to be relative ones, such as

127

not stressing a particular syllable enough, or not dropping the voice enough in order to make a rise.

Correct allocation of *stress*, and a clear distinction between stressed and unstressed syllables, is the basis of rhythm in English. It is arguably the most important of the prosodic systems for foreign learners to master, as it serves to make some words more prominent than others. Danish operates with a similar system of stress allocation to English, but this does not mean there are no learning difficulties. Common Danish errors of stress placement include the following:

1. Stressing the wrong element in a noun phrase, eg the first word instead of the second in *prime minister*.
2. Failing to put the main stress on the first element of words such as *pick-up*, *feedback*, which have been loaned into Danish and given a different stress pattern.
3. Pronouncing syllables which should be unstressed with a pure vowel instead of the weak, central vowel, eg in *but, Thomas,* saying [bʌt, tɔmæs] as opposed to [bət, tɔməs].

In all three cases, the rhythm of the utterance will be adversely affected.

Assessing the prosody of whole utterances means evaluating the *general impression* created by the stress, rhythm and intonation. This is rather subjective, but something that all oral examinations attempt, often without very clear criteria for evaluation. An IL study could assess the general impression of the prosody on a number of parameters. These could be pitch range, the pitch of unstressed syllables, glides, clear pragmatic and discourse marking, rhythm and phrasing. Learners could be placed on a 5-point scale with most native-like at one end and heaviest foreign accent at the other.[7]

It is only fair to repeat that little systematic observation or analysis has been done on prosody learning, whether at the level of detail or of general impressions. The few studies reported (Tarone 1978, Gårding 1981) involve instrumental analysis of a very technical nature. An essential preliminary is the choice of data type for analysis, and here we suggest that *reading aloud* is used only with extreme caution. Prosody is used differently in reading aloud and in conversation,[8] and the goal for the vast majority of Danish learners is being able to converse in English rather than to read aloud. This is not to say that reading aloud may not have its pedagogic uses (eg careful imitation of a good reading), but the task of converting a written text into spoken language with the appropriate prosody, which marks the relationship between sentences and carries all the nuances of meaning, is extremely demanding. The main advantage of using texts for reading aloud in IL studies is that the texts can be selected so as to oblige learners to use specific phonemes, stress patterns and intonation contours. But this is a different task from using them in conversation.

7.4 Studying the learning of specific sounds

We turn now to the learning of individual sounds, and show how the methods of error analysis and performance analysis can clarify problems in the learning of these. We report on 3 studies, which form part of a study of the use of obstruents (plosives, affricates and fricatives) in the PIF corpus.[9]

EXAMPLE 1. *PIF obstruent error analysis, unprepared speech*
This is an example of an error analysis designed to find out which obstruent errors were frequent in a corpus of impromptu, ie unprepared speech. The details of the analysis can be presented by following the procedural steps recommended in chapter 18.3.

1. Pronunciation problem: all obstruents.
2. Data type: film summaries, recorded in a language laboratory, after subjects had watched the 5-minute film twice. Learners could structure their descriptions as they wished.
   Learner group: a cross-section of half the PIF population, ie 58 learners from beginner to advanced.
   Corpus size: roughly 10.000 words.
3. Each learner's entire text was transcribed, using sheets with the tramline system demonstrated in chapter 19.
4. 3 native speakers listened to the tapes and identified all obstruent errors, writing on the transcripts the errors that they could hear.

129

5. Two investigators, one Danish and one English, coordinated the results from the error identifiers.

Prior to calculating the frequency of different error types, a check was made of the phonetic environment of each error, ie adjacent sounds preceding and following the error. Each obstruent was sub-classified according to whether it occurred initially, medially or finally. Final plosives occurring before an unstressed syllable, eg *lot of,* are in an identical position to medial plosives, eg *better,* and were therefore processed separately from final plosives in other phonetic environments.

When the errors were added up, a clear pattern emerged. Apart from the final lenis /z/, the only frequent error was a fortis plosive occurring before an unstressed syllable. The much higher figure for /t/, as compared with /p/ and /k/, reflects the much greater frequency of this plosive. Table 11 highlights the two frequent error types by giving them separate boxes. The figures for sounds in the lowest box are so low that they have not been sub-classified, and figures below 10 occurrences have been excluded.

Analysis of the sounds substituted for the target sounds revealed that, almost invariably, for the sounds in the first box a lenis plosive had been used instead of a fortis one, and in the second box a fortis fricative instead of a lenis one. In both cases this corresponds to mother tongue practice in these phonetic contexts. This is clear evidence of the psycholinguistic process of transfer, and contrastive analysis can account for the type of substitution made (see 19.4.1).

Many other points emerge from a qualitative analysis of the data, for instance, the mispronunciation of /θ/ most often occurs when the sound is in the vicinity of an /s/, indicating a confusion between the two, but this is not captured by the quantitative results.

It might have been possible to count the errors occurring for each target sound at each level of learner, but the amount and type of data in question made such a task problematical, because the texts were of different lengths and content, and learners were free to structure them in whatever form they liked.

Table 11: Obstruent error count, unprepared speech

Obstruent type		Total number errors
Fortis plosive before unstressed syllable	final /t/ before an unstressed syllable, eg *lot of, get a*	128
	/t/ with lateral release, eg *kettle*	30
	medial / t/ , eg *better, water*	29
	/p/ and /k/ in similar contexts to those for /t/, eg *cup of, clock and*	16
Final lenis /z/	/– z/, eg *was, his*	90
Other	/ð/ eg *this*	33
	/θ/ eg *thin*	29
	/b, d, g/ mostly word finally	23
	/p, t, k/ in other contexts than above	20
	/v/ eg *over, very*	16
	/tʃ/ eg *watch*	13
	/dʒ/ eg *strange*	11

We now move on from a crude error count to looking at errors as a proportion of total occurrences of a particular sound. This is undertaken in performance analysis, as in our second example, which is a follow-up on example 1.

EXAMPLE 2. *PIF dental fricative performance analysis, unprepared speech*

1. Pronunciation problem: dental fricatives.
2-6. As in example 1, except for
    Learner group: 12 learners at each of grades 6, 8, 10, 12.
    Corpus size: included below in table 12 (approximate number of words spoken by the 12 learners at each level).
7. All occurrences of dental fricatives were counted up, as were all errors, for each of the two dental fricatives, initially, medially and finally. Error types were noted.

Table 12. Dental fricative performance analysis

Level	6		8		lgs		3gs	
Approximate no. of words	1525		1160		2115		2210	
Initial /θ/	10	5	29	12	28	6	38	3
Medial /θ/	3	1	0	0	12	1	18	1
Final /θ/	4	4	0	0	1	0	1	0
Initial /ð/	163	21	132	13	214	8	218	5
Medial /ð/	8	0	7	1	6	0	9	0
Final /ð/	20	12	11	7	19	3	20	1

Note. For each level the figures in the left hand box are for occurrences, in the right hand box for errors.

This table documents the progress across 6 years of school learning, from grade 6 to grade 3gs, of 12 learners of English. The general trend is, not unexpectedly, a progressive reduction in the number of errors. The figures for errors as a proportion of the total number of occurrences of the target sound could have been expressed as percentages, but to do so would have the effect of concealing the fact that dental fricatives are much more frequent initially than medially or finally. The figures for actual occurrence give a very clear picture of how frequent or infrequent these sounds are in English, information which was to some degree implicit in the figures in example 1. (We discount the possibility of the figures being influenced by learners avoiding using particular sounds.)

The figures show that there are definite difficulties in articulating /θ/ at the 6th and 8th grades; the errors substituted are /s/ and /f/ initially, as in *think;* and /t/ before /r/, as in *three.*

The figures for /ð/ are in many ways very similar to those for /θ/. The tendency is for the initial sound, as in *then,* and the final sound, as in *with,* to be replaced mostly by /d/ and less frequently by /z/.

The data in examples 1 and 2 were obtained from analysis of language produced freely: after watching the film, subjects simply said what they wanted to about the film. Clearly there are quite different speech production processes involved when working from the visual prompt of a written text, as is the case with reading aloud. In the PIF project a performance analysis of obstruents in a reading aloud task has been undertaken, and some of the results of this can be given as a way of demonstrating some of the principles of pronunciation analysis of this kind. Obviously if learners all read the same text it is much easier to make comparisons between learners at different levels or between different learners in the same group.

EXAMPLE 2. *PIF obstruent performance analysis, reading aloud*
1. Pronunciation problems: /t/ and /dʒ/.
2. Data type: tape-recordings of readings of a page from a modern novel, recorded in a language laboratory.
   Learners: one intermediate group of 12 learners at level 1gs, one advanced group of 8 university students.
   Corpus size: for each learner a text of 166 words.
3. Transcription: not relevant.
4. 3 native speakers listened to the tape and identified all obstruent errors, noting down the errors that they could hear. Experts took the final decision on error type.
5. Errors are expressed as a percentage of all occurrences of each sound. Learning sequences can be read off.

In the more complete analysis, figures for all obstruents have been analysed. /t/ has been singled out for presentation here as it was the most frequently occurring error in the film descriptions (see example 1), and because there is a very complex picture behind the gross figures of the performance analysis. The affricate /dʒ/ has been selected because it is the phoneme which recorded the highest error percentage of all in the reading aloud task.

The following table lists results for the two levels for these phonemes.

Table 13: Error percentages for /t/ and /dʒ/,
performance analysis, reading aloud

Sound \ Level	lgs	university
Initial /t/	0	0
Medial /t/	33	13
Final /t/	14	4
Initial /dʒ/	46	11
Medial /dʒ/	73	44
Final /dʒ/	100	44

So far as *learning sequences,* or the order in which sounds are learnt is concerned, the following conclusions can be drawn:

– initial /t/ is no learning problem at these levels,
– final /t/ is learnt before medial /t/,
– /dʒ/ is learnt in the sequence initial – medial – final.

The results for medial /t/ indicate that a fairly high proportion of intermediate learners, one third, and 13 % of advanced learners, make errors. These figures for the reading support the findings on medial /t/ from the film description. (But for a more detailed analysis see below).

The results for /dʒ/ indicate that even for advanced learners the sound is difficult, particularly in final position. In the film descriptions it was only in final position that there was a high proportion of errors: for these groups of learners, over 50 %. In the reading task, the figures for errors perceived by our error identifiers are far higher when the relevant word is in stressed rather than unstressed position.

/t/ is a *frequent* sound, whereas /dʒ/ is extremely rare. This means that /t/ has a high functional value in English, being used to identify many words and keep them distinct from others, whereas /dʒ/ does so to a much lesser extent. In terms of learning the system of English, there can be no doubt that /t/ is more important, and that relative frequency makes it a conspicuous indicator of Danish »accent«.

7.5 Explaining pronunciation errors

In examples 1, 2 and 3, the general tendency is for the errors to be predominantly due to *transfer* (see 11.3.2). There are rather more errors of other kinds at the lower levels, not reported here, specially in reading aloud. But transfer seems to operate in complex ways with such closely related languages as Danish and English, as the following analysis shows.

In the reading text elicited from 94 PIF learners, there were seven occurrences of medial /t/, meaning 94 × 7 occurrences of medial /t/ in the whole corpus. Of these, 24 % were identified as being errors. However the picture is far from uniform when the figures for each lexical item are studied. Of the 94 occurrences of each item (1 item per learner), the following percentages were identified as errors:

mister	1
eastern	4
waiting	11
party	18
graduated	29
later	50
later	54

How can the spread in these figures be explained? We regard the difference between the figures for the two occurrences of *later* as being insignificant. But one would expect in particular *waiting* and *later* to record roughly the same proportion of errors, particularly as these words all occur sentence finally, in other words in the same position as regards sentence intonation. Plausible explanations for the variation in the figures are as follows:

– In *mister* and *eastern* the /t/ is neutralised, due to the preceding /s/, so that a /t/ or a /d/ is equally good.

- Danish has several words in which *-ting* is the second part of a compound (»Folketing«), and loans (»marketing«) in which the /t/ behaves as though it is initial, hence aspirated; transfer works to the learner's advantage in *waiting*.
- *party* is a loanword from English in Danish, and often pronounced in an anglicized fashion.
- The only cases where there are no factors facilitating a fortis rather than a lenis sound are *graduated*, which occurs in mid-sentence, and *later*, which on both occasions is sentence-final, which probably gives *later* a greater perceptual prominence, hence a greater likelihood that an error may be perceived; in addition, Danish has several words in which the final syllable, unstressed, consists of a lenis plosive and a similar vowel to the English, eg *fætter, sætter.*

Thus it seems that for the same phonetic category, medial /t/, transfer can work both to learners' advantage (eg *waiting* and *party*) and to their disadvantage (*later*). The phoneme therefore needs to be seen in conjunction with lexical information and stress. This is a more linguistically-informed way of looking at the problem than merely shrugging one's shoulders and concluding that learners behave inconsistently. It might be that learners learn individual words with a specific pronunciation, rather than phonetic rules; these are evidently trickier when they cut across mother tongue categories, as the plosives do. Or that both types of learning occur.

What this discussion of medial /t/ also shows, even more than the comments on the other examples of error and performance analysis, is the need for *quantitatively* based studies to be combined with *qualitative* studies (cf the discussion on methods in 19.1).

It is also necessary to be extremely careful in the use of both terminology and concepts. Even such a basic concept as »word-final phoneme« may conceal regularities, because at times word-final plosives are in the same phonetic environment as word-medial plosives. As was seen in example 2, the most general feature of errors with fortis plosives was that they occurred before a weakly stressed syllable, whether word medially (eg *better*) or word finally (eg *lot of*).

Explaining learner errors in terms of transfer is a *learner-internal* explanation (cf 18.2.3.). The PIF data cannot be explained by reference to such *learner-external* factors as the way teaching was conducted, as the project did not investigate these. On the other hand the obstruent study shows that some of the English sounds which have no counterpart in Danish, for instance /tʃ/ and /θ/, do not seem to present much of a problem to learners after 4 years of English; whereas in areas in which the sound systems of Danish and English partially overlap, such as medial plosives, errors persist. It is quite possible that the attention of learners has been consciously directed to new, »difficult« sounds, whereas the fortis/lenis distinction in medial plosives is one to which they have not been sensitised to the same degree.

Footnotes to chapter 7

1. The term »received« pronunciation indicates that it originally implied a social judgement, whether the speaker could be received into the »right« society. It is not an official standard. For discussion, see Gimson 1980.
2. For a survey of work in this area, see Edwards 1982.
3. For a presentation of varieties of Standard English, and a plea for tolerance of a mixture of dialects, see Trudgill and Hannah 1982.
4. What we are calling the 'unmarked' form is referred to as »the 'typical' neutral intonation« by Brown/Currie/Kenworthy 1980.
5. See the two articles by Bolinger in Bolinger 1972.
6. These judgements are attributed to Lloyd James, K. Sørensen and J. D. O'Connor. See references in Phillipson 1978.
7. See Phillipson 1978 for an outlined plan for such work.
8. See references in Crystal 1969, and Brown 1977.
9. Phillipson and Lauridsen 1982.

Chapter 7. Follow-ups

1. Select a text of which a native speaker recording is available. Record some learners reading the same text aloud. Use the native speaker version as the yardstick against which to measure the prosody of the Danish learner. Do your findings confirm a failure to use weak forms, sufficient pitch movement, specific intonation contours? How close is the text to the style of spontaneous (ie not read) language? Would the learner prosody have the same shortcomings in other spoken language contexts?
2. Make a recording of the free production of a small group of learners. Select one

phoneme or a set of phonemes for a performance analysis (see 7.4 and chapter 18). If you analyse the same obstruents as those reported on in this chapter, are your findings similar? How far are the errors attributable to transfer and how far to other causes? The task could be repeated after a period of some months' teaching and results compared.

3. Danish learners of English sometimes have a resistance towards adopting RP intonation, which they find posh. Discuss whether this should have any impact on teaching goals. Consider ways in which learners can be made more conscious of the effects of inadequate prosody.

4. Discuss the following statement: »It might be that learners learn individual words with a specific pronunciation, rather than phonetic rules ...« (this chapter)? Is there a case for phonetic interrules in foreign language teaching?

Chapter 7. Sources and further reading

For an introductory work on variation in British English see Hughes and Trudgill 1979. Wells 1982 is an exhaustive work on the pronunciation of English around the world. Key works on prosody are referred to in footnotes 4, 5 and 8; of these the simplest presentation is Brown 1977. Davidsen-Nielsen 1981 is intended for Danish university students.

For interlanguage phonology, see Tarone's survey article in Richards 1978, and a summary of principles in Phillipson and Lauridsen 1982, chapter 2.

On contrastive analysis, see James 1980, chapter 4. Davidsen-Nielsen's textbooks, 1970 and 1975, are contrastive in approach, as is the section on pronunciation in Davidsen-Nielsen/Færch/Harder 1982.

For a thought-provoking psychological perspective on pronunciation learning, see Stevick 1976, particularly chapter 4.

Chapter eight:
Production, fluency and reception

In the preceding chapters, we have described different aspects of communicative competence without attempting to describe the way these interact with each other in actual communication. In this chapter we shall present a model of speech production and reception which integrates the elements presented in isolation so far.

For the sake of simplicity we shall refer to speakers and listeners but not explicitly to writers and readers. This does not imply that what is said about production and reception holds good only for spoken communication. On the contrary, the underlying processes are fundamentally similar, even though the channel and the time factor differ.

8.1 Speech production

Imagine a communicative event in which John (a young man) approaches a stranger (an elderly gentleman) in the street in order to ask for a light. Describing the production of John's speech involves specifying the links between his communicative intention and the sounds that he utters. This necessarily involves identifying

- the speech acts he intends to perform
- the modality of these acts
- the textual structure of the acts
- the appropriate referential content
- an appropriate syntactic and lexical form for the acts
- the pronunciation necessary for the transmission of the words.

If one thinks in sequential terms, John first has to make a plan for the actional, referential and interpersonal aspects of his communicative intention, then select appropriate words, put these in an appropriate order, and convert these elements into sounds. In addition to finding the right words in relation to these goals, he has to pay attention to the discourse context that the utterance fits into. In this communicative event, John is going to initiate the conversational exchange, so it would be natural for his requesting act, the core phase, to be preceded by an opening phase (these concepts were introduced in chapter 4).

John is in a position to choose from (at least) the following for his opening phase:

hey
good afternoon (+/– sir)
excuse me
I'm sorry to trouble you but

To initiate a communicative event involving a stranger in the street, in a form which is marked as being polite, it is likely that John would select either the third or fourth form.

Similarly, for his requesting act, John can choose between a range of ways of expressing this (as in the »money« example in chapter 3). He must select the referential content (where the key elements might be *you* + *have* + an object), mark for a question, select which word for the object to use *(lighter/light/match)*, and arrange the words in the syntactically correct order. The necessary words could be as follows:

excuse   me   do   you   have   a   light.

This formula now has to be converted into the appropriate phonetic form at the level both of individual sounds:

/ɪkskjuːz miː dʒə hæv ə laɪt/

and of stress and intonation:

The model of the speech production process presented in figure 10 attempts to capture the successive decision-making steps. Speech production involves moving from the top to the bottom of the model. The setting and discourse context are relevant at all levels.

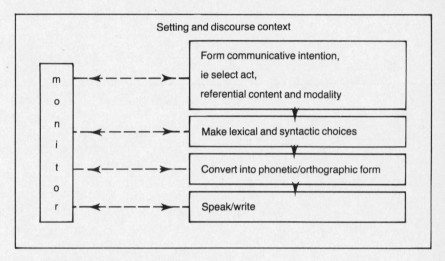

Fig. 10: Model of speech production

MONITORING is a process of checking the form of what is said (or is to be said) for correctness, as well as checking that the communicative effect of one's speech is in accordance with the original communicative intention. Monitoring takes place constantly, consciously or unconsciously, and depends on contextual and personal factors. In situations in which there is a pressure on the speaker to produce language at a reasonable speed (for instance in face-to-face interaction), there is clearly less time for monitoring than in situations in which there is no direct contact between the interlocutors. This accounts for the well-known fact that learners generally express themselves more correctly when they write than when they speak, because the writing situation allows them to monitor more carefully the various steps in the production process. Differences of personality may account for the fact that in one and the same situation different learners monitor to different degrees depending on how much they focus on correctness.

Monitoring takes place in either of two ways:

- *self-monitoring:* the learner monitors her own speech production, including the outcome of this (ie speech/writing)
- *other-monitoring:* the learner monitors the reaction of her addressee(s) in order to detect signs of lack of understanding or misunderstanding.

Self-monitoring takes place either before an utterance is produced or after delivery of the utterance. In the latter case, monitoring may result in self-repairs, as discussed in chapter 4. The importance of self-monitoring has been demonstrated in experiments in which speakers are artificially prevented from listening in to their own speech. The effect of this is almost inevitably speech with a great deal of stuttering.

Other-monitoring is dependent on immediate feedback such as verbal and non-verbal uptaking as well as on the way addressees continue the discourse. If there is little coherence between a speaker's initiating act and the addressee's responding act, the speaker may interpret this as an indication of lack of understanding and initiate a self-repair.

Singling out the different phases of speech production like this might create the false impression that speakers first plan and then produce one utterance after another. In reality, speakers usually start planning what to say next and how to do so before actually having finished uttering a preceding unit: planning and execution typically occur simultaneously. One result of this is a smooth transition from one unit to another, an essential aspect of fluency.

8.2 Fluency

The term »fluent« is defined in the Oxford Concise Dictionary in relation to speech as meaning

»copious, coming easily, ready;
expressing oneself quickly and easily«.

This definition indicates that in everyday English the notion of a fluent speaker may cover *either* someone who says a lot (»copious«) *or* someone who speaks freely and easily.

In foreign language pedagogy the term »fluency« is generally restricted to the second of these two meanings, although obviously someone who talks a lot will mostly speak easily. Essentially fluency involves the capacity *to be able to put what one wants to say into words with ease*. This is the broad sense in which we shall refer to fluency. Speed of delivery does not in itself constitute fluency since tempo is usually adjusted to different factors in the communicative event.

Fluency has to do with how well the speaker is able to link the units of speech together smoothly and without strain. These units can belong to any of the following levels of the linguistic system: individual sounds, words and their combination, semantic units. Consequently, one might talk about different types of fluency depending on which level one is referring to:

> *semantic fluency:* linking together propositions and speech acts
> *lexical-syntactic fluency:* linking together syntactic constituents and words
> *articulatory fluency:* linking together speech segments.

In chapter 4 we have already considered the linking together of propositions and speech acts, which we there termed coherence. As this term covers the way semantic units are linked, we shall restrict the term FLUENCY to the levels of articulation, lexis and syntax, and use coherence for the semantic level.

Symptoms of *non-fluency* are pauses, false starts, self-corrections, repetitions. These are observable products in non-fluent speech which indicate difficulty in the *process* of speech production. There may be different causes for such non-fluency. Not knowing *what* to say or *how* to say something may result in non-fluency at the lexical-syntactic level; difficulty in pronouncing particular sounds may result in articulatory non-fluency (pathological conditions such as stuttering are a special case of this). Fluency is a relative concept, partly dependent on personality, and influenced by social and psychological factors such as confidence, fatigue, familiarity with the context, and degree of preparedness. Before going on to look at some

143

examples of fluent and non-fluent speech, in the mother tongue and a foreign language, we shall consider the psycholinguistic processes of speech production in more detail.

In the terms of our speech production model, a fluent speaker is someone who is able to move from top to bottom of the model without running into problems, so that the resulting speech product has smooth links between all the units at each level. In the example introduced earlier in this chapter, the utterance

excuse me   do you have a light

consists of two parts. The second part could function on its own, so there can be no doubt that the major break is between »me« and »do«. The words to the left and to the right of the break form two tone groups and would in fluent speech be pronounced as such, with appropriate stress and intonation.

If we restrict our attention to the second part of the utterance, and assume the insertion of one pause, there are the following possibilities:

(1) do   you have a light
(2) do you   have a light
(3) do you have   a light
(4) do you have a   light

Let us consider the effect of each of these on the perceived fluency of the speaker.

In both (1) and (4), the pause divides up elements which are syntactically more closely related to each other than to other elements in the utterances: *do* is an integral constituent in the combined subject and verb phrase (auxiliary and main verb); *a* is intimately related to *light*, together with which it forms the object noun phrase. Pauses as placed in (1) and (4) therefore violate the integrity of major syntactic units. If a native speaker needs to pause at such points of strong linking, there is a tendency to preserve the links by repeating the preceding item:

144

(1a) do   do you have a light
(4a) do you have a   a light.

We might say that the placement of a pause at a point of strong linking decreases fluency as perceived by the hearer in that it makes it
more difficult for her to utilize pauses for the identification of major
syntactic constituents. Native speakers are often aware of this, when
they pause at points of strong linking, and *compensate* by repeating the
preceding item. We could therefore characterize (1a) and (4a) as
examples of COMPENSATORY FLUENCY.[1]

In (2), the pause occurs between the subject (preceded by the
auxiliary *do*) and the predicate, at a point of weaker linking than the
pause in (1), though not as weak as the link between the (subject +
verb phrase) + (object), the point where the pause occurs in (3). *If
the speaker needs to pause once, the best place is immediately before
the object as in (3).* To compensate for the more problematic placement of the pause in (2), the speaker would have to use the full vowel
[u:] in *you,* possibly lengthened. If a reduced vowel is used ([ə] or
[ʊ]), followed by a silent pause, the effect will be non-fluency, probably hesitancy.

What the examples illustrate is that pausing is possible at all points
in the utterance, but that speakers need to compensate in various
ways for pausing at points of strong linking. As well as the repetition
of a word, compensatory fluency can also consist of gambits (eg *you
know, sort of, I mean*), and filled pauses (eg *er, erm*) as opposed to long
unfilled (ie silent) pauses.

Learners may not be too skilled at compensating for their in-
evitable need to pause at odd places in order to monitor or to retrieve a word. The reason why such speech strikes the listener as
non-fluent is that the comprehension process becomes disturbed, as
it cannot utilize the pauses as cues of syntactic/lexical structuring.
One therefore has to be extremely careful when relating pauses (as
well as speed) to fluency: pauses do not in themselves indicate lack of
fluency, as little as speed indicates the opposite. For pauses to lead to
low fluency they have to diverge from a 'normal' pause pattern, be
excessive in duration or number, or diverge from the pattern of
lexical, syntactic and articulatory links.

The following text, which is the first part of a conversation,

145

contains many indicators of non-fluency as well as of compensatory fluency:[2]

Text 14

A er look i – do – er w I I – felt I really must get round the department because I am becoming more and more the faceless man who's totally unknown to everybody – er by even by sight – erm – er and I did it you know in my first year here – er – but
5 erm – that was about five years ago – and so I thought I'd pop up again this this this er winter but I feel much more – erm sort of gently – and I wasn't going to spend any more time looking at laboratories – er unless somebody has got some I mean here I was told that I jolly well had to look round the er rooms
B mm
A because ...

A is a highly educated native speaker of English, a university lecturer. The problems he seems to have in this particular context appear to be due to him not having completely planned what to say before starting speaking, which results in poor coherence as well as a marked lack of smoothness at the lexical-syntactic level: false starts (lines 1, 8); repetitions (lines 1, 6); frequent filled pauses (*er, erm, I mean, you know*) and unfilled pauses (throughout). It is highly likely that he is a fluent speaker in other contexts, such as giving lectures, where the content and even the choice of words has been thought through beforehand.

Contrast this extract with one from a transcript of a film description:[3]

Text 15

at the beginning of the film it's indicated (clears throat) that the – the character – in fact the only one in the – the whole film – erm feels himself to be some kind of fiasco – erm he's got a piece of paper – er – on his back saying fiasco – – after we've been in-
5 truce introduced to him we see – er – I think it's called a s er dream pictures – we see – er our main character lying on a bed – and – what he's dreaming about on a big screen – in fact we're follow hi following him into his dreams

Although this text also contains a fair amount of pauses, filled and unfilled, the effect is not one of non-fluency, as the learner is quite skilled at compensating for the problems she has. As we discussed above, syntactic units are preserved because the learner repeats words which belong to the unit after she paused: »the – the character«, »the – the whole film«. Another way in which the learner compensates is by explicitly marking why she feels a need to interrupt herself: »the character – *in fact* the only one ...«; »We see – er – *I think* it's called ...«. It is chiefly the false starts and self-repairs of lines 5 and 8 and the lexical uncerntainty of lines 5–6 which are indications of typical learner problems, and which prevent her from being characterized as fully fluent.

As a final example, consider the following text produced by a learner at an intermediate level.[4]

Text 16

the – clock – ring – and he and it's morning now (clears throat) he's very – erm (clicks tongue) strained – – he's not wo er wide awaken eller awoken yet but – he – (clicks tongue) he (clicks tongue) is very fused and so on he – he can't – d the – clock ring and ring –

The extract contains examples of all the features of non-fluency mentioned above: pauses at strong linking points, false starts, repetitions, which in combination make for a very faltering delivery. In contrast to the native speaker this speaker's low fluency is primarily caused by linguistic problems which she is incapable of solving smoothly.

To round off this discussion we want to state what fluency is *not*. As we already mentioned a couple of times, fluent speech is not synonymous with *fast speech* (though naturally much fast speech is also in fact fluent).

Secondly, fluency has sometimes been used in relation to *written language,* as a rough label for a text which is easy to read because it is well constructed. There is an inconsistency here, as one would not describe someone as being a fluent writer in the same way as people can be called fluent talkers. When applied to the spoken language the description »fluent« applies to the process of producing speech, whereas in relation to written language we are almost invariably interested in the product, rather than the writing process. We therefore recommend that when analysing written texts, where the focus is on the structure of the text, it is more appropriate to use such concepts as coherence and clarity, lexical and syntactic cohesion, narrative structure and argumentation. The notion of »fluency« should be reserved for speech.

A third possible confusion has been the tendency in language teaching circles to regard fluency as somehow *an alternative to correctness*. This is a false opposition. A speaker can be fluent and incorrect, fluent and correct or, of course, not fluent at all (irrespective of relative correctness).

8.3 Speech reception

At the other end of the communication chain we have the listener, trying to reconstruct the speaker's communicative intention by decoding the message. The terms PERCEPTION and COMPREHENSION are often used in this connection, the distinction between the two being that 'perception' refers to the processes used by the listener in order to identify units of phonology and orthography (ie, units at the lowest level in the speech production model), whereas 'comprehension' refers to processes at the higher levels, processes which enable the listener to reconstruct the speaker's intended meaning. As it is difficult to maintain a clear-cut division between these two, we use the term 'comprehension' to refer to alle the processes involved in decoding speech.

One way in which speech comprehension may take place is that the listener first identifies the minimal phonological segments (sounds). These are then gradually added together to larger units (syllables, words, sentence constituents) until the largest units have been identified. Borrowing a term from computer simulations of speech processing, this type of comprehension process can be referred to as BOTTOM-UP PROCESSING. This term is readily understood if one relates what has just been said to the production model presented in 8.1.

The basic principle of bottom-up processing is that listeners exclusively use the incoming flow of sound and their linguistic know-

148

ledge in speech comprehension. This would correspond to the situation in which a person switches on the radio in the middle of a programme and starts decoding the first utterance heard. It would probably only take a few words before she would be able to start guessing at what word class the next word was likely to belong to and perhaps even predict the semantic field of the word. This element of principled guessing is important in most comprehension situations, and is relevant at all the levels of the model of speech production. It is implausible therefore that the one and only way in which speech reception works is from the bottom of the model upwards, in other words that it is speech production in reverse. It is more likely to work through a synthesis of all the levels, irrespective of sequence, but with a tendency to work from the top downwards. As an instance of principled guessing on the basis of limited input, consider the following example:[5]

Text 17

NS   do you have a lot of work after school
L   er I'm – (sigh) – every Wednesday I – (sigh) – I er – I – don't know what er – – (sigh) I – a newspaper er
NS   aha you you you take a newspaper around to people aha
L   yeah

The native speaker's guess is based on a combination of features in the setting and discourse context. As the native speaker has produced an initiating act (a request for information), he can expect the learner's act to be a response to this, ie an informative act functioning as a reply. As the initiating act refers to work after school, it is to be expected that the content of the learner's reply will relate to this topic. These are textually based considerations. Given these, the native speaker can proceed to situationally based considerations such as: what are likely activities for a 13-year-old boy that involve newspapers and take place once a week? It is easy to see how the native speaker manages to comprehend the learner's utterance in spite of its extremely fragmentary character. One could say that the native speaker fills in the lower level units (syntax, words, sounds) on the basis of a prior identification of units at a higher level (communicative intention, specified in terms of speech act and content). This is

149

essentially TOP-DOWN PROCESSING: from top level comprehension supported by a crucial low level item such as »newspaper«, what is missing can be inferred.

Guessing can be equally important at the lower levels of vocabulary and syntax. Listeners know that in English, determiners are normally followed by adjectives or nouns, prepositions by noun phrases, auxiliary verbs by main verbs, some main verbs by adverbials and others by one or two objects, etc. The range of possible words can be further limited by means of semantic considerations (»yesterday I ate an enormous ...«. Possible: *hamburger/ice-cream/meal*. Impossible: *happiness/deck chair/education*). Even at the phonological level certain sounds are typically followed by some sounds and not by others (eg in English a syllable initial stop consonant by a vowel or a liquid but not by a fricative or a sibilant).

The examples of speech reception so far show a hearer inferring on the basis of incomplete input. As described in chapter 5, the process of INFERENCING involves making informed guesses as to the meaning of (part of) an utterance in the light of all the available linguistic cues in combination with the hearer's general knowledge of the world, her awareness of the situation and her relevant linguistic knowledge. Inferencing can play a significant role when only part of an utterance has been understood, for instance when a hearer is not familiar with all the words used by a speaker. This is, of course, a frequent experience of learners. Even so it is difficult to find clear-cut examples of a learner inferencing in the PIF conversations, since the native speakers are more than ready to self-repair or respond to repair requests. Consider the following extract from a conversation with a 10th grade learner:[6]

Text 18
NS do you think there are any ways of solving the unemployment problem in Denmark?
L solving
NS you know finding solutions for it er you know – erm any ways of changing things so that there is less unemployment
L – there must be some but they haven't found it in the government

The learner's repair request (»solving« with rising intonation, supported by a questioning facial expression) elicits a paraphrase (»finding solutions«) which does not enable the learner to grasp precisely what is being asked – »solving« and »solution« are probably unfamiliar lexical items. When the native speaker simplifies (»ways of changing things«, »less unemployment«), the learner is able to correctly infer what was being asked. This seems to imply that part of the native speaker's initial question, perhaps the entire utterance less the word »solving«, was understood.

Inferencing is an important element in the comprehension of speech, both when what is said is incomplete and when only part of what is said is understood instantly. Comprehension is of course a question of degree. Comprehension of a single utterance may be:

total (either instantaneously or delayed, if the addressee needs time
    to piece the message together)
partial (part of the communicative intention escapes the addressee)
zero (the entire message fails to get across because one or more fundamental aspects are not interpreted appropriately).

PARTIAL COMPREHENSION is a useful concept when working with learner language. It may apply at any level of the model of speech production: It is possible to misunderstand the implications of a particular intonation, to grasp only the referential meaning of a lexical item and miss some cultural connotations, or to understand only part of the referential meaning, as in the extract below.[5]

Text 19
NS have you got football boots proper football boots
L (whispers) boots
NS boots like – what you wear on your feet when you play football
L (deep sigh) these (pointing to his shoes)

The learner obviously does not understand the lexical item »boots« and probably only gets as far as »something you wear on your feet«.

Footnotes to chapter 8

1. The notion of »compensatory fluency« has been developed by Lilian Jensen in an analysis of fluency in the speech of Danish learners at Gymnasium level (Jensen 1982).
2. This example comes from the Lund/London corpus of spoken English (Svartvik/ Quirk 1980).
3. PIF informant no 147, university student.
4. PIF informant no 94, grade 10.
5. PIF informant no 104, grade 6
6. PIF informant no 89, grade 10.
7. PIF informant no 120, grade 6.

Chapter 8. Follow-ups

1. Using a tape-recording of a learner, play back the tape with the learner, bit by bit, and ask her to correct herself. Note the kinds of error which are corrected, eg errors of grammar, lexis, pronunciation, and which are not. Discuss with the learner whether she remembers instances of monitoring during production of the tape.
2. Make a recording of a learner telling the same story first in Danish and then in English. Check where the pauses are put, in particular whether they occur at points of strong linking. Are the pauses silent or voiced? Could they be a source of irritation to others?
3. Shannon's prediction game (1951) involves guessing, letter by letter, the written symbols in each successive word in an unknown utterance. Divide in pairs. The A-students have been given the same English utterance which the B-students are to guess. A-students say yes/no to each guess. A-students record the number of guesses needed for each letter. This can be done in the form of a chart like the one below.

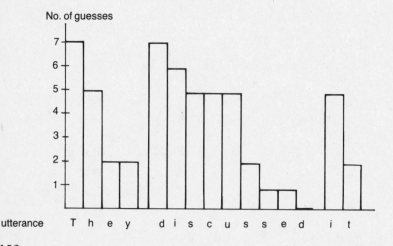

Immediately after completing the task, A interviews B about her inferencing strategies. A and B then study the chart together, comparing it with B's own account and relating her inferencing strategies to top-down and bottom-up processing.

4. Take a short cloze test intended for your own proficiency level. Mark it. Discuss in groups which items were selected on the basis of top-level inferencing (such as speech acts) and with which items you were conscious of having used cues from lower levels (such as morphology and syntax). Discuss the suitability of cloze tests as tests of English as a foreign language.

5. Ask a number of teachers of English how they would define fluency. Compare and discuss answers. Discuss the following claim: »Teachers' beliefs about fluency are more important than formal definitions of it«.

Chapter 8. Sources and further reading

For a brief introduction to the principles of speech production and reception see McDonough 1981. Much more comprehensive, with experimental evidence, is Clark/Clark 1977.

On monitoring see Laver 1970, Morrison/Low 1983 and, for a more restricted view, Krashen 1981, 1982.

Despite its title, Leeson 1975 covers many more aspects of speech than fluency. Dalton/Hardcastle 1977 is a specialist book for speech pathologists. For a study of fluency in the Gymnasium, how the term is used, and an elaboration of compensatory fluency, see Jensen 1982.

For introductory books on the teaching of comprehension, see Dirven 1977 and Allen/Corder 1974, chapter 4.

Chapter nine:
Communication strategies

In discussing fluency we pointed out that people do not always succeed in converting their communicative intentions into speech without running into problems. We also described a number of ways in which speakers may *cover up* for these problems without their fluency being affected. In this chapter we address ourselves to the related question of what possibilities speakers have for *solving* problems in communication. Although our focus will be on learners, much of the description will be valid for native speakers as well, especially when involved in asymmetric communicative events (either among themselves or with IL speakers).

Foreign language learners often experience a discrepancy between what they would like to say, their communicative intention, and what they know how to say in the foreign language, their IL knowledge. A similar discrepancy occurs in speech reception whenever learners are incapable of securing total comprehension (cf. chapter 8). In order to bridge the gap between communicative needs and limited communicative resources, learners may make use of COMMUNICATION STRATEGIES. This term covers problem-solving devices that learners resort to in order to solve what they experience as problems in speech production and reception.

9.1 Strategies in production

When learners cannot find the word or expression needed, the choices open to them are to give up completely, to reduce the original communicative intention, or to try to solve the problem by making creative use of the communicative resources available. Accordingly a distinction can be made between *reduction strategies*, the most extreme form of which is giving up, and *achievement strategies*, by which learners try to achieve what they actually intend to say. In the following extract from a PIF conversation the learner makes extensive use of achievement strategies:[1]

```
NS   do you erm how do you go to school – – erm do you er go to school by bus
L
```

```
NS   –
L        yes sometimes er sometimes I take my er – er – what's it called – er
```

```
NS   er your                        oh              what does it look like –
L    – er – my – cykel – er (laugh) "knallert" – ['knælə]  – er (laugh)
```

```
NS                              (laugh)
L    you know er Puch – kn Puch – (laugh) you know so – er some people –
```

```
NS                    mm – (laugh)
L    er have er a cykel       (laugh) er – – no I can't explain it – you know
```

```
NS                    aha                              aha yer
L    some people have a car –      and some people have a bicycle –
```

```
NS                                                        oh a
L    and some people have a er – erm – a cykel there is a m motor –
```

```
NS   bicycle – with a motor –                    no no it's –  a
L                      motor – is that a bicycle –        oh
```

```
NS   motorcycle – yer – so you have a bi-cycle I mean or a bicycle and a
L    bicycle yer er
```

```
NS   motorcycle –        (laugh) aha – and you you have a motorcycle –
L              oh yer –                                    yer ...
```

9.1.1 Achievement strategies

The learner in text 20 has the problem that she does not know the English word *moped* for Danish *knallert*. Instead of giving up and thus abandoning the topic she makes a series of attempts at conveying to the native speaker what she wants to say. We can list her attempts:

1. cykel
2. knallert
3. ['knælə]
4. Puch
5. some people have a ...

What we see illustrated here is two main types of ACHIEVEMENT STRA-TEGIES: strategies which make use of the learner's L1 (1, 2, 3, 4) and strategies that try to reach a solution by making creative use of the learner's IL knowledge (5). We shall discuss each of these in some detail, as well as two other types of achievement strategies, inter-actional and non-linguistic strategies.

L1 based strategies
It is convenient to distinguish between three types of L1 based strate-gies, two of which are represented in text 20.

Category	Description	Example	Comment
code-switching	learner borrows one or more words from L1, aware that it/they are not English	my "knallert"	Danish word for moped
anglicizing	learner tries to make a Danish word sound English, thinking it may now be English	[knælə]	modification of Danish word "knallert" to English pronunciation
literal translation	learner makes a word-for-word translation from the mother tongue	I take myself in the neck	Danish: "Jeg tager mig selv i nakken" = I pull myself together

Fig. 11: L1 based strategies

There is a considerable risk of such L1 based strategies not being comprehensible. In the case of the three quoted examples, none of them was understood by the native speaker in the contexts in which they were used. L1 based strategies may be a safer bet when the vocabulary has entered both Danish and English from the same foreign source (eg *spaghetti, restaurant,* and a lot of the technical or specialised vocabulary based on Latin and Greek).[2] For the same reason the learner's attempt to use *Puch,* an assumedly international brand name, was no bad idea. Had the native speaker known some-thing about mopeds (which she apparently did not), she would probably have been able to understand what the learner was trying to say at this point.

IL based strategies
Both 'anglicizing' and 'literal translation' make use of the learner's IL knowledge. They have, however, been classified as L1 based because the point of departure in each case is a form in the learner's L1. With the four types of strategies listed below, there are few traces of the learner's L1 in the strategy.

Category	Description	Example	Comment
paraphrase	learner explains by means of other English words, often focussing on characteristic properties or functions of intended referent	some people have a car – and some people have a er bicycle – and and some people have a er cykel there is a m motor ...	she tries to explain moped as a category of transport between bicycle and car
generalisation	learner assumes that her original goal can be reached by using a generalised IL term	people from all country	original goal: young people from all parts of the world
restructuring	learner is unable to complete initial sentence pattern, breaks off and starts in a different way	I have four – I have er three sisters and one brother	learner realizes that she does not know the English for Danish *søskende* ('sisters and brothers')
word-coinage	learner constructs a new IL word	funny-dress ball	fancy-dress ball

Fig. 12: IL based strategies

IL based strategies have a better chance of being understood than L1 based strategies. The main risks with IL based strategies are that extensive use of paraphrasing and restructuring strategies may make considerable demands on the addressee's patience. Generalization strategies may create an impression of vagueness. However IL based strategies offer the greatest scope for making creative use of one's communicative resources in a way which is maximally efficient, short of knowing the appropriate word or expression. The fact that the native speaker in text 20 drew the erroneous conclusion that the learner was talking about a motor-cycle is more a consequence of her lack of relevant knowledge of the world (mopeds are not significant in British culture) than of the learner failing to paraphrase exactly what she had in mind.

Interactional strategies

One choice open to the learner in situations in which there is direct contact with the addressee is to appeal for help.

Category	Description	Example	Comment
appeal	learner invites addressee to help her out directly or indirectly	my sweater is – er what colour is this	points to her sweater

It is easy to see that the strategy of appealing is closely related to what we termed self-initiated, interactional repair in chapter 4. The difference is that with repair work as we described it, the speaker first tries to express her intention in one way and then realizes that there is a problem, whereas the above example of an appeal contains no 'first attempt' which then needs repairing. This slight difference between repairs and at least some appeals should not, however, obscure the fact that there are strong similarities between interactional repairs and the use of interactional communication strategies.[3]

Non-linguistic strategies

In the example of an appeal above, the learner supports her verbal request by pointing to her sweater. This combination of linguistic and non-linguistic strategies such as gesture and facial expression is common in situations in which there is visual contact between the interactants. Occasionally, non-linguistic strategies are used instead of linguistic attempts, especially by beginners.

9.1.2 Sequences of achievement strategies

In the following extract from an intermediate learner,[4] we see gesture supplementing linguistic strategies. The text is chosen to illustrate how learners at this level often make use of L1 based, IL based, and non-linguistic communication strategies, and that a sequence of strategies is needed to reach the goal. The topic is why people move out of Copenhagen. The learner has a Danish concept in mind (»parcelhus«), and does not know an English equivalent for it.

Text 21

	transcript	comment	communication strategy
NS	why do you think they do that?		
L	mm they want a "parcelhuset"		code-switching
NS	uhuh what's that?		
L	erm it's a house erm it it's not an apartment	gesture indicates plot of land	paraphrase + non-linguistic
NS	mm		
L	but it's a big house where just THEY live	gesture shapes house	paraphrase + non-linguistic
NS	oh I see a a sort of totally detached house		
L	yeah		

The first paraphrase the learner uses is a negative definition, »it is not an apartment«, which puts the native speaker on the right track. With the additional linguistic information in the second paraphrase, plus the gestures, she is able to supply what she believes is the words the learner was needing. It is impossible to decide whether the learner actually recognizes the words »a totally detached house«, ie has it in his vocabulary, or whether he takes a bit of a gamble,

159

hoping that the native speaker has understood what he intended to say.

It is interesting to observe that the sequence of strategies in text 21 is similar to the sequence we listed for text 20. In each case the learner starts off with L1 based strategies but has to change to IL based strategies to convey her communicative intention.

9.1.3 Identifying achievement strategies

How can we know that a learner makes use of achievement strategies? With interactional strategies there is obviously no problem as the strategy itself is overtly marked as a request. Evidence for other types of achievement strategies is explicit as well as implicit, and we consequently distinguish between explicit and implicit STRATEGY MARKERS. In text 20 the learner says »what's it called« (learner line 2), while looking away from the native speaker (ie she is not appealing), and »no I can't explain it« (learner line 5). Both of these *explicitly* reveal her uncertainty. Supporting evidence for the achievement strategies in text 20 is the learner's repeated attempts to express one and the same intention. This is usually a reliable indication of the speaker experiencing a problem.

Signals of uncertainty such as pauses, laughs, hesitations, false starts, sighs, clicks and heavy breathing may be used with caution by analysts as *implicit* strategy markers. The problem is that as we pointed out in chapter 8, many of these signals have important functions in »normal« speech. The analyst therefore needs a combination of uncertainty signals in order to be reasonably sure that what follows these may be the result of a communication strategy. Text 20 contains many instances of this (filled and unfilled pauses, laughs, hesitations and false starts).

It follows that it is not always possible to identify achievement stragegies in learner language performance in a rigorous fashion. A fair amount of interpretation is needed. More valid results can be obtained by consulting the learner immediately after she has produced an utterance and asking her to introspect about (1) what problems she experienced and (2) how she solved them. Experience with *introspection* shows that this is a technique which has to be used with considerable caution. In particular, you cannot expect learners to be able

160

to describe how they solved their problems unless they have been instructed about communication strategies beforehand.

Let us complete this discussion of how to identify achievement strategies by briefly pointing out an approach which *cannot* be recommended. One might reason that as communication strategies are used when a learner does not know how to express herself in the foreign language, there might be a direct link between the use of communication strategies and *errors*. However, there is no simple relationship between strategy use and errors.

The result of a communication strategy *may* be an error, as when a learner says *animal hut* for *cage,* referring to what her canary lives in. But often strategies do not result in errors, as will have appeared from our discussion of IL based and interactional strategies.

Similarly, the occurrence of errors in IL performance is not necessarily the result of the learner having made use of a strategy. When a grade 6 learner says »can I English can I 'lidt' [æmərɪkænsk]« it is just possible that he experiences a problem in how to say 'American', but it is less than probable that he is aware of any problem relating to the use of *can I ..., can I ...* (modelled on Danish syntax), or that the use of Danish *lidt* ('a little') is the result of a conscious problem-solving procedure. Errors cannot be regarded as indicators of communication strategies.

9.1.4 Reduction strategies

So far we have concentrated on strategies by which the learner tries to get her communicative intention across. However, many learners tend to choose the opposite way out, ie to reduce their communicative goal.

REDUCTION may take place at both the pragmatic and the referential level. Reduction at the *pragmatic level* is a typical feature of many intermediate and even advanced learners, who have difficulties in marking appropriately for politeness and social distance (cf chapter 3). One reason for this may be that learners do not pay sufficient attention to the importance of expressing speech acts appropriately because in the »traditional« foreign language classroom they only produce language at one level of formality. When placed in different situations, they are forced to reduce compared to the way they would express themselves in their L1.

Reduction may also occur at the *referential level*. The degree of reduction varies from saying nothing at all about the topic introduced, ie *topic avoidance,* to saying something approximating to what one would like to say, ie *meaning replacement*. Here is an example of meaning replacement:

intended communicative goal:	»Macbeth is a despairing and unbalanced ruler with a lust for power«
realized message:	»Macbeth is a very bad tyrant«.

When a learner produces utterances like this, the effect may well be that her interlocutors find her imprecise, vague or even naive. Vagueness, which is typical of much learner language, may be due to meaning replacement or caused by the learner overusing generalisation, eg using superordinate terms such as »flower« for »tulip«, and »thing« to refer to everything under the sun. In our analyses, generalisation seems sometimes to blend into meaning replacement.

9.2 Strategies in reception

In the section on speech reception in chapter 8 we discussed the process of *inferencing*. Addressees draw on their cultural and linguistic knowledge, problems are clarified as the situation evolves, and conscious and subconscious inferences are drawn. Inferencing is consequently a normal reception process, but learners may have to rely more on inferencing procedures than native speakers.

A learner experiencing real difficulty in comprehending an utterance, ie a learner who is unable to infer meaning, may resort to an interactional strategy. In terms of repairs, the learner would request the interlocutor to self-repair, ie the repair would be an other-initiated interactional repair. The repair request could be either of the following types:

(1) *general repair request,* learner expresses lack of understanding in general, without specifying what the comprehension problem is (»I don't understand«, »what«)

162

(2) *specific repair request:* learner specifies at what point in the discourse the comprehension problem occurred (»*where* did she go?«).

General repair requests are typically expressed by means of routinized formulae like »what« or »what mean you« (common in the IL of elementary Danish learners of English). The utility value of such formulae for beginning learners is no doubt significant, and although native speakers often just repeat their turn verbatim after a general appeal (though more slowly and distinctly), there are instances in which a general repair request is followed by a specific repair. Both possibilities are illustrated in the examples below from the PIF corpus:

NS: y you don't want to visit England particularly
L: what
NS: you don't WANT to visit England particularly
L: no

NS: how long how much time do you spend at the stables
L: what
NS: how how much time do you spend with the horses
L: I don't know erm

A more reliable way, however, of eliciting a specific repair is to utter a specific request:

NS: is it an exchange
L: I don't know what that is
NS: it means ...

NS: d'you like going to the cinema
L: to the what
NS: the cinema
L: yeah

The division into production and reception strategies is not watertight. A hybrid strategy, *pleading ignorance,* is interesting in that it demonstrates how reception problems become indistinguishable from production problems. »I don't know« serves the double function of constituting a minimal reply in itself, without initiating a repair-sequence, and concealing a comprehension or production problem.

9.3 Communication strategies and proficiency levels

Various studies have been undertaken of the ways in which strategies are used by learners at different levels of proficiency in the foreign language.[5]

At *lower proficiency levels,* learners make extensive use of L1 based achievement strategies like code-switching, as is to be expected. Often non-linguistic strategies are substituted for linguistic strategies. As for appeals, it is worth noting that some learners use them extensively and others hardly at all. Learners who do not use appeals would benefit from being made aware of the advantages of asking for help instead of just giving up or using a Danish word.

At *intermediate levels,* learners use a larger repertoire of strategy types, although individual learners often have their own preferences for specific types. There is some evidence (Bialystok/Fröhlich 1980, Brodersen/Gibson 1982) that those learners who have the most limited linguistic skills are also the least efficient strategy users. This is hardly surprising, as a prerequisite for using the more efficient IL based achievement strategies is the presence of IL knowledge.

At the intermediate proficiency levels, learners fall roughly into two groups: those who generally try to use achievement strategies, »*achievers*«, and those who do the opposite, »*reducers*«. Why do some learners achieve and others reduce? We believe that there are at least two major determining factors. First, there is the learner's personality. A person who is careful and who never runs risks, if these can be avoided, may prefer reduction strategies rather than risk making mistakes. The second factor is the learner's experience of communication in the foreign language classroom. It is fair to assume that teachers who encourage their learners to chance their arm, who prefer an erroneous attempt to no attempt, will tend to encourage »achievers«, whereas teachers who focus on correctness, on form rather than on content, will »produce« »reducers«.

Finally, at *advanced levels,* one might expect to find few communica-

164

tion strategies, because learners who have proceeded this far might be expected to have a closer fit between their IL resources and their communicative needs. However, it could be argued that the better one's proficiency in the foreign language, the greater one's communicative ambitions. For this reason one might still expect a fair number of strategies, even in the speech of advanced learners. In the conversations of advanced learners in the PIF corpus, it is difficult to find strategies which are clearly marked as such by the presence of (explicit or implicit) strategy markers. What happens at these levels might be that learners are more like native speakers in that they are better at anticipating problems and at solving these during the normal planning of speech. As a result there is no sign of problem-solving at the points in the learner text at which there might be recourse to a strategy.

Notes to chapter 9

1. PIF informant no. 73, grade 10.
2. There is evidence that 9th grade learners have considerable awareness of which L1 words are loan words, cf Brodersen/Gibson 1982.
3. Whether one characterizes a specific instance of learner performance as a repair or an interactional strategy is very much a question of whether one is interested in the *discourse* category of repairs or in the *psycholinguistically* oriented category of communication strategies.
4. PIF informant no. 89, grade 10.
5. The most systematic of these is reported in Bialystok/Fröhlich 1980. Our description is based partly on this, partly on analyses of the PIF conversations, see Haastrup/Phillipson 1983.

Chapter 9. Follow-ups

1. Following the instructions in follow-up 3, chapter 2, identify the achievement strategies used and classify them according to the categories introduced in this chapter. Are there problems of classification? How are the strategies marked? Is there a pattern of strategy use by particular learners?
2. Record a communication task and go over the recording with the learner immediately afterwards, asking her to identify communication problems and strategies (tape-record the introspection discussion as well). Prepare a transcript of the original recording and identify strategies by means of strategy markers. Compare this with the learner's own identification of problems and strategies.

Are there examples of reduction strategies? of achievement strategies which are not accompanied by strategy markers?

3. Divide a group of learners into two. Provide one group with a list of Danish words which they do not know the English equivalent of (or which do not have exact equivalents). Ask one learner at a time to explain the word in English to the other group, who assist in guessing what is referred to. Having completed the task, the group listen to a tape-recording of it and note down the explanations used. This is used as a basis for a discussion of types of interlanguage based strategies and the effects that these might have on native speakers.

4. It might be argued that learners are already strategy users in their L1. Discuss how this could be utilized in foreign language teaching. Are there any obvious ways of organizing teaching so as to enable learners to develop appropriate achievement strategies?

6. Consider ways in which compensatory fluency can be increased in advanced learners in connection with strategy use.

Chapter 9. Sources and further reading

Færch/Kasper 1983b contains a comprehensive collection of studies ranging from discussion of criteria for defining and classifying communication strategies to empirical investigations of the occurrence and function of strategies. The problem of how to identify communication strategies is discussed in two studies. The book also contains an extensive bibliography.

Sproglæreren published a series of articles in 1982 on communication strategies. Brodersen/Gibson 1982 contains a description of an experiment in teaching communication strategies in the Folkeskole.

Chapter ten:
Communicative competence

Communicative competence has tended to be something of a vogue term in language teaching circles in recent years, with all the hazards that new fashions involve. The term has often been used without clear statements of what is covered or excluded by it. The purpose of this chapter is to clarify what is essential to the concept "communicative competence", partly by pulling together some of the many threads from earlier chapters, partly by introducing three new dimensions. One of these, the question of what impression different types of interlanguage make on native speakers, is of general relevance to communicative competence both in and out of school. A second dimension, which covers the relationship between learners' general cognitive and social development and their language proficiency, is of particular relevance to foreign language teaching in schools, as is the final dimension, learners' metacommunicative awareness.

10.1 The components of communicative competence

Historically the term communicative competence evolved as a result of a shift of emphasis among theorists in linguistics, a move away from the rules of language form, traditionally associated with grammar, vocabulary and pronunciation, towards an emphasis on the ability to use language.[1] The essential components are the ones that we have presented in earlier chapters in the book. Provisionally we can state that communicative competence consists of the following:

	Components
Communicative competence	phonology/orthography
	grammar
	lexis
	pragmatics
	discourse
	communication strategies
	fluency

The components relate to each other in the following way:

(A) Phonological/orthographic, grammatical and lexical knowledge are commonly referred to as LINGUISTIC COMPETENCE. What it is important to note is that linguistic competence in no way represents an alternative or counterpart to communicative competence. It is impossible to conceive of a person being communicatively competent without being lingustically competent.

(B) Pragmatic and discourse knowledge provide the link between linguistic competence and actual *language use* in specific situations. These components account for speakers' capacity to act by means of language in ways which are appropriate to their communicative intentions, to the contexts in which they communicate, and to the discourse into which their verbal contributions fit. The combination of linguistic competence and pragmatic and discourse knowledge will be referred to as PRAGMATIC COMPETENCE. (We use this for want of a better term, and need to stress that pragmatic competence covers more than pragmatic knowledge, as described in chapter 3).

(C) STRATEGIC COMPETENCE refers to speakers' ability to solve communication problems by means of strategies. It can therefore be considered compensatory relative to other types of competence: the activation of strategic competence presupposes an inability to make use of parts of linguistic or pragmatic competence.

(D) *Fluency* refers to speakers' ability to express what they want to say with ease. As with strategic competence, fluency is superimposed on linguistic and pragmatic competence. But whereas strategic competence presupposes a lack of (accessible) knowledge, fluency covers speakers' ability to make use of whatever linguistic and pragmatic knowledge they have.

The relationship between the various components of communicative competence can be represented as in fig. 13.

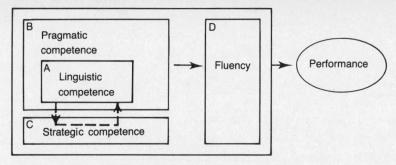

Fig. 13: Components of communicative competence
(the letters refer to the text above)

Before we exemplify this by discussing the relative importance of the various components in two hypothetical communicative events, a few general points concerning communicative competence need to be made.

The fact that linguistic competence is an essential part of pragmatic competence does not imply that learners first have to master all the rules of grammar, vocabulary and pronunciation before they can proceed to pragmatic and discourse knowledge. The belief that it is necessary to learn linguistic competence first in schools, and that pragmatic competence can be left to post-school communication, a stance often associated with traditional foreign language teaching, is indeed questionable. In point of fact English teaching in Denmark throughout this century has, at least at the elementary levels, always been concerned with developing learners' ability to communicate in English. It has aimed at giving them the wherewithal to understand and use English within a particular cultural tradition, to put them in a position to use the skills and knowledge acquired in school later in life. The recent emphasis on "communicative competence" is therefore very much a question of focussing *more* on communicative competence rather than introducing something entirely new. Unfortunately, some of the proponents of communicative competence, and publishers needing to promote new teaching materials, have tended to distort the issues by presenting communicative competence as somehow an alternative to, for instance, grammar. This can be seen in the following excerpt from an ad:

169

"Teaching in the Folkeskole until the 9th class is designed to build up communicative competence, and *for this reason* there is no concentration on grammar or written work."[2]
(our translation and underlining)

This quotation contains two fundamental misconceptions, firstly that grammar is unimportant for communicative competence, and secondly that communicative competence is only concerned with the spoken language. A related unjustified restriction of communicative competence is the belief that it applies to production only. Communicative competence in fact covers listening and reading as well as speaking and writing.

For teachers of English there have been plenty of descriptions of linguistic competence available for most of this century, whereas it is only in recent years that pragmatic and strategic competence have been at all adequately defined and described. The increased insight into these has resulted from research into how language is actually used and in particular how learners perform. Descriptions of communicative competence can be of use in many ways, for instance in specifying learner goals, in analysing texts, and in planning and structuring learning activities. Neither the communicative events presented in chapter 2, nor the two to be discussed below, can be adequately described without concepts which go far beyond what traditionally constituted "linguistic competence". But at the same time, linguistic competence is essential.

A related point is that emphasizing the need for learners to master rules of grammar, vocabulary and pronunciation/orthography for them to be communicatively competent does not imply that this linguistic competence has to be correct in all respects. The issue of correctness *is* obviously important for learners' communicative competence, as we shall discuss below. There is however an unfortunate and widespread misconception that teachers who stress linguistic competence are preoccupied with correctness, whereas teachers who give high priority to pragmatic competence have a more lenient attitude to errors. We want to emphasize that it is perfectly possible for a teacher to hold simultaneously the view that learners ought, for instance, to master highly productive syntactic rules and the view that learners cannot be expected to apply *all*

170

grammatical rules correctly.

It is impossible to specify communicative competence in any absolute sense; it needs to be done relative to the socio-psychological characteristics of individuals, to their communicative needs and to the situations in which they communicate. IL users are generally in a situation which in significant respects (see chapter 17) differs from that of native speakers. In order to state what is required for Danish learners to be communicatively competent in English, it is necessary to relate communicative competence to the communicative events in which learners participate, to their communicative intentions, and the social roles which their interlocutors (native speakers or other IL speakers) assign to them. An important consequence of this is that it is false to equate communicative competence in native speakers with communicative competence in IL speakers.

By restricting our coverage of communicative competence to the components listed above, we have ignored the fundamental fact that communicative competence never exists independently of SOCIAL COMPETENCE. L1 communicative competence is part of language users' capacity to interact with other members of the same speech community. Pragmatic knowledge is a particularly clear instance of communicative competence interacting with social competence. Speech act knowledge constitutes part of a more general knowledge of what acts (verbal and non-verbal) are possible in social groups, just as expressing speech act modality appropriately presupposes a basic ability to identify relevant social roles and the status associated with these. It is therefore obvious that for learners to be able to communicate with people from different communities (the social norms of which may differ from those of the learner's own community), and to understand textual products from that community, it is necessary to possess not just communicative but also social competence.

Whereas the link between communicative competence and social competence is a fairly obvious one, the relationship between general *cognitive abilities* and communicative competence is less clear. Cognitive and linguistic (L1) development are intimately related in primary and secondary socialisation, but it is impossible to claim the same for foreign language learning. It is intuitively plausible that learning a foreign language is facilitated if the learner has advanced cognitive abilities (eg can abstract, generalise, draw analogies, etc.), but at the same time it is possible that such cognitive abilities are fostered by foreign language learning. There is research evidence in the field of bilingual education which indicates that this may be so (Swain/Lapkin 1982).

10.2 Exemplifying communicative competence

To demonstrate the use of the components identified so far, and the integration and interaction of these, we will present two hypothetical communicative events which exemplify the kinds of situation that intermediate to advanced Danish users of English may be involved in.

Communicative event 1. A Danish medical student reading an anatomy textbook in English
As is the case with most higher education studies in Denmark, this student finds that some of the obligatory textbooks are written in English. At school she read plenty of English and American literature, but only a limited amount of non-fiction, mostly journalistic and social-historical texts. Her new anatomy textbook, however, is a dense presentation of a wealth of factual material. It is a totally different genre from what she is used to. Luckily she is highly motivated (she will also be examined for detailed understanding of the content).

Reading the text makes demands on her *receptive* competence in English; she makes notes in Danish. There are many unfamiliar *lexical* items, but these are well covered in the dictionary, even the more technical terms. However as she has as yet little experience of dissecting the human body in the laboratory, much of the content is rather remote from her experience. The task is cognitively demanding (in the terms of our speech production model, she has difficulty with top-down processing). As she is fairly new to her studies, her *pragmatic* competence, when reading scientific English texts, is limited, in particular her capacity to follow the structure of the arguments, relationships such as generalisation, exemplification and conclusion. The textbook makes great demands on her discourse knowledge, for instance how to interpret markers of cohesion between sentences, relationships of contrast, condition, result and many of the other characteristic features of scientific discourse. In short she lacks experience in handling the kind of expository prose that is common in academic textbooks. As reading is essentially a private activity, and as she is working on her own, she has only her own resources to draw on when making a synthesis of all the elements (pragmatic, discourse, lexical and grammatical) which together express the writer's communicative intentions.

172

Communicative event 2. Scandinavian teenagers in informal discussion at a peace movement gathering

The discussion begins with polite greetings, smiles, embarrassed pauses and a good deal of uncertainty about how they should get going. Present are one Finn, one Norwegian and a Dane. They agree on speaking English when it emerges that the participants are unable to understand each other's mother tongues. Once these introductory steps are over the Finn gets the business part of the discussion going by presenting a proposal for action. Making a coherent presentation makes great demands on her *pragmatic* competence, but as she is very familiar with the subject of planning peace demonstrations, the necessary *lexical* items can be *fluently* activated. The Dane and the Norwegian have no trouble in understanding the Finn, as they are familiar with the vocabulary and the sort of arguments presented. This is so, even though the Finn makes *grammatical* and *pronunciation* errors: she does not seem to be consciously monitoring for correctness, but rather concentrates on getting her points across, at times drawing on her *strategic* competence (she uses paraphrases and gesture) to fill in some lexical gaps. The Norwegian has been eager for some time to interrupt, but the Finn has held the floor successfully, making it clear by means of gambits and intonation that she has not finished. When there is a silent pause, it is the Dane who successfully takes over the initiative, coming in swiftly and politely with a request for the Finn to clarify whether she was making a suggestion or merely stating a fact: there were gaps in the Finn's *pragmatic* competence, as a result of which she had expressed herself ambiguously. It transpires that the Norwegian was anxious to clarify the same point, but that he has much less experience in participating in this kind of discussion than the Dane, who is therefore more confident than the Norwegian in operating in English.

These are very fragmentary descriptions of the two imagined communicative events, but they hopefully serve to make a number of points clear. All the components of pragmatic competence as listed earlier are necessary in any communicative event; different aspects of these components, as well as of the additional components of strategic competence and fluency, are drawn upon in different communicative events; some tasks make greater demands on particular components of communicative competence than others.

10.3 Dimensions of communicative competence

So far, our description of the components of communicative competence has been equally valid for communicative competence in a native language and in an interlanguage. With the exception of fluency, which we have restricted to spoken communication, all the components are necessary for anyone to be communicatively competent. We now discuss a number of 'dimensions' which are also relevant in a characterization of communicative competence, but which are of particular interest for descriptions of *communicative competence in a foreign language,* especially when the foreign language is taught as a school subject.

10.3.1 Communicative competence in a foreign language as assessed by native speakers

We pointed out earlier that the relationship between communicative competence and correctness is not a straightforward one. An important issue in the description of learner communicative competence is whether it is possible to state what effect learner divergence from a native speaker norm has on native speakers. This is an area where teachers are at a serious disadvantage. Often they are so familiar with learner language that they can understand most learner utterances, not least those containing transfer from L1. But how do native speakers react to the speech of learners? How significant are errors for comprehensibility? What do native speakers find distracting in learner language?

One way of providing answers to these questions is to use TOLERANCE TESTS. These are tests which elicit native speaker (in this case, British) reactions to samples of English produced by foreigners (here, Danes). Tolerance tests attempt to assess the effect that learner language has on native listeners, to specify which aspects of communicative competence are particularly important, and what impedes communication.

The risks that learners run are essentially of two kinds:

- learner language may be *incomprehensible*
- learner language may *distract* the attention of the listener away

174

from the message and onto the form in which the message is expressed.[3]

In chapter 19 (19.5) we shall summarise a tolerance test which focussed on the comprehensibility of learners' written language. The main finding of this study was that lexical errors impede comprehension far more than grammatical ones. We shall here present a tolerance test of spoken language covering distraction as well as comprehensibility[4].

The corpus consisted of extracts from authentic conversations between a young Englishman with no knowledge of Danish and Danish intermediate learners. The learner texts were processed in two ways: a linguistic performance analysis was undertaken, and the tolerance of 300 British informants to extracts from the conversations was tested. For the linguistic analysis all lexical, grammatical and phonetic errors were identified. On the basis of this an error density measure (the ratio between the number of errors and the total number of word tokens) was calculated. A test was then constructed consisting of extracts lasting 2–3 minutes from the tapes of five learners, who between them spanned the top, middle and bottom of the error density spectrum. The tolerance test involved the British native speakers assessing the learners on a five-point scale for 14 bi-polar criteria, covering *language aspects* (eg good/bad grammar), *personality* characteristics (eg tense/relaxed), the *content* of what was said (eg interesting/boring), and *comprehensibility* (eg easy/difficult to understand).

One of the significant findings of this study, which involved a considerable amount of computer-assisted statistical analysis, was that native speakers were able to make significant judgements for each of the four factors, in other words that each of the learners was rated separately for language, personality, content and comprehensibility.

A second finding was that there was no evidence that a particular category of error (eg lexical) impaired comprehensibility more than others. In continuous text, such as conversation, there are many other cues which the addressee can make use of in order to reconstruct meaning. Thus one learner stated: "in 1933 the boys and girls get together in one [kɔːps] but er mostly there are girl troops

175

or scouts and boy scouts." Pronouncing the word "corps" as [kɔːps] did not lead to misinterpretations – though probably to a good deal of mirth – because in the context words like "scout organization" and "patrol" had also been used. Errors which were most likely to lead to actual misunderstandings or low comprehensibility were discourse level inadequacies such as incorrect use of conjunctions or pronominal reference across sentences. The authors conclude that, because there is no direct correlation between measures of correctness and of comprehensibility, whether an error will lead to poor comprehension or not will not so much depend on whether the error is of a particular kind (eg lexical, grammatical or phonetic), as on the linguistic context in which the error occurs. The negative effect of lexical errors may be alleviated by contextual support, whereas with discourse errors this is less likely.

A third finding was that low comprehensibility was related to extensive use of hesitation phenomena. It is reasonable to conclude that poor fluency, whatever the cause of it, leads to limited comprehensibility. In the light of this finding the authors draw the conclusion that in interaction with native speakers, and given contextual support, it may be more important to be fluent than correct.

As regards how far deviation from the target language code is distracting, it is hypothesized that distraction is directly predictable from the number of errors which an interlanguage text contains, regardless of error type.

The study does not provide definitive answers to questions about the relative importance of each constituent of communicative competence in relation to the reception of learner language but, to summarise, the results seem to imply:

– that none of the components of communicative competence can be ignored
– that lexis and inter-sentential cohesion, when used erroneously, are likely to lead to breakdowns of communication, but that in continuous discourse, such as interactional communication, isolated lexical errors may be clarified by contextual support
– that poor fluency impedes comprehensibility
– that a high density of errors, of whatever kind, is distracting.

10.3.2 Context-reduced or context-embedded language

As we have just seen, one and the same error, eg a lexical error, may have very different consequences depending on the context in which it occurs. Any sample of language use could be placed on a continuum at one end of which there is no support for understanding the language provided by the situational context, whereas at the other end there is a great deal of contextual support. At the CON-TEXT-EMBEDDED end of the continuum, language is supported by a wide range of paralinguistic and situational cues, and meaning is actively negotiated and created by the participants. Comprehension is checked through immediate feedback. CONTEXT-REDUCED communication, on the other hand, relies primarily on linguistic cues to meaning and requires mastery of the symbolic system conveying the message.

For children, communication at home, with friends and in the playground is generally context-embedded, whereas school activities like reading and writing are much more context-reduced. The latter involve operating almost exclusively with abstract linguistic cues for such purposes as to narrate, to explain, to gain knowledge, to generalize, to enter a fantasy world, etc. An important aspect of success in school is learning to operate with context-reduced language.

In foreign language learning at the beginning stages, a basic problem is that the learner has limited experience both of the relevant linguistic code and of the contexts in which the language is used by native speakers. The text-based tradition of English teaching in the Danish Gymnasium attempts to develop language proficiency while introducing learners to an English-speaking world which is foreign linguistically, culturally and often also historically. It is therefore not surprising that those learners who are relatively more dependent on context-embedded language in their L1 have trouble in developing communicative competence in relation to texts of which they can only grasp the linguistic and cultural content with difficulty. More recent teaching methods and materials acknowledge this problem by providing much more contextual support for language than was the case 20 years ago, through illustrations, video, etc. Still, it is important to remember that one of the end-goals of foreign language teaching, except perhaps for a minority of learners, is to be able to use the foreign language not only in context-rich, but also in context-reduced situations like reading and writing. It is therefore no solution in the long run to alleviate the task for learners by providing only context-rich environments for language learning.

10.3.3 Metacommunicative awareness

In our discussion of the components of communicative competence, we referred to the various types of "knowledge" which the individual must possess in order to be communicatively competent. We need to emphasize that "knowledge" is used here in a broader sense than in everyday language, where "knowledge" carries strong associations of consciousness. Communicative competence sometimes refers to the ability to communicate, to be proficient in communication, without the speaker having much understanding of the principles which underlie this proficiency. But communicative competence can also be regarded as referring both to knowledge in the sense of being *able* to communicate and to knowledge *about* communication. We believe that communicative competence, when it is an objective in foreign language teaching within general education, should incorporate more than just foreign language proficiency. Learners should also develop what we shall refer to as METACOMMUNICATIVE AWARENESS, conscious knowledge about the components of communicative competence, their interdependence and social functions.

In the same way as communicative competence encompasses linguistic competence, the notion of metacommunicative awareness has as one of its components metalinguistic knowledge, knowledge about grammar, phonology and lexis. It is therefore easy to see that there is nothing revolutionary about the idea that metacommunicative awareness should be a teaching objective within foreign language teaching. All teachers have probably found themselves trying to pass on to their learners knowledge about rules of grammar and pronunciation. But two points need to be made, to avoid misunderstanding.

Firstly, when teaching rules of grammar and pronunciation, only very restricted areas of metacommunicative awareness are co-

178

vered. Indeed, one can argue that the areas covered are not *in themselves* terribly relevant, unless they are related to pragmatic and social considerations. Metacommunicative awareness assumes a focus on *pragmatic* competence.

Secondly, the teaching of meta*linguistic* knowledge is typically motivated by the belief that conscious knowledge will assist learners in developing their proficiency in the foreign language. This means that metalinguistic knowledge is taught as a means to an end (proficiency), not as an end in itself. Whether this is a good teaching approach or not in relation to proficiency is debatable (see chapter 11), but not directly relevant here. What we want to stress is meta*communicative* awareness as a teaching objective in itself, irrespective of whether or not this awareness will help improve proficiency.

Our plea for metacommunicative awareness in foreign language teaching might be countered by the following argument. Metacommunicative awareness should first be developed in relation to the code which learners know best, namely their L1, in which case it is the responsibility of L1 teachers to prepare the ground for foreign language teachers by raising the learners' consciousness about L1 communication. However, there is evidence that such consciousness-raising may work better if the process is initiated in an area in which the person is not directly involved (eg L2 communication), but which is similar to situations the individual can recognize from personal experience (L1 communication). This point is well expressed by the American anthropologist Muriel Saville-Troike (1982, 4–5):

"One of the best means by which to gain understanding of one's own 'way of speaking' is to compare and contrast these ways with others, a process that can reveal that many of the communicative practices assumed to be 'natural' or 'logical' are in fact as culturally unique and conventional as the language code itself. A valuable by-product which emerges from this process is an essential feature of all ethnography: a sense of cultural relativism."

Footnotes to chapter 10

1. The concept of "linguistic comptence" is usually ascribed to the American linguist Noam Chomsky (see eg Chomsky 1965). One of the first major criticisms of this concept was by Dell Hymes, the American anthropologist, who emphasized the need for extending competence to comprise various aspects of language use (see Hymes 1972a).
2. The ad was printed in "Gymnasieskolen" in 1981.
3. We prefer the term "distraction" to "irritation", which was coined by Johansson 1973.
4. This study is summarised in Albrechtsen/Henriksen/Færch 1980.

Chapter 10. Follow-ups

1. Consider a number of more polemical articles on communicative competence and foreign language teaching in journals, eg *Sproglæreren,* and assess how the concept is used. Are some of the disagreements due to conflicting views on what is covered by the term "communicative competence"?
2. Analyse the declared goals for foreign language teaching in Folkeskole and Gymnasium and the relevant official guidelines in terms of the components and dimensions of communicative competence presented in this chapter. Could a more specific statement of goals for various levels of proficiency be envisaged? The present-day goals could be contrasted with those in earlier legislation, and changes traced.
3. "In order to state what is required for Danish learners to be communicatively competent in English, it is necessary to relate communicative competence to the communicative events in which learners participate, to their communicative intentions, and the social roles which their interlocutors (native speakers or other IL speakers) assign to them". Is this feasible?
4. Write out communicative event 2, section 10.2, as a textual transcript of what the participants might actually have said. What additional information on the event do you need in order to perform this task?
5. It might be claimed that social competence in Denmark and Britain does not differ significantly and therefore does not constitute a learning problem. Is this so?
6. Is it a reasonable goal to set for all learners of English that they should be able to communicate in context-reduced situations? Could one envisage collaboration between teachers of Danish and English to achieve this?

Chapter 10. Sources and further reading

For general surveys of the history and uses of "communicative competence", see Canale/Swain 1980, Canale 1983, Munby 1978 ch. 1 and Andersen/Risager 1981. There is a more explicit link to pedagogical applications in Piepho 1974, Breen/Candlin 1980, Edmondson/House/Kasper/Stemmer 1982, and Savignon 1983. See also the references in chapters 13 and 14.

On the principles of tolerance testing, and details of a number of ingenious experiments, see Johansson 1973 and chapter 18.

Theory-building in relation to bilingual education, in particular the elaboration of context-free and context-embedded language, and cognitively demanding operations, is principally the work of Cummins, see Cummins 1980, 1981. For a consideration of parameters in the spoken language, in relation to assessing the communicative competence of adolescent native speakers, see Brown 1981.

Part II:
Language learning

So far the emphasis in this book has been on the forms that language can take, the functions that language can perform, and on the processes and strategies involved in language use. Together, these components constitute a person's communicative competence, as outlined in chapter 10. The question to which we now turn in part II is *how* learners develop communicative competence in a foreign language. This involves psychological as well as social considerations, because foreign language learning, like the acquisition of the mother tongue, takes place through the interaction of learner-internal processes and learner-external factors. In chapter 11 we concentrate on ways of characterising this interaction and illustrate it with reference to some teaching methods currently in use in Denmark. In chapter 12, we discuss some socio-psychological variables which have a potentially determining impact on the learning process.

Chapter 11:
Learning a foreign language

Earlier chapters, particularly chapters 3–7, have focussed on language, on linguistic *products*. Chapters 8–9 dealt with some *processes* involved in speech production and reception. And as these chapters show, it is no simple matter to identify and describe mental processes: we have no direct access to what goes on in the brain when people communicate. Although there is hope that the neurological mechanisms underlying speech production and reception will eventually be identified, psycholinguists are at present forced to rely heavily on indirect evidence, on inferring from observation of product-level phenomena to underlying processes.

The problems one encounters in describing language *learning* reflect the general problem of how to get at the level of mental processes when the only access to this is through the observation of individuals from the outside. But in addition, the analyst interested in the processes of language learning has to disentangle these from receptive and productive *communication* processes. This would be a simple matter if the two types of process occurred in clearly differentiated situations, what we might for the time being refer to as "communicative situations" and "learning situations". Although there are differences between situations the primary purpose of which is communicative, eg a job interview, and situations which are created to promote learning, eg English teaching Monday mornings between 8.55 and 9.40, there is a considerable overlap between "communicative situations" and "learning situations". Indeed, one might argue that the major part of native language acquisition and, frequently, a considerable part of second language acquisition, is a by-product of the individual communicating with friends, family and colleagues. Similarly it can be argued that one takes a very restricted view of communication if one rules out the possibility of educational situations also being "communicative". So rather than distinguish between "communicative" and "learning" situations, we prefer to draw a distinction between educational and non-educational situations, both of which are communicative. Relative to foreign language learning, an EDUCATIONAL SITUATION is a communicative situation which is created in order to promote learning. In a NON-EDUCATIONAL SITUATION, communication is the predominant goal.[1]

This distinction does not help us to identify learning processes as distinct from communication processes, but it helps us to formulate the problem in a precise way. Assuming that both educational and non-educational situations are communicative, and that learning often takes place in either type of situation, we must accept that learning processes have to be described not in isolation but as interacting with receptive and productive processes of communication, and that communication and learning processes operate simultaneously, though at different levels of consciousness. If the wish to communicate is in focus, at a less conscious level there may be a process of learning taking place simultaneously. In some situations, eg in connection with certain classroom activities, the priority of the two types of process may be reversed so that learning is in focus, or there may be no communication process in any real sense of the word. However, most foreign language learning, even in the context of the classroom, probably takes place indirectly, as a by-product of communicating in the foreign language.

11.1 Input – intake

One major factor in foreign language learning is the language which learners are exposed to. The nature of this foreign language INPUT will vary with the type of situation in which the language is encountered. A Danish schoolchild learning French may well be exclusively dependent on the input that the classroom provides, simply because no French is ever heard or read outside it. By contrast, learners of German in certain parts of the country may watch German television, meet German-speaking tourists, or travel south of the border, all of which can provide communicative situations which represent a different type of input to what is experienced in the classroom. The English language impinges on Danish children in 101 ways outside school: youth culture, American clothes and food, sport, television, cinema, tourism, technology, etc. There is constant exposure to the language and indeed the cultures from which it originates. Danes are familiarised with English sounds, with concepts and words. All these are experienced directly, without the mediation of the mother tongue, as the following imports into Danish testify: *allright, burger, cornflakes, cowboy(bukser), babysitter, pub, soft ice, world cup,* etc.

Some of the input can be interpreted directly by means of the knowledge the learner already has of the foreign language (the learner's 'interlanguage' knowledge, see chapter 17). This means that the psycholinguistic rules (cf chapter 6) which a native speaker has used in order to produce the language are matched by rules in the learner's IL system. The learner can also interpret input by means of inferencing strategies (see chapter 8), by making qualified guesses as to the meaning of input ('top-down processing'). The result may be total or partial comprehension, or there may be a residue of input which is incomprehensible.

In figure 14, (a) and (b) cover COMPREHENSIBLE INPUT, input which the learner can interpret either by means of a direct application of existing IL knowledge or by the activation of inferencing procedures. (c) covers incomprehensible input.

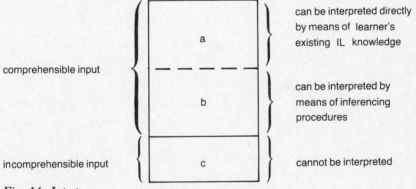

Fig. 14: Input

The concept of comprehensible input applies to processes of *communication*. We can now take a step into *learning* and say that it is a prerequisite for learning new rules, words, etc., both that input is comprehensible and that input goes beyond what can be directly interpreted by means of the learner's existing IL knowledge.[2] We have all had the experience of listening to a foreign language we do not know and which we can make no sense of whatsoever. Clearly, no new learning takes place unless we can assign (tentative) meaning to at least parts of such input: input-based learning (see below, 11.4.2) presupposes comprehensible input. On the other hand, it is obvious that if the language the learner is exposed to contains nothing but speech acts, words, grammatical structures and intonation patterns which are familiar, it is difficult to see that the learner could learn anything new. Foreign language learning presupposes input which is made comprehensible by means of inferencing and not by the direct application of a psycholinguistic rule. To continue with our metaphor from computer science, we can refer to those parts of input which satisfy the conditions we have just specified for learning to take place as INTAKE: intake is input which affects the learner's existing knowledge of the foreign language. In figure 14, (b) refers to intake.

11.2 Processes in foreign language learning

"Comprehensible input" and "intake" are necessary preconditions for learning to take place, but they do not clarify what the learning processes themselves consist of. How much is known about these? Today there is general agreement among psycholinguists that some ways of characterising language learning processes which were popular some years ago do not explain *all* aspects of foreign language learning. A good example of this is the process of IMITATION, which occupies a central place in behaviourist psychology. According to this, a child acquiring language observes a stimulus-response sequence such as someone acknowledging receipt of something by saying "thank you", and follows suit in equivalent circumstances by imitating this linguistic activity. The imitation involves at least three stages:

(1) the individual stores in memory the 'model' utterance (in our example, the speaker's "thank you")
(2) the individual produces an 'imitated' version of this utterance
(3) the individual compares her own version with the stored model utterance.

Some types of foreign language learning emulate this process by having learners repeat samples of the target language. Imitation

188

figures prominently in audio-lingual teaching materials, a typical activity being language laboratory drills. For instance, in the following four-phase drill, the learner hears sentences one and three on tape, and is expected to produce sentence two on the basis of the stimulus in one and to repeat the model utterance which three represents.

Four-phase drill

1. (tape) John is angry today. Yesterday.	Stimulus
2. (learner) _____ (John was angry yesterday.)	Response
3. (tape) John was angry yesterday.	Model utterance (ie correct response)
4. (learner) _____ (John was angry yesterday.)	Repetition of model

Psycholinguists have pointed out the many limitations of imitation (see eg Clark 1975, Hatch 1983). Firstly, it is easy to find examples of language produced by children which cannot be explained in terms of imitation, because it is unlikely that adults ever produced such utterances. This is the case in utterances such as "Louise comed yesterday", in which the child generalises a regular verb ending.

Secondly, a condition for individuals to store information for more than a few seconds, in their LONG-TERM MEMORY (see Stevick 1976), is that the stored information is related to information already there. Imitation itself cannot therefore explain learning. If information is only stored in SHORT-TERM MEMORY, the part of memory which can only process a very restricted number of items at a time, then individuals could only imitate fairly short utterances and then only immediately after they have been received (as in a four-phase drill, for example).

Thirdly, an important aspect of language learning is interpretation. This can be easily seen in relation to the acquisition of deictic expressions, such as the first and second person personal pronouns or adverbs of place, which reflect the communicative role of speaker and hearer. The correct use of neither "this is my coat" nor "come here" could be learned through imitation.

For these and numerous other reasons, psycholinguists have concentrated on developing alternative ways of accounting for language learning, which focus more on the cognitive operations involved in the learning process. One such approach will be presented, but before leaving imitation we should point out that the fact that imitation cannot explain all aspects of language learning does not imply that there is no place for imitation in language learning. It may well be important in the learning of certain aspects of language, such as those parts which are learned unanalysed, in wholes ("Gestalts"), for instance prosody or routine formulae.

The model we present sees foreign language learning as primarily a cognitive process of *hypothesis formation* and *hypothesis testing*, supplemented by processes of *automatization* and *consciousness raising*. To illustrate what we mean by these terms, consider the following example. A Danish learner of English at an elementary level needs to refer to 'week-end' in replying to a question asked by her teacher. She hypothesises that the word *week-end* (pronounced ['viːgenɔd]), used in Danish, may also be used in English. This is the stage of hypothesis *formation*. She therefore, in reply to the teacher's question, uses the word with the Danish pronunciation. This is the stage of hypothesis *testing*. The teacher corrects the word by repeating it with the English pronunciation. The learner interprets this as confirmation of her initial hypothesis as regards the existence and usage of the word in English, but understands that it needs revision with respect to pronunciation. On future occasions, the learner attempts to imitate the teacher's pronunciation when using the word. Soon the learner is capable of retrieving and pronouncing the word without experiencing any problems in so doing, i.e. she has *automatized* her knowledge of the word *week-end*. At this stage, the learner is likely to be conscious of the fact that some words currently used in Danish are both formally and semantically equivalent with English words, in other words, the learner's *consciousness* about cognates has been *raised*.

11.3 Hypothesis formation

11.3.1 The nature of hypotheses

If we say that foreign language learning is primarily a process of hypothesis formation and testing, we need to clarify what we mean

190

by HYPOTHESES. Let us first emphasize that by hypotheses we do not imply something which the learner is necessarily conscious about. Hypotheses *may* be consciously formed, as could be the case when a learner guesses that *eventually*, like the Danish cognate word *eventuelt*, can be used to express possibility, which it cannot. But if we restricted 'hypotheses' to what learners were conscious about, the model would soon fail to account for other instances of foreign language learning, as there is clear evidence of learning taking place without learners being conscious about the individual steps they are taking. Let us consider an example from the PIF corpus.[3]

A learner in his second year of learning English wrote a text in which he is describing a cartoon film: a man's hand gets stuck successively to an alarm-clock, a telephone, and a coffee pot. The text contains the following occurrences of the present progressive:

the watch ringing	he's flying out
his hand sitting	he's sitting
the telephone sitting	he's singing
the can (= pot) flying	
the can going	

On the face of it, the learner masters the correct English rule (subject + BE + verb + *-ing*) in a certain number of cases, but otherwise uses a deviant, IL specific, rule. As learners at more advanced levels never leave out the auxiliary before the *-ing* form of the verb, we can assume that the learner's IL will change and that learning will proceed from the stage reflected in the data just quoted to a stage which is in accordance with correct English usage. Consequently, we can assume that the learner's IL system at the time of using the forms listed above contains a hypothetical rule for the formation of sentences containing *-ing* forms. Our guesses as to what such a hypothesis might be are:

(1) *-ing* forms following pronominal subject require an auxiliary verb whereas those following nouns do not

or

(2) *-ing* forms are used as finite verb forms, but a pronominal subject of an *-ing* form has a specific form *(he's)*.

191

Whether (1) or (2) is the more correct way of representing the learner's hypothetical rule is not relevant here. What we want to illustrate with the example is that it is at least likely that the learner in question is not aware of the existence of a hypothetical rule. We therefore take it that learners are often unconscious about the hypotheses they form, and that these hypotheses are not defined relative to conscious beliefs but relative to the cognitive representation of the learner's interlanguage knowledge. Hypotheses are cognitive representations of knowledge which are ready to change if confronted by evidence that they are inadequate. Those parts of an interlanguage system which contain hypothetical rules/items and which are ready to incorporate new hypotheses are said to be PERMEABLE. The opposite of permeability is FOSSILIZATION, which refers to a state where the cognitive representation is inflexible, and the relevant parts of the system are generally unwilling to incorporate new hypotheses.[4] A prerequisite for foreign language learning to take place is that the learner's cognitive representation of her interlanguage knowledge is permeable.

11.3.2 Where do learners' hypotheses come from?

One important source for hypothesis formation is input, interpreted by means of inferencing strategies which utilize the learner's L1 or other languages different from the relevant foreign language, as well as the learner's existing interlanguage knowledge. A different type of hypothesis formation is exemplified by *week-end* and *eventually*, discussed above: the learner wishes to express something she does not have the appropriate interlanguage knowledge for, and makes use of productive communication strategies. These, like the receptive procedure of inferencing, typically involve the activation of L1 (as in the two examples just mentioned), or of L2. The net result is that no matter whether the learner reaches a hypothetical rule because she has to make sense of incoming data by inferencing or because she does not have the direct linguistic means for expressing what she wants, she is likely to activate her L1 or her interlanguage knowledge. Hypothesis-formation based on L1 will be referred to as transfer, whereas the term generalization refers to hypothesis-formation based on interlanguage knowledge.

192

(a) Generalization

This is the process of extending existing interlanguage knowledge to new contexts. Let us consider a learner's interlanguage rules for the function of the expanded tense as reflected in text 22, chapter 18. The text contains two errors with respect to this: "high jackers are often getting ..." and "sometimes are the police trying ...". We assume that the learner has already established the rule that reference to verbal actions of limited duration is expressed by means of the expanded tense. The learner needs to refer to what is in fact verbal action of limited duration, but with the modification that the action occurs frequently or regularly. The learner, consciously or not, generalizes her existing interlanguage rule to these contexts. The result of this is that she establishes a new (hypothetical) rule, which is in fact a modification of her already existing rule. The rule happens to be erroneous relative to the target language norm, and it is likely that she will revise it at some point, either because of target language input she receives, which will not follow this rule, or because she will receive corrective feedback to her own production (her teacher might decide to put a red line against the examples just discussed).

(b) Transfer

Carrying over a form from the mother tongue or from other foreign languages into IL is referred to as TRANSFER. The role of transfer in foreign language learning is probably one of the most debated topics among researchers. Whether the L1 is regarded as a help or a hindrance in L2 learning has important implications for foreign language pedagogy.

There are two factors which are particularly important for L1-based hypothesis formation.

1. The amount of *formal and functional similarity* between the L1 and the L2, with respect to the various linguistic levels and to the different components of communicative competence (consider the differences between on the one hand Danish and English, and on the other hand Danish and Greenlandic). This factor of "objective" distance between languages is not in itself relevant for whether or not learners *will* transfer, but rather determines what the outcome of a transfer-based hypothesis will be. If there is a considerable overlap between the two languages, a greater number of transfer-

193

based hypotheses will be correct than if there is less overlap between the two languages.

2. Whether or not the learner is *willing to transfer*. The fact that L1 and L2 are closely related with respect to a certain feature is no guarantee that learners will transfer, just as there is no guarantee that learners abstain from transferring within areas of no overlap.

What, then, determines whether learners decide to transfer or not? First of all, the perceived distance between the L1 and L2 is undoubtedly important. Learners probably in the very early stages of foreign language learning develop an assessment of how closely the two languages are related at various linguistic levels. Second, it has been shown that there are certain areas of the L1 (eg idiomatic expressions, cf chapter 5) which learners are generally unwilling to transfer because they consider them marked or language-specific. Third, the learner's metacommunicative awareness of L1 may play an important part. Certain areas of language lend themselves more to conscious awareness than others: learners are probably more aware of words and of morpho-syntactic rules than of pragmatic and discourse phenomena or prosodic features in their L1. It is conceivable that low metacommunicative awareness promotes transfer, and that learners therefore more readily transfer pragmatic, discourse and prosodic features than lexical and morpho-syntactic rules.

11.3.3 How do learners try out their hypotheses?

Hypothesis-testing can take place in both educational and non-educational situations, and can be achieved in either of two ways: (a) by the learner scrutinizing spoken or written input for examples which can confirm or reject hypotheses in the learner's IL system; or (b) by the learner interpreting feedback to speech which she (or a different learner) has produced. We shall deal with each in turn, and concentrate on hypothesis-testing in educational situations.

(a) Input-based hypothesis testing

Both teaching materials and the language produced by the teacher and by other learners may contain instances of rules and items which a learner has formed hypotheses about. Necessary conditions for the learner to make use of such information are that the learner (1) *identifies* such occurrences; (2) *interprets* them correctly; (3) *draws the necessary conclusions,* either to give the cognitive representation of the relevant rule a less hypothetical status, in the case of positive confirmation, or to revise the hypothetical rule, in the case of partial confirmation or dis-confirmation.

In the *identification phase*, learners processing incoming speech activate existing hypothetical rules and match these against the rules underlying the input. But as comprehension may take place as a top-down process (cf chapter 8), without the recipient activating all the relevant knowledge sources, it is possible for the learner to overlook input which could help her test hypothetical rules. This provides one explanation for the well-known fact that frequently occurring rules in English such as "the 3rd person -*s*" or the rules for the function of simple and expanded tenses often do not seem to influence learners' wrong hypotheses about the rules. A learner may process and completely comprehend 100 sentences containing examples of finite present tense verb forms with -*s* and still, in her own production, leave out the -*s*. It is just conceivable that the learner, in processing these sentences, never reaches a stage where she tries to assign a function to the -*s* ending, ie that she does not in fact identify the -*s* as relevant in relation to her own hypothetical rule. What the teacher would very often do for such learners, write 5 examples on the blackboard with -*s* and 5 without, and ask the learners to identify the difference, can be characterized as "guided identification". The teacher helps the learners get through the first stage of hypothesis testing so that they can concentrate on the second and third stages, interpretation and conclusion.

In the *interpretation phase*, learners try to decide whether their existing hypothetical rules and items need revision or can be given a less hypothetical status. Here we have to accept that learners may develop their IL through a succession of erroneous hypotheses, that the revision of one hypothetical rule does not of necessity lead directly to a correct rule. The use of the simple or progressive present

195

tenses in English can again serve as an illustration of this. An initial hypothesis might be that the -*ing* form is used as a finite verb much like the Danish present tense. At this stage, simple present tenses would not exist. As the learner receives more varied input than "I'm V-ing so and so", she hypothesizes that -*ing* forms are used for limited activity taking place "now". This is obviously a better hypothesis than the preceding one but still not the correct foreign language hypothesis, as the learner may produce sentences like "then he is walking towards the window, then he is opening his book, and then he is writing down what the teacher is saying". This hypothesis may therefore give way to the revised hypothesis that reference to a succession of actions is expressed by simple verb forms. The important thing for the learner is of course that she goes on developing her hypotheses in the direction of the target language. And for the teacher that she does not simply see the learner as *still* making errors within one and the same area, but that she tries to analyse whether the errors the learner makes indicate a development in the right direction. One could say that the teacher also needs to interpret the input she receives from the learner in order to decide on what action to take.

If the identification and interpretation phases are responsible for which parts of the input get assimilated into the learner's IL system (what we referred to as "intake" earlier), the *conclusion phase* is concerned with the processes seen from the learner's end, with what happens to existing IL knowledge when new knowledge is introduced. We shall focus on one specific aspect of this. Revisions of a hypothetical rule are often introduced gradually, preserving traces of the old cognitive representation of the rule. One well-known fact about learners' foreign language production is that it often exhibits variability in the use of a given L2 rule. Learners make errors when they become excited, or when they write their home assignment at the breakfast table, errors which they would not make if their language production was more careful (ie in situations which allow for monitoring to take place, cf chapter 8). Cases like these demonstrate that earlier cognitive representations are preserved alongside revised versions of the same hypotheses, and that there may be an intimate relationship between different versions of one and the same rule and characteristic features of the communicative situation in which the learner activates the rule for productive purposes. Two factors seem particularly relevant in this connection: (1) the degree of consciousness involved with respect to the rule; (2) the degree of automatization of the rule. As we return to these two issues below, let us just point out for the present that the reason why previous versions of hypothetical rules become activated in unmonitored situations is probably that they are more highly "automatized", ie that they can be activated and converted into behaviour without a great deal of mental energy. In educational situations, it is likely that learners' corrections of hypotheses are caused by the teacher's explicit feedback, which may have the consequence that the revised hypothesis is more conscious. If we assume that there are limits to how much mental energy language users can spend, it is easy to understand why easily activated rules are used in situations in which energy is concentrated on planning *what* to say rather than *how* to say it.

Before we proceed to looking in detail at how learners interpret feedback to their own productive use of the IL, mention should be made of an important type of hypothesis testing which we have not considered above, namely learners seeking information on specific points of language from authoritative sources like dictionaries, grammar books, teachers, fellow students or native speakers. This type of hypothesis testing presupposes a high degree of consciousness as well as, frequently, the existence of metacommunicative knowledge (so as to understand information presented in terms of a metalanguage like the description of a grammatical rule in a grammar book).

(b) Interpreting feedback

The following example illustrates a different way in which learners obtain information about the adequacy of their hypothetical IL rules and items:

Pupil:	from – oh – [ai'li:nz] father
Teacher:	[i'leInz]
Pupil:	[i'leInz]

The hypothesis-testing process here involves two phases:

(1) a learner produces an utterance which contains a hypothetical element (in this case, the pronunciation of the name Elaine)
(2) an interlocutor, in this case the teacher, provides feedback.

FEEDBACK can be POSITIVE, informing the learner that what she said was correct. Or it can be NEGATIVE or "corrective", pointing out that the learner's turn contained an inappropriate element and possibly informing the learner about the correct form. Negative feedback can be considered more useful to the learner than positive as it helps eliminate other possible, but erroneous hypotheses. There is, however, some evidence from experimental psychology that learners do not necessarily act according to what is most efficient from a narrow cognitive point of view (ie negative feedback), and that they prefer positive feedback.[5] The teacher's task is therefore to make sure that *both* types of feedback are provided, to take into account both cognitive and affective factors.

Whereas negative feedback is on principle possible whenever a learner's utterance contains an error, it is far more difficult for the teacher to decide when to give positive feedback. It is necessary to estimate whether the learner is trying out a hypothesis leading to correct language, and therefore *needs* confirmation. Or whether the learner is just producing "correct" language on the basis of a well-established rule and therefore does not *need* positive feedback – although it may still be welcome, and useful to other pupils, who have not yet established the rule in their IL.

In the "Elaine" example, the reason for the teacher's feedback is *linguistic:* she corrects the pronunciation of a name. Other examples of linguistic feedback are:

Pupil: she told him that Elaine was leaving and er
Teacher: yes that she had left yes
Pupil: and there was a letter to him

Pupil: it is about Benjamin's father's ['kəupænənʃip] – – companion-
ship
Teacher: I think you would say partnership
Pupil: partnership
Teacher: yeah

The teacher also frequently provides feedback on the *content* of what the pupils say, as for example when discussing a literary text:

Pupil: Benjamin had raped her father's wife
Teacher: had he
Pupil: no but his father says
Pupil: well I I think that she got her own ideas – – she
Teacher: why do you stress think – you say I THINK that she's got her own ideas – –
Pupil: I don't know er I don't er I don't know er I just know of her what the author tells me so I can't do anything but think

In all of the examples we have quoted, the teacher provides feedback DIRECTLY, she explicitly takes up the problem in a special turn. Corrective feedback of this sort would be classified as "other-initiated", interactive repair work in discourse terms (cf chapter 4). Teachers sometimes consider it beneficial for the smooth development of talk in the classroom not to interrupt the pupils by producing feedback turns and instead delay their feedback to their own turn. This feedback may still be given directly, ie by explicitly taking up the problem, but often the feedback is provided in an INDIRECT way. One way of doing this is exemplified by the following exchange:

Pupil: in their mind I think he behave himself like that if you can say so
Teacher: yes so maybe here we have you remember that we have – eer talked about the way he breaks the rules – again and again he behaves in – a way ...

The teacher manages to incorporate a correction of the learner's error in her own turn.

Feedback can be formulated in *metacommunicative* terms, ie in terms of explicit rules. Or feedback can be given by the teacher simply providing the correct utterance, without further explanation. The example just quoted of indirect feedback is a good illustration of feedback which contains no metacommunicative information (a characteristic feature of indirect feedback in general). (See also text 13, chapter 6).

199

11.4 A model of foreign language learning

The following figure summarises the main points made so far about foreign language learning seen as a process of hypothesis formation and testing.

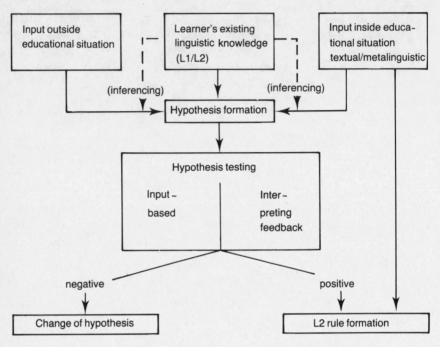

Fig. 15: Foreign language learning seen as a process of hypothesis formation and testing

In the figure we have added one process to those covered already, the one represented by the arrow that combines "Input inside educational situation" with "L2 rule formation". This is to allow for the possibility of "direct teaching". The teacher or the teaching materials introduce a new target language rule or item, eg a word, which the learners then practise. Clear-cut instances of this are to be found in connection with vocabulary teaching, where the teacher may decide to introduce words not encountered in texts (for instance words belonging to a relevant semantic field). As regards grammar, teachers generally prefer to let learners meet sentences exempli-

200

fying a grammatical rule several times in context during which learners start hypothesis formation before they formulate a rule which then makes explicit what the learners are on the way to accomplishing themselves.

11.5 Types of knowledge, automatization and consciousness-raising

In studies on L2 learning, a distinction is often observed between EXPLICIT and IMPLICIT linguistic KNOWLEDGE. One, simplified, way of accounting for this difference is to say that implicit linguistic knowledge is what the individual can use but not describe, whereas explicit linguistic knowledge is knowledge which the individual can describe but does not necessarily use. A typical example of implicit linguistic knowledge is the pre-school child's knowledge of her L1, although one is often surprised at even very young children's ability to describe linguistic rules. Explicit knowledge in the extreme is found in cases of rote-learning, eg when somebody can rattle off a long list of prepositions in German which take the dative case, but does not know the precise meaning of half of them and has great difficulty marking the noun with the correct case. It is clear that this crude distinction between implicit and explicit knowledge does not capture all those cases of knowledge which the individual can *both* reflect on and use automatically.

Let us first take a closer look at what we have referred to as explicit linguistic knowledge. When the teacher gives the rule about prepositions in English quoted above (the 'instead of' example in chapter 6, text 13), she is trying to establish one type of explicit linguistic knowledge in the learners' heads. This is explicit knowledge formulated within a (simplified) form of the metalanguage we can refer to as English grammatical description. Such metalinguistic knowledge is an important part of foreign language learning/teaching, whereas it may be less developed with respect to individuals' L1, though this depends on school tradition in L1 teaching.

Explicit linguistic knowledge, however, need not be knowledge which individuals can formulate within a metalanguage. There are degrees of explicitness. Metalinguistic knowledge represents the highest degree of explicitness. Less explicit knowledge may be formulated in everyday language ("we use *små* in Danish if we talk about more than one") or occur in situations where the individual can decide that something is *not* correct, without being able to give reasons. Rather than operate with a dichotomy between explicit and implicit knowledge, we therefore propose the following continuum as a more satisfactory way of characterising types of linguistic knowledge in terms of consciousness:

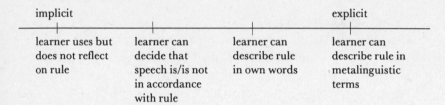

implicit			explicit
learner uses but does not reflect on rule	learner can decide that speech is/is not in accordance with rule	learner can describe rule in own words	learner can describe rule in metalinguistic terms

One might argue that there is no difference between the two leftmost categories, that somebody who can use a linguistic rule can also decide whether something is right or wrong. The reason why there is no such one-to-one relationship between actual language use and acceptability judgments is that awareness of linguistic norms may interfere with the individual's ability to reflect on her own verbal behaviour. It is well-known that people sometimes systematically use a linguistic rule which they would, if asked directly, categorically claim to be unacceptable and not believe that they themselves use.[6]

There are two important questions to raise in connection with a discussion of types of linguistic knowledge:

(1) How much of the continuum can a certain rule (more precisely, a psycholinguistic rule) occupy? In other words, is it possible for rules to be both maximally implicit and explicit at the same time? Or do some types of linguistic knowledge rule out the presence of other types?

(2) Supposing that learning sets in at *one* point on the continuum, what are the possibilities for the learner to extend this knowledge into other areas of the continuum?

Opinions differ considerably among researchers on these questions. One view is that implicit knowledge is of a completely different type from metalinguistic knowledge: implicit knowledge has to be 'acquired', explicit knowledge has to be 'learnt'. They may coexist, but serve very different functions in communication: implicit linguistic knowledge is at the basis of speech reception and production, whereas explicit linguistic knowledge is used for monitoring these processes. This is the view most categorically advocated by the American researcher Stephen Krashen (see eg Krashen 1982).

A different view is that there is nothing in principle that prevents a certain rule from being represented both at the extreme implicit and at the extreme explicit ends of the continuum simultaneously: learning can proceed either from implicit knowledge to more explicit knowledge, or in the opposite direction. The process of developing more consciousness about implicit knowledge is part of the general process of CONSCIOUSNESS-RAISING. A process in the opposite direction – the learner gradually developing an ability to use a certain rule for productive and receptive purposes without being aware of this – is usually referred to as an AUTOMATIZATION process.

We can illustrate the processes of consciousness-raising and automatization, relative to foreign language learning, in the following way:

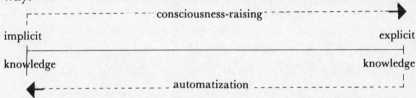

The view we have just described is held by many European researchers and is largely in accordance with Soviet psycholinguistic theory.[7] We consider both automatization and consciousness-raising important elements in a comprehensive model of foreign language learning, in addition to the processes already discussed (hypothesis formation and testing, imitation).

11.6 Foreign language learning related to classroom activities

We finish off this chapter by relating the process of foreign language learning to three classroom activities, a translation exercise, teacher-guided discussion of a literary text, and role play. These are activities which illustrate the different processes at work.

11.6.1 Teacher conducts translation exercise in the classroom

Before the lesson, the pupils (grade 10) have prepared a translation into English of ten sentences, all dealing with the problem of inversion. The teacher asks one pupil to write her translation on the chalkboard, and invites the rest of the class to comment on it. This leads into a discussion (in Danish and English) of different aspects of inversion in Danish and English, and the teacher finishes off the teaching sequence by outlining on the chalkboard the most relevant rules for inversion in English.

Which of the types of learning discussed above are likely to occur in this situation? Most of the processes seem to be represented. The pupils can form and test hypotheses, they can imitate the teacher's corrections, establish explicit (metalinguistic) knowledge. The only thing they are not likely to do is automatize their IL knowledge. From a superficial point of view this looks like a fairly good learning situation, and translation was in fact one of the cornerstones of the so-called 'grammar – translation method'. Closer inspection reveals that what the learners are likely to learn is fairly restricted. When the translation task is structured around a linguistic problem, here inversion, learners do not practise the coordination of *various* types of linguistic knowledge or pragmatic and discourse sides of communicative competence. Also important is the fact that the teaching situation *itself,* ie the interaction between the pupils and between pupils and teacher, adds very little in terms of language learning to what is the objective of the teaching sequence, learning specific linguistic rules and practising these in a given (and in this case restricted) context.

11.6.2 Teacher guides discussion of a literary text in class

The pupils (grade 1gs) have been asked to read the last chapter of Charles Webb's *The Graduate* at home, with the instruction only to check those words in the dictionary which prevent them from reconstructing the overall meaning of the text. The teacher's objective is partly to check the pupils' understanding of more difficult passages in the text, partly to complete the analysis of the book which they have been working with for the last two weeks. The teacher asks most of the questions, sometimes directing the same question to different learners when she is dissatisfied with the reply from the pupil addressed first. The pupils occasionally interrupt each other and the teacher, partly to express lack of understanding ('repair requests'), partly to express disagreement. The pupils generally seem active and willing to contribute to the discussion.

Considering language learning relative to *this* situation, we find a dramatic change in emphasis from the first example discussed. In the text discussion, automatization is very much in focus, perhaps not so much within speech production (as it is only one of the 24 pupils who speaks at a time) as within speech reception. There is ample scope for hypothesis formation and testing and for imitation, but as the teacher tries not to repair too much and, when she does repair, to do so indirectly, there is little consciousness raising involved. However, one of the teacher's objectives for the textual analysis is to discuss characteristic features of the dialogues in *The Graduate*, and there is therefore scope for consciousness raising.

11.6.3 Pupils role-play in small groups, followed by general discussion in class of pupils' experiences in role-playing

The teacher's objective for this lesson is to teach the pupils (grade 8) ways of complaining in English and how to counter complaints by using a range of modal verbs and other modality markers (cf chapter 3). In the previous lesson a drama text had included a number of complaints, and the learners were made aware of this speech act. The class is divided into groups of four, three pupils role-playing and the fourth noting down examples of complaints and complaint rejections. After the role-playing session, the observers write their observations on the chalkboard, and the teacher joins the class to discuss the examples. In this discussion, different forms of complaints and complaint rejections are included as well as other matters, eg morphology and lexis, whenever relevant.

This situation, with its two phases (small-group interaction and clasroom interaction) incorporates all the language learning processes mentioned above: hypothesis formation and automatization in the role-play situation itself; hypothesis testing partly in the role-play situation (with other pupils), partly in the classroom situation (pupils and teachers); consciousness raising in both the role-play situation (because of the distance created by role-playing) and in the classroom (with the possibility of building up metacommunicative awareness within the area). But it needs emphasizing that the main reason why so many learning processes are covered is that in our example the teacher does not use role-playing simply in order to create variation in teaching but, very deliberately, to reach certain teaching objectives. If role-play is not carefully planned and followed up, there is the risk that all the learners do is form hypotheses, test these against other pupils' hypotheses, and increase automatization of both correct and incorrect rules.

Footnotes to chapter 11

1. See also section 2.4 in chapter 2. Frequently used terms are *formal situation* for what we have referred to as 'educational situation', and *informal situation* for 'non-educational situation'. We avoid these terms because in everyday usage, non-educational situations are often referred to as more or less formal.

2. It is necessary to emphasize that this is a *necessary*, though not a *sufficient*, condition: as all language learners have probably experienced, it is not the case that one learns whenever one is forced to making sense of input by means of inferencing strategies. For reasons that are still badly understood, one may repeatedly be in a situation in which one is forced to infer the meaning for instance of a word, without apparently learning the word in question. Cf also the discussion in section 5.6 of what it means to know vocabulary.

3. See Færch 1979.

4. We use the term *fossilization* in a broad sense, irrespective of whether the relevant area of the IL system is or is not in accordance with a target language norm. The term is often used in a more restricted sense, to refer to those areas of the system which are incorrect and resist change. See eg Selinker 1969.

5. See McDonough 1981.

6. One consequence of this is variation in native speaker performance in different contexts, described in a series of pioneering studies by the American sociolinguist William Labov (see particularly Labov 1972).

7. See for instance Leont'iev (1971), (1974), *Osnabrücker Beiträge zur Sprachtheorie* vol. 10 (1979), *Tværsproglige Blade* 2/1 (1982).

Chapter 11. Sources and further reading

McDonough 1981 is a good, up-to-date and easily read introduction to foreign language learning, covering many more areas than we do in this and the following chapter. The book considers both behaviourist and cognitivist learning models, as does Clark 1975. Knapp-Potthoff/Knapp 1982, part I, provides a comprehensive discussion of principles of foreign language learning, with an emphasis on insights provided by IL studies. Hatch 1983 contains a wealth of information on research into second language acquisition; for the reader who wants an exhaustive and up-to-date description, the book is indispensable.

Comparisons between L1 and L2 learning are contained in all of the preceding studies. McLaughlin 1982 is useful on this topic. For imitation, see Stevick 1982.

The function of transfer in foreign language learning is discussed in some of the contributions to three anthologies: Gass/Selinker 1983, Dechert/Raupach (in press) and Kellermann/Sharwood Smith (in press).

Automatization and consciousness raising as processes in foreign language learning are treated in various publications. For different views, see Krashen 1981, 1982, Bialystok 1982, Sharwood Smith 1982. Also relevant are the Soviet studies referred to in footnote 7.

On neurolinguistics, see Ellegård 1982. For a review of the relevance of neurolinguistic research to language teaching, see a series of contributions to *TESOL Quarterly* 1982/3 and Diller 1981, part 1.

Chapter twelve:
Individual variation

Our description of foreign language learning in chapter 11 might give the impression that learning can be reduced to "input", "intake", "cognitive operations", "automatization", etc. In our examples of teaching activities that concluded the chapter, the focus was on the *teacher's* objectives and on what the learners might be expected to achieve, if they made full use of the learning possibilities created by the teacher. Learning, however, is not a process of passively receiving what the teacher pours into an empty receptacle ("mug and jug" pedagogy, Rogers 1969), it requires both an active contribution from the learner and an ability to learn.

Learners' success in foreign language learning is often regarded as being crucially dependent on the learner's willingness to learn, or MOTIVATION. A second determining factor is reckoned to be the language learner's ability, or APTITUDE. These are very general terms, and need to be narrowed down before any explanatory power in relation to language learning can be attributed to them. What we shall try to do in this chapter is to sort out the contribution of some factors which influence learners' motivation or account for their aptitude, and to describe some of the empirically-based educational research undertaken to determine the significance of a number of factors, in particular the age variable and various psychological traits.

12.1 Attitudes

It is clear that there is a fairly strong link between achievement or success in foreign language learning and the learner's attitude, whether to the school subject, to a particular foreign country, or any other decisive aspect related to the language. A positive attitude is synonymous with increased motivation, and generally produces better results. On the other hand, it may be early success in learning which has generated the positive attitude. So that while it is probably an advantage to identify closely with the content or methods of a subject, it is false to regard attitude or motivation as in any way a causative variable (Burstall 1975).

In any case there may be other intervening variables which are more significant. If you are a boy in a society which accepts the widespread dogma that "girls are better at foreign languages than boys", as is the case in many countries, this is almost bound to lead to boys performing less well than girls, as has been documented in a British project on the learning of French in the primary school (ages 7 to 11). This correlated with the boys having less positive attitudes to French (Burstall et al 1974), a clear instance of societal attitudes producing under-achievement.

When considering such results, one needs to look carefully at what exactly is tested, how this is done, and at the social context. A comprehensive survey article on the relationship between sex and language learning casts doubt on the validity of the British results (Ekstrand 1980). In Denmark, social attitudes to foreign language learning are quite different, as success in English is important both in the education system and in many professions, and this is likely to influence the motivation of both boys and girls.

We could try to relate classroom interaction patterns to our model of language learning processes. If it is the case that girls tend to be more orderly in classrooms, talking less than boys in teacher-centred discourse, asking fewer awkward questions and generally accepting the framework laid down by the teacher to a greater extent than the boys[1], then one might expect this to mean that the girls have less chance to test hypotheses, stretch their language and develop their communicative competence. Is this so? The question has not been investigated so far, but it would certainly be interesting to explore sex-specific interaction patterns in the foreign language classroom.

Another factor which could be of importance for motivation is the fact that sex roles are reinforced by the stereotyping which characterises teaching materials (Freudenstein 1978, Lautrop 1980). All too often the target culture is presented through traditional sex roles, ie with women confined to the home or subordinate positions. Although it is true that the English-speaking world is male dominated, teaching materials tend to be unduly unjust to women, which aggravates the sex stereotyping which is already part of the hidden curriculum, both in terms of the roles adopted in the classroom and the selection of reality which learners encounter. As the values of the peer group are extremely influential, one can be sure that stereotyping contributes to learner attitudes, but less sure about the precise way in which different individuals' cognitive or affective traits are affected.

Considering the social bias of secondary and higher education in Denmark,[2] it would be surprising if there was no correlation between learners' social background and success in foreign language learning in schools, especially in view of the fact that foreign language teaching at advanced levels is typically geared towards developing more academically oriented skills. We know of no studies of this topic which can shed light on English teaching in Denmark and can only speculate that the following may be ways in which social class influences success in learning English:

- parental attitudes to school and academic success, to the English language, and to the culture of Britain and the USA
- the level of literacy in the home, the degree to which use is made of books, writing, intellectual pursuits
- the degree of contact of the home with foreign cultures, professionally and socially, travel, guests
- financial strength permitting a privileged home context, travel abroad.

12.2 Age

It is a popular belief that the younger the learner, the easier and better the learning of a foreign language. This is founded on the widespread observation that children who go to live in a foreign country "pick up" the language effortlessly when they are exposed to it and use it. People above the age of puberty have relatively more trouble, and they usually retain a foreign accent. There is also wide variation in the degree of success of language learning amongst adults.

In the 1950s and 1960s there was extensive interest among educators in starting foreign language learning progressively earlier, from age 7 or even before that. There was a conviction that the learning should be organized so as to take avantage of the innate bio-

210

logical capacities that were assumed to exist for children prior to adolescence. In Denmark the issue never became an educational hot potato in the way that primary school French did in the United States and Great Britain.[3] The Danish authorities have fixed grade 5 as the time when the first foreign language, English, is started. In Sweden and Finland the first foreign language is started in grade 3, in Norway in grade 4.

One way of handling the age factor is to see this as a question of differences in what the brain can do. Prior to adolescence, the two major hemispheres of the brain specialize (LATERALIZATION is the neurophysiological term) so that one hemisphere (for most people the left) assumes control over a number of analytic processes which are essential in language use.[4] First language acquisition therefore takes place at a time when the brain is more flexible than after lateralization. This had led psycholinguists to suggest that there exists a CRITICAL PERIOD ("optimal age") for language acquisition prior to lateralization (Lenneberg 1967), which would explain the frequently observed shortcomings of foreign language learning after early childhood.

There is now, however, fairly substantial evidence that younger children are not generally as efficient foreign language learners as adolescents or even adults – with the exception of the development of articulatory skills.[5] It seems as if the more highly developed analytic skills after early childhood provide shortcuts for language learning, so that adolescents and adults can make much faster progress than children, at least during the first stages of foreign language learning.[6] Furthermore, it is now widely recognized that it is necessary to see the age factor in conjunction with other factors, rather than as a purely neurophysiological variable. This can be seen from results obtained in a Swedish project, EPÅL ("Engelska på lågstadiet"), which has investigated the effect of starting English earlier in schools in Sweden (see Holmstrand 1980).

The project investigated in great detail the achievement of two large groups of learners, an experimental group that started English in the first grade, and a control group who began in the normal way in grade 3. The total number of hours of instruction was the same for each group by the end of grade 6, meaning that the early starters had their time more thinly spread over the 6 years. At this point the proficiency in English of both groups, measured in a range of tests, was basically the same. This the project investigators interpreted as meaning that it is perfectly feasible to start a foreign language as early as at age 7. However, the project could not document the dramatic advantages that were expected through the early start. These seem to have been cancelled out by the organizational limitations. The intensity of learning for the early starters was as follows: $\frac{1}{2}$ hour per week in the first year, $1\frac{1}{2}$ hours per week in the second, 2 hours a week in the third and fourth years, 3 hours a week in the fifth and sixth. The project concludes that the optimal age theory is very debatable, and that the advantages of an early start are restricted to the acquisition of the sound system of a foreign language.

It is hardly surprising that the optimal age research has led to no conclusive results. It is impossible to treat a single factor like age in isolation from other factors which have to do with the learner's cognitive, affective and social development, and with educational objectives and curriculum organization. At least the following are relevant:

- the intensity of learning (the number of hours per week)
- the total time spent on the foreign language
- the extent to which linguistic skills in the mother tongue are well developed
- the level of cognitive or intellectual development of the learners
- the motivation of learners, which is generally influenced by their parents' attitudes to the language but not their knowledge of it
- whether the foreign language is being taught as a school subject in the traditional sense, or is being used as a medium through which other subjects on the curriculum are learnt (cf chaper 16).

Any decision to change the age at which learners begin English in Denmark should be based on a consideration of all these factors, and a clarification of what implications there would be for the subject throughout the school system.

212

12.3 Aptitude

The question of language learning aptitude has not been very important in the European educational tradition, whereas aptitude tests
are widely used in North America. Carroll, one of the pioneers in
aptitude testing, lists the following as essential components (1981):

- *phonetic coding ability,* comprising ability for sound discrimination
  as well as sound imitation
- *grammatical sensitivity,* the individual's awareness of syntactic
  structures and grammatical functions in the native language
- *rote-learning ability* or ability for memorisation
- *inductive language learning ability,* the individual's ability to develop
  meaning inductively.

If such 'abilities' are regarded as *fixed,* either because they are
assumed to be innate or to have developed during primary socialization, aptitude testing could have devastating consequences for those
individuals who were found to score low on the tests, because
teachers' expectations are often self-fulfilling. If the teacher *expects*
particular learners to have low foreign language aptitude they may
treat them accordingly. A less problematic outcome of such results
would be if they are used for preparing differentiated learning activities (see chapter 16). If, on the other hand, language learning aptitude tests are regarded as measuring mental faculties which can be
influenced or *changed,* individuals who score low on the tests can be
helped to increase their aptitude (for a discussion of this, see Wesche
1981).

Carroll's four components are all language-related: neither
non-verbal intelligence nor other general psychological variables
are included. Broader in scope are investigations into the characteristics of "the good language learner", carried out in a Canadian
research project (Naiman/Fröhlich/Todesco/Stern 1975). A series of
studies were undertaken to identify which learner variables correlated positively with success in foreign language learning. These
variables, among others, were:

FIELD INDEPENDENCE: ability to identify items independently of the context ('field') in which they occur

CATEGORY WIDTH: preference for including many items in one broad class or fewer items in several classes

TOLERANCE OF AMBIGUITY: ability to endure conflicting information, eg in comprehension, and wait for disambiguation, rather than jump at one solution

EXTROVERSION: having a personality which is outgoing, talkative, sociable.

Using standardised psychological tests for measuring these variables, and comparing results with results obtained on two proficiency tests (one measuring speech production on an elicited imitation task[7], one measuring listening comprehension), it was found that "field independence" correlated highly with the results of both proficiency tests of the grade 12 learners, the highest of three levels investigated. Neither "extroversion" nor "category width" seemed to correlate with the proficiency results. As regards "tolerance for ambiguity", this was found to correlate positively with the listening comprehension task, but not with the production task.

The finding that field independence and tolerance for ambiguity correlate positively with at least the comprehension test is hardly surprising, in the light of our description of top-down/bottom-up processing and of inferencing. It is perhaps more surprising that neither degree of extroversion nor category width seemed to correlate with the proficiency results.

What implications could follow from results like these? One interpretation is that the learner variables in question *are* valid, that they are isolated constituents of aptitude for learning foreign languages. This interpretation would entail that field-independent learners are better in general at learning foreign languages than field-dependent learners.

A different interpretation would see the results as reflecting the specific type of teaching which the learners have been exposed to.[8] Teaching at the advanced levels of the educational system is likely to place considerable emphasis on analytical skills, as these are needed in higher education. This would favour those learners who are more analytically inclined (field-independent) and discriminate against

214

those who are more Gestalt-type, ie who process language as 'wholes'. According to this interpretation, it would be impossible to conclude that field-independence in itself indicates language learning aptitude. All one could say is that field-independence leads to success if teaching places special emphasis on this.

12.4 Implications

Two important points have emerged in our discussion of individual variation. The first is the impossibility of identifying and studying one single variable in isolation from others, for instance the age factor. The second is that the precise nature, origin and contribution of both motivation and aptitude in foreign language learning is unclear. Explanations in terms of innate dispositions are not just ideologically unpalatable but can also not be substantiated by neurophysiology. Social psychological research into attitudes may shed light on such factors as stereotyping but cannot size up the importance of any cognitive or affective variable in foreign language learning.

To demonstrate the problems involved in assessing the validity of research results, let us revert to the findings of the Canadian investigation reported earlier. In this there was a positive correlation between field independence and success in foreign language learning. Some American test results (reported in Hatch 1983, 223) show that women are generally more field dependent than men. One could therefore be tempted to conclude that American men are better language learners than American women – which is exactly the opposite not only of what is generally believed about the foreign language learning ability of both sexes, but also of the relatively few research findings on sex-specific differences in foreign language learning (see Börsch 1982 for an overview). By contrast, in the Canadian experiment *no* significant differences were found between male and female informants with respect to field dependence/independence (Naiman et al 1978, 49).

There are two implications from these apparently conflicting results. First, one cannot conclude categorically that women are more field dependent than men. If women are found to be highly field dependent, this reflects a female-specific socialization process, and not an innate (= universal) neurophysiological characteristic. One

215

therefore needs to be extremely wary about generalising research findings concerning individual variables from one social context to another.

Second, even granted that the American women investigated were more field dependent than male informants, this does not imply that they would necessarily be poor language learners, although they might well score low on the two Canadian proficiency tests. What these measure is a very restricted area of communicative competence, and there is good reason to assume that the tests particularly favour analytical skills in the foreign language.

We therefore have to conclude this chapter by emphasizing that just about the only fact which is indispensable about individual variation in foreign language learning is that it exists. Two possible conclusions can be drawn from this. One would be that as learners differ so much, we should ensure more homogeneous classes by streaming the children according to some criterion of 'ability'. The second would be that teaching must be changed in such a way that all learners can benefit from it. The first solution is alien to an egalitarian ideology of education, so it is the second which needs careful consideration, and which represents a real pedagogic challenge. It is therefore not surprising that such topics as teaching mixed-ability classes and individualisation loom large in teacher training. We shall return to this problem in chapter 16.

Footnotes to chapter 12

1. There is some evidence for this in Larsen/Nielsen 1982. See also the publications of the project "Språk och kön i skolan", Lärarhögskolan, Malmö.
2. See *U 90,* Ministry of Education, Copenhagen, 1978, pages 66–70, and references there to publications from the Danish Statistical Office and the Social Research Institute.
3. See, however, for Danish investigations Florander/Jensen 1969, Mylov 1972.
4. For recent discussion of lateralization, see Walsh/Diller 1981; Hatch 1983, chapter 11.
5. See contributions to Krashen/Scarcella/Long 1982 and Hatch 1983, 192 ff.
6. This is the position of Krashen/Long/Scarcella 1977.
7. For the technique of elicited imitation, see Naiman 1974.
8. Cf McDonough 1981, 132 f.

Chapter 12. Sources and further reading

On motivation, se McDonough 1981, chapter 10. For the concepts instrumental and integrative motivation, developed in the Canadian context, see Gardner/Lambert 1972.

On age, see Krashen/Scarcella/Long 1982, and Hatch 1983, chapter 10.

On aptitude, see Diller 1981, and Hatch 1983. Naiman et al 1978 is a good example of an empirical investigation into aptitude.

For research into male/female factors and education, see a special number of *Nyt om Uddannelsesforskning*, 1982/4.

Part III:
Language teaching

The focus in parts I and II of the book has been on the learner, the components of communicative competence, the processes underlying learning, and some possible determining factors. In part III we switch to the teaching that the learner encounters.

Chapter 13 is concerned with the formulation of aims in foreign language teaching. The official and rather general aims in Denmark are contrasted with a much more detailed specification of language learning goals.

In chapter 14 principles for the selection and organisation of teaching content are presented. One way of analysing teaching activities and relating them to language learning processes and the components of communicative competence is proposed.

Chapter 15, on evaluation, suggests what qualities to look for in a language test, and mentions some innovations in exams in Denmark.

Chapter 16 considers a number of pedagogic principles which are influencing the way foreign language teaching is evolving, and considers innovations which are consistent with the principles elaborated elsewhere in the book. The chapter concludes by suggesting how teacher education should develop in order to live up to the challenge of qualifying foreign language teachers adequately.

Chapter thirteen:
Aims

In this chapter we first discuss some of the purposes that English serves in Denmark, and the aims of English teaching as specified in official documents. The chapter concludes with a description of an alternative way of specifying aims, developed by researchers associated with the Council of Europe's "Threshold Level" project.

13.1 English in Denmark, second or foreign language?

When considering the status of non-native languages it is useful to make a distinction between 'second' and 'foreign' languages. A SECOND LANGUAGE is one which has some specific functions within a society, and which is learned after the mother tongue. In Britain and the USA English is a second language for the immigrant and ethnic minority groups for whom English is not the mother tongue, and who need English in many spheres of life (eg business, politics, education) but not in others (eg home life, religion). Similarly in many formerly colonized countries, the colonial language has been retained after independence for certain purposes. English was thus a second language in multilingual Tanzania both before and after independence, but Swahili has gradually taken over in education and public life.

A FOREIGN LANGUAGE is one which has no internal function in the learner's country and which is learnt in order to communicate with native speakers or interlanguage users of the foreign language. A clear case in point would be the position of Russian in Denmark, which is primarily learnt in order to decipher Russian texts.

A language learnt as a second or a foreign language can function as a LINGUA FRANCA, a language used between people with no common language and for neither of whom it is a first language. Thus a Danish engineer is likely to confer with a Japanese colleague in English. English served as a lingua franca for the 3 Scandinavians in the peace demonstration example in chapter 10.

While there is normally an integration of cultural and linguistic goals in both foreign and second language learning, it has been suggested (Richards 1978) that a lingua franca can be learnt with less emphasis on the culture from which the language originated. This, however, is a position which many researchers disagree with.

Danes need English to communicate with native speakers of English as well as with interlanguage users of English, both within Denmark and abroad. Furthermore, it is arguable that English has become so significant in so many spheres of life in Denmark that it is on its way to acquiring the status of a second language. This is the case if English is needed not just for foreign travel or as a mark of a certain level of general education, but as a condition for full participation in Danish society, in connection with politics, technology, business, the media, sport, etc.

13.2 English as a school subject

In recent years there has been a keen debate about the number and status of foreign languages taught in schools in Denmark.[1] One camp have argued that because of the increased importance of English in Danish society and worldwide, it would be more reasonable to ensure that all Danes have a good proficiency in one foreign language (English) rather than a smattering of several foreign languages. The goal of foreign language teaching would therefore be to change Denmark into a bilingual society, with English as the second language. Another camp have argued that the tendency for English to become dominant should be counterbalanced by teaching other foreign languages, that a basic knowledge of a range of foreign languages enables the individual to follow up later in life whichever language is needed. A third possibility would be for individuals to choose which one of several foreign languages they should study in depth, to ensure that Denmark also has strong cultural links with, for instance, the French-, Spanish-, or Arabic-speaking worlds.

It is worth pointing out that the dominant position of English – hence of English teaching – in Denmark is relatively new. Up to World War II pupils in primary education could choose between English and German, and it is probable that more pupils studied German than English then. One consequence of this is that although

English teaching has been obligatory since 1937 in primary schools, there is still a large group of people (aged roughly 55 upwards) who have had no English as part of their formal education. This is why adult education not only has to cope with "false beginners" but also with true beginners of English.

Decisions on foreign languages in education are political, and are taken with reference to societal goals, individuals' needs, economic interests, the qualifications of teachers, changes in international orientation, etc. Some attempts have been made to document foreign language needs, mostly in the form of surveys of which languages are needed by industry and for what purposes,[2] and studies of the actual use learners make of foreign languages in life after school.[3]

In general education, the aims for specific subjects have to be seen within the framework of broader educational aims, since school subjects are expected to contribute to these aims in various ways. This relationship becomes clearer if one contrasts the general aims for the Folkeskole and the specific aims for English (fig. 16).[4]

The description for English tells us something about the overall, very general intentions that politicians and experts have for English teaching in Denmark. But they reveal very little of a specific kind which can be used by teachers. For this, one has to turn to the official guidelines ("Undervisningsvejledning") for English in the Folke-skole, which state that

> "The aim is that pupils develop the ability to *use* the language ["et brugs-sprog"]. The language should be a means of communication and self-expression of practical value."

This official interpretation of the general regulations quite unambiguously puts communicative competence as the teaching objective for English at the Folkeskole, with an emphasis on proficiency.

To exemplify aims at a more advanced level, we turn to the specification of these for the modern languages specialisation in the Gymnasium.[5] Here there are two overall aims:

> I "The teaching aims at improving the ability to understand and use the English language in its spoken and written forms."

223

General aims	Aims for English
1. The task of the Folkeskole is, in co-operation with parents, to make it possible for the pupils to acquire knowledge, skills, methods of work, and forms of expression which contribute to the all-round development of each child.	1. The aim of the teaching is for pupils to develop proficiency in understanding spoken English, in speaking the language, in understanding the content of an English text, and in using the written language.
2. The Folkeskole must, throughout its work, seek to create situations of experience which encourage pupils to work independently, increase their urge to learn, open up their imagination, and develop their ability to analyse and make judgements in an independent way.	3. The teaching should promote the pupils' desire to use the language and their interest in making progress in the language.
3. The Folkeskole prepares pupils for involvement and participation in a democratic society, and for joint responsibility for the solution of shared tasks. The school's teaching and entire daily life must therefore be founded on freedom of thought and democracy.	2. The teaching should enable pupils to become well informed about the life and culture of the countries where the language is spoken, so that they acquire a more solid foundation for international understanding.

(Our translation)

Fig. 16: Aims, Folkeskole

II "At the same time it should provide the pupils with insight into characteristic aspects of the culture of the countries which use the English language as a means of expression, particularly England and the USA."

The official guidelines stress that the cultural goal is very important. There is an attempt to consolidate this through regulations for how many pages of fiction and non-fiction texts have to be read in the three years, and which literary genres should be included. As regards the linguistic goal, it is conspicuous that there is no mention of metacommunicative awareness and that specifications of the skills aspect of communicative competence are vague and limited to linguistic competence and fluency (with a few concessions to pragmatic and discourse knowledge). The guidelines explicitly state that working with texts provides the best method for developing learners' oral proficiency.[6] This illustrates the close interrelationship in the Gymnasium between cultural and linguistic goals.

The general impression of the specification of aims for English teaching for both Folkeskole and Gymnasium is that they are described in an extremely vague and general manner. An alternative and much more explicit way of formulating goals will be presented in the next section.

13.3 Specifying teaching aims – the Threshold Level approach

In an attempt to specify a level of foreign language proficiency which could serve as an aim for elementary foreign language teaching in Europe, researchers associated with the Council of Europa developed a method for specifying communicative goals in terms of a combination of linguistic and pragmatic categories.

According to the *Threshold Level* (van Ek 1975), a specification of language learning aims has to involve the following components:

1. the *situations* in which the foreign language will be used, including the topics which will be dealt with;
2. the language *activities* in which the learner will engage;
3. the language *functions* which the learner will fulfil;
4. what the learner will be *able to do* with respect to each topic;
5. the *general notions* which the learner will be able to handle;
6. the *specific (topic-related) notions* which the learner will be able to handle;
7. the *language forms* which the learner will be able to use;
8. the *degree of skill* with which the learner will be able to perform.
(van Ek 1975,5)

Of these, "functions, "notions" and "language forms" are particularly important and well described.

THRESHOLD LEVEL FUNCTIONS, in the following T-functions, are very different from "speech functions" as described in chapter 3. T-functions are more closely related to speech acts described out of context (as in chapter 3).The main *groups* of functions in the T-level description are the following:

1. imparting and seeking factual information
2. expressing and finding out intellectual attitudes
3. expressing and finding out emotional attitudes
4. expressing and finding out moral attitudes
5. getting things done (suasion)
6. socializing
(van Ek 1975,19).

Specifying "notions" is an even more open-ended task than specifying functions. The T-level description makes a point of the notions included being exemplary and open-ended. The notions are arranged into 14 semantic fields:[7]

1. personal identification
2. house and home
3. trade, profession, occupation
4. free time, entertainment
5. travel
6. relations with other people
7. health and welfare
8. education
9. shopping
10. food and drink
11. services
12. places
13. foreign languages
14. weather
(van Ek 1975, 14–16).

Each of these is further subdivided, and a list of words is provided for each of these subclasses, specifying whether the word should be mastered for receptive purposes (marked R in the list below) or for both receptive and productive purposes (marked P). Thus the semantic field "Relations with other people" contains the subcategories listed below. We include selected examples of words belonging to some of the subcategories:

friendship/aversion	*friend* P
	to like P
	to dislike R
	to like + negation P
invitations	... (19 words and expressions)
correspondence	... (18 words and expressions)
club-membership	... (4 words and expressions)
political and	*politics* P
social views	*party* P
	government P
	to govern R
	conservative P
	socialist P
	communist P
	king P
	queen P
	... (21 words and expressions in all)

(van Ek 1975, 91–93).

To illustrate how the specification of language forms operates, we have selected the function "requesting others to do something", belonging to the group "getting things done (suasion)":

requesting others	Would you (please) + VP P
to do something	Could you (please) + VP P
	Please + VP P
	Would you be (so kind as to ...) (kind enough to ...) R
	Would you mind + V_{ing} ... R
	Can I have + NP + V_{ed} (,please)? P

(van Ek 1975, 43).

As compared with the description of communicative competence in chapter 10, the following aspects are not incorporated into descriptions of the T-level for English:

– speech act modality
– discourse
– strategic competence

- fluency
- accuracy (affecting comprehensibility and distraction)
- context embeddedness
- metacommunicative awareness.

Some of these aspects, eg accuracy, fluency and the lack of specification of speech act modality[8], are discussed in van Ek (1975). Some have been incorporated into the more recent T-level descriptions for French and German[9] (eg discourse and speech act modality). Of the remaining aspects not covered, the most revealing gap is strategic competence. There is an in-built discord between the notion of strategic competence and the principles on which the T-level is founded. Strategic competence as a teaching goal involves preparing learners to communicate in a range of situations which may not have been anticipated in the teaching. Whereas the T-level descriptions rest on the assumption that learners' communicative needs must first be identified, following which there is a specification of the language that is needed.[10]

13.4 A specification of aims – help or hindrance?

The T-level provides an exhaustive description of most of the components of one level of proficiency. This represents one extreme position in the specification of teaching aims. By contrast the official aims for the Folkeskole and Gymnasium are so broadly defined that it is difficult to see from the descriptions of the goals alone what English teaching in Denmark is expected to achieve. This represents the other extreme in the specification of aims.

It might be thought that any specification of communicative competence as detailed as the T-level description puts textbook-writers, learners and teachers into a straightjacket which leaves little room for manoeuvre, that it is more of a hindrance than a help. Whereas the present situation in Denmark allows ample opportunity for learners and teachers to negotiate their own aims, as a prior step to deciding on a syllabus and methods. While we are sceptical about the value of defining aims as rigidly as in the T-level, we suspect that it may be something of an illusion to believe that vague aims are really a help for learners and teachers.

228

One reason why we are dubious about the value of such freedom is that in order to make use of it, teachers need experience and training in all aspects of foreign language pedagogy, in addition to a very high level of proficiency. Otherwise there is a risk that teachers will be uncertain about aims and, relying largely on intuition and tradition, they may resort to familiar activities (eg reading aloud, translation, well-tried grammar exercises) or keep strictly to a textbook. More clearly specified aims might help learners and teachers towards a greater freedom in deciding on ways in which to reach these aims.

A second reason is that teachers are responsible to pupils, parents and society at large for seeing that learners pass through the exam filter. There is consequently a risk that examinations come to be considered the authoritative interpretation of the aims, that exams to some extent replace clearly specified aims. If aims were more clearly defined than is the case today, though not in as rigid a way as is done in the T-level, the backwash effect of exams on teaching might be somewhat reduced.

Footnotes to chapter 13

1. A conference on foreign language teaching in Denmark was held in Copenhagen in February 1982 with representatives of the political parties, the labour market, educational establishments and the language teachers' associations. See the special issue of *Sproglæreren* 1982 summarizing the conference. See also a joint publication of all the language teachers' associations, "Ud med sproget", published as a special issue of *Gymnasieskolen,* January 1980.
2. See Høedt 1980.
3. See Looms 1981 and Haastrup 1981.
4. General aims according to the Folkeskole Act, 1975. Aims for English in the official guidelines for English in the Folkeskole, Undervisningsministeriet (Ministry of Education) 1976.
5. Undervisningsministeriets bekendtgørelse 322, 16 June, 1971, § 5.
6. The official guidelines for English in the Gymnasium, Undervisningsministeriet (Ministry of Education) 1971, 31.
7. These are the so-called "specific" topics. In addition to these, the T-level description contains a list of "general notions" like existential expressions, logical relations and quantitative words.
8. Cf the following quote: "It would be pointless to prescribe *how* learners should be able to fulfil a language function or to express a notion; the only thing that can

be stipulated is *that* they should be able to do it." (van Ek 1975, 34).

9. See Coste et al 1976, Baldegger et al 1980.

10. However the need to enable learners to go on learning is acknowledged in van Ek 1976, 20.

Chapter 13. Sources and further reading

English as a second or foreign language is covered in Strevens 1980 and Brumfit 1982. On principles for language planning in society see the survey article by Kennedy 1981. On language policy in Scandinavia, Germany and North America, with particular reference to bilingualism and ethnic minorities, see Skutnabb-Kangas 1983.

The status and role of foreign languages in Denmark is analysed in Kristiansen 1981. On the general educational framework which foreign language learning in Denmark fits into, see Bencke/Hansen/Wahlgren 1981 and Harsløf 1983.

For a summary of work sponsored by the Council of Europe in a wide range of contexts, within a framework of communicative language learning systems development, including aims definition and threshold levels, and plans for future work, see Council of Europe 1981. For the threshold level for modern language learning in schools, see van Ek 1976.

Chapter fourteen:
From aims to teaching

In order to progress from overall aims to actual teaching, it is necessary to divide the aims into subgoals. There are many levels involved in this, from specifying the goal one intends to reach after a school year to deciding on the specific objectives of individual lessons. The principles used in establishing subgoals and in sequencing these into a SYLLABUS involve several criteria, which will be discussed in section 14.1.

Once a syllabus has been chosen and the objectives of the individual lessons identified, there are still numerous decisions to be made, on the choice of materials, teaching methods and classroom organization. In order to demonstrate the range of the issues involved in foreign language teaching methodology, we shall present an exercise typology which moves from highly controlled exercises to free production, and a check-list for evaluating teaching methods and classroom organization in terms of language learning and communicative competence.

14.1 Principles of syllabus design

In this section we describe three principles for organizing teaching content, linguistic, pragmatic and thematic syllabuses. Following this we relate the three principles to English teaching in Denmark.

In a LINGUISTIC SYLLABUS,[1] the structuring principle is grammatical and, to a lesser degree, lexical. The learner is introduced to the grammatical structures and the vocabulary of the foreign language in a step-by-step manner, moving from what are considered to be fairly simple structures and vocabulary to more complex items. Many course books are built up around a linguistic syllabus. We can show how this principle works by taking a beginners' course (Alexander 1967) and considering how modal verbs are introduced.

231

The first occurrence of modal verbs is in lesson 29, in which *must* is introduced ("what must I do?"). Lesson 43 introduces *can*, as below:

Learner's book:

MARY: *Cán you máke the téa, Jóhn?*
JOHN: *Yés, of cóurse, I cán, Máry.*

MARY: *Cán you sée it?*
JOHN: *I can sée the téa-pot, but I cán't see the téa.*

Teacher's book:

Content and Basic Aims

Patterns and structural words	Vocabulary		
	Nouns	*Verbs*	*Expressions*
Can you ... (= Are you able to) Yes, I/you etc. can ... No, I/you etc. can't ... (He) can't ... but (he) can ... It's behind/in front of ... Are there any (cups) ...? Is there any (coffee) ...?	cupboard dear kettle tea-cup tea-pot	boil find hurry (up)	Yes, of course, over there there it is here they are

General Remarks
Note that *can* is introduced as a secondary linguistic feature in this lesson. The main intention is to contrast uncountable nouns with countable nouns in the plural and to practise the use of *any* and *some*.
(Alexander 1967, 85–86)

As can be seen, no distinction is made between *can* expressing 'ability' (the use of *can* in the specification of "content and basic aims") and *can* used in a request ("can you make the tea, John").

The modal verb *could* is not introduced until lesson 103, after the past tense has been dealt with. *Could* is first introduced with reference to 'ability'/'inability', then (lesson 107) in requests ("could you show me another blue dress").

Alexander (1967) has a strict progression in the introduction of linguistic forms, but introduces different functions simultaneously because these are expressed by the same formal means (*can*). Different ways of expressing the same speech act (request) are introduced at widely different points because one is treated as a 'present', the other as a 'past' tense form.

The linguistic progression used in a course book like Alexander's rests on (intuitive but usually ill-defined) considerations of linguistic simplicity and complexity. The assumption is that certain structures are inherently simpler, and easier to learn, than others, irrespective of the mother tongue of the learner.[2] But as we emphasized in chapter 11, L1 transfer is a highly relevant factor in FL learning, and it is therefore reasonable to require that a linguistic syllabus pays *some* attention to structural similarities and differences between learners' L1 and the L2. This is impossible to live up to with teaching materials which are prepared for distribution world-wide, like Alexander's.

A PRAGMATIC SYLLABUS uses speech acts as the main structuring principle.[3] Just as a linguistic syllabus takes the learner through the grammatical structures of the language, a pragmatic syllabus takes the learner through a succession of speech acts. For instance, in an intermediate course book organized along these lines, the speech act *permission* is dealt with by learners asking for, giving, and refusing permission in a number of situations, as below (Abbs/Freebairn 1979a):

Ask for, give and refuse permission

(formally)	May I come and see the flat?	Yes, of course.
		Yes, certainly.
(informally)	Can I come and see you?	Yes, sure.
		Yes, do.

1. *Work in pairs. Ask for permission to do these things:*
   open the door   close the door
   borrow your book   turn on the light
   use your telephone   turn on the television
   Ask for and give permission, first formally, then informally.

May I use your phone?	Well, actually, I'm expecting a phone call myself.
Can I use your phone?	Sorry, but I'm expecting a call.

2. *Work in pairs. Ask for and refuse permission, first formally, then informally. Use a different reason each time.*

May I ...?	Well, actually ...
Can I ...?	Sorry, but ...
come and see you this evening	I've got guests for supper.
	I want to go to bed early.
smoke	this is a no-smoking room.
	I feel sick when people smoke.
telephone you at work	I haven't got a phone.
	my boss doesn't like it.
open the window	it's very noisy when it's open.
	I've got an awful cold.
borrow your car	there's no petrol in it.
	I need it myself.
play your new Abba record	I lent it to my sister.
	the record player is broken.

3. *What do you say to:*
   a friend when the room is hot and you've got a headache?
   a stranger when you need to make a phone call in his house?
   a stranger when you want to look at his newspaper on the train?
   a friend when you want to talk to him/her alone?
   Act these situations with a partner.

In this lesson the speech act *permission* is practised with different linguistic forms (*can I, may I*) and related to speech act modality explicitly (formal/informal). The learner is also expected to relate these modalities to different interlocutors (friend/stranger).

Just as pragmatic competence includes linguistic competence, pragmatic syllabuses invariably pay considerable attention to linguistic form, even when linguistic considerations have been subordinated to pragmatic ones. The authors of the material excerpted above relate the functions explicitly to the grammatical forms which most commonly occur in the relevant speech act. They are listed together as follows in the teacher's book (Abbs/Freebairn 1979b):

Asking for and giving permission – formally and informally	*May I come and see the flat?* *Yes, of course./Yes, certainly.* *Can I come and see you?* *Yes, sure./Yes, do.*	Modals: *May/Can* + verb phrase
Asking for and refusing permission – formally and informally	*Well, actually/Sorry, but I'm expecting a telephone call myself.*	*Well, actually/Sorry, but* + verb phrase

When considering our examples of teaching materials following respectively a linguistic and a pragmatic syllabus, it should be pointed out that Abbs/Freebairn 1979a is *not* intended for beginning learners. It can therefore be assumed that basic structures and vocabulary have already been introduced, and that the focus on pragmatics and discourse involves re-arranging what has already been learnt, as well as providing the learners with new metacommunicative information of a pragmatic kind. Careful linguistic grading is obviously much more called for in a beginner's course, like Alexander's, even given a pragmatic orientation.

Most course books produced since the mid-70s claim to follow a pragmatic syllabus. This reflects an awareness that a linguistic syllabus is inadequate to reach the goal of communicative competence. However some authors seem to be reluctant to admit to using a combination of criteria, linguistic and pragmatic, in their syllabuses. This is probably due to the same misconception as in the linguistic-versus-communicative competence strife referred to in chapter 10, namely that any interest in linguistic competence is outdated.

A third principle on which a syllabus can be designed is a THEMATIC one. This could involve choosing a group of people or a family in order to provide continuity in a course book for beginners, or it could be a theme such as "the liberation struggle in southern Africa" or "race relations in Britain" at a higher level. Themes are chosen because of the light they can shed on the culture of an English-speaking country and for their appeal to the participants. Clearly such themes are one way of living up to the cultural aims of foreign language teaching. Equally clearly, the linguistic and pragmatic dimensions of a thematically structured syllabus cannot be ignored, and ideally the three structuring principles form a coherent whole. In other words it is not enough if the theme is motivating, there also has to be a probability of progress on the linguistic and pragmatic fronts as well.

It might be felt that a thematic syllabus is inappropriate at the level of the Folkeskole, because with beginners, linguistic and pragmatic structuring principles should dominate, provided that the topics covered are stimulating enough. However, even at this level, the thematic content is of vital importance, not merely in retaining learners' motivation, but also because all teaching materials project an image of some aspects of the English-speaking world and contribute to learners' awareness and understanding of it.[4]

At the Gymnasium level it may be fairly unproblematical for teachers and learners to negotiate and agree on the themes that can serve as a structuring principle for a given period of time. The question then is how to ensure an integration of the linguistic, pragmatic and thematic goals, which is no easy task. Not surprisingly, many teachers pursue thematic goals through the study of relevant texts, and separately pursue linguistic and pragmatic goals through grammar exercises, translation and composition work, and the like. At its worst this results in a watertight division between two types of activity, textual study and language practice, with no clear links or cross-fertilisation between the two.

Irrespective of whether several syllabuses are being pursued in parallel, or whether they are integrated into a coherent whole, it is important to consider what syllabus the individual learner follows. Individuals learn at their own tempo, and have different starting-points and learning styles. Ideal learning conditions are created in such a way that learners progress to greater mastery of the thematic issues and simultaneously develop greater communicative competence, these being interrelated. If students all work together on a theme, group work can offer more specialized or even individualized support for linguistic and pragmatic competence goals. Some may practise listening comprehension, working with a tape, while others are producing a written product. Variants of this approach

236

are used quite widely in the top forms of the Folkeskole, and might perhaps be used more extensively in the Gymnasium.

14.2 Exemplifying teaching methods: "An Exercise Typology"

Grewer/Moston/Sexton 1981 provides a framework for the classification of exercises in foreign language teaching. The underlying principle is that exercises help students develop proficiency in the foreign language by bridging the gap between highly controlled types of language use and free participation in classroom communication. This is an important point to be aware of in foreign language teaching: learners have to be carefully prepared in order to function freely in classroom discussion and group work in the foreign language. Grewer/Moston/Sexton 1981 offers a wealth of suggestions for exercise types at each of four phases. To illustrate the typology, we provide a brief characterization of each of these phases, illustrated by an example.

Phase A: "Organizing Information"
The exercises in this phase are designed to help learners to make sense of texts they either listen to or read. They are a means of checking that the main points and ideas have been understood. In the following example, learners watch a TV film and are then expected to pair off the words quoted on the right with the name of the person who said the words:

Do you remember the film?
Who said what?

A	Darren Burn	1	It's quite hard work for Darren, too.
B	Mr Burn	2	Keep smiling. Head down.
C	Mrs Burn	3	I'd hate his private life to be taken over.
D	Joanna	4	It's wonderful what you can do with a voice.
E	Ray	5	Never heard of him.
F	Promotion Manager	6	Just an ordinary boy, who liked the open air.
G	Producer	7	I am not exploiting him.
H	the kids	8	I'm not going to be able to travel on the tube any more.

| I | the pop-music papers | 9 If Darren has any chance of having a hit record we will sink in that sort of money. |

Do your pairs match?	A	B	C	D	E	F	G	H	I

(From: Speak for Yourself, Image-makers, 1.6)

Phase B: "Implanting Skills"

Learners are trained to react to different types of text, and then gradually to express their own ideas and feelings in the foreign language. A range of simulated situations and role-playing is involved, and the exercises progressively switch from the world of native speakers to the learners' personal experience. The example we have chosen is from a stage in which both reception and production are being built up, as the explanatory introduction indicates.

In the first part of this exercise the student hears a succession of sound effects on tape, and has key words in writing for each of 12 stages in a story. In the second part of the exercise the student uses the noises and the key words in order to narrate the story. The exercise is intended for a language laboratory, in which case the learner's attempts at telling the story are tape-recorded.

Noises: Listen carefully
1. *Birds singing .../... countryside sounds*
2. *Fast car .../squeals into the bend .../... noise of a crash*
3. *Female voice screaming .../... crying ...moaning*
4. *Quick footsteps on the pavement ../... gravel*
5. *Heavy breathing*
6. *Sound of a doorbell, repeated three times*
7. *Loud, violent knocking on a door*
8. *Noise of a window breaking*
9. *Opening a window .../... curtains being pulled apart .../... someone jumping into a room*
10. *Telephone dialling. A voice answering the telephone*
11. *Noise of a crowd outside ...–...?*
12. *Ambulance siren, coming closer and stopping*

Announcer: Part 2. Well, did you get the story?
Listen again and this time you say what you could hear.

(From: FWU Teacher's Notes to 'English for Today', Book 2, p. 32)

Phase C: "Developing Skills"

Learners are expected to make more productive use of language, but still within simulated situations. Our example is of a training exercise designed to lead to increased awareness of the language used in order to convey specific intentions.

Card Game

Make two sets of cards: a set of 'intentions' and a set of 'language' cards. Then listen to the tape. You are walking along the street. As you walk, you overhear bits of conversation. As you hear each extract, put down the right language card, and your partner should try to cover it with the correct intention card.

Intention	Language
1. *Making a suggestion*	A. You haven't said anything yet. What do you think?
2. *Showing enthusiasm*	
3. *Greeting*	B. What time's your train?
4. *Showing sympathy*	C. He's about your age, but a bit taller, and thinner.
5. *Asking for information*	
6. *Giving an opinion*	D. She left school when she was fifteen.
7. *Describing a person*	
8. *Asking for an opinion*	E. Why don't you go and see a doctor?
9. *Showing disagreement*	
10. *Expressing anxiety*	F. Heh! That's marvellous!
11. *Denying*	G. I just don't know what to do.
12. *Giving information*	H. Hello, Mike. Fancy seeing you here!
	I. I think it was a very stupid thing to do.
	J. No, that's not right, that's not right at all.
	K. It wasn't me who did it.
	L. Oh, I am sorry, I really am.

(From Challenges, Something to Say, Chain G)

Phase D: "Using Skills"

The learner should be able to take full part in interaction in the classroom, react to and discuss texts, and participate in group discussions. The exercises help learners to do this, primarily by increasing their metacommunicative awareness.

Probably there are many reasons for your opinions. Here is a list of some of the things you may want to say.
You can, of course, say other things.
In the classroom discussion, use your notes and give your opinion.
Prepare what you want to say carefully.
Make sure that the reason you give fits the opinion you have.

Here are some phrases which can be useful in a discussion:

As an introduction	Well, I think ...
	It seems to me ...
	What I think is ...
Interrupting someone	Hold on, ...
	Hang on, ...
	Just a second, ...
	Wait a minute, ...
	Yes, but ...
Expressing doubt	Well, I'm not sure that's right ...
	Maybe, but ...
Expressing agreement	That's right.
	You're (He's) right there.
	That's what I think.
	Quite right.
Denying something	That's completely wrong.
	That's not true.
Taking the floor	Let me finish.
	I haven't finished.
	The other thing I wanted to say was ...

(From: Ugly Brutes, 21.4)

14.3 Analysing the communicative and learning potential of classroom activities

There is a strong element of trial and error involved in most teaching, and it is important both for teachers and learners that they can afford the price of experimentation. As well as trying out new approaches and activities, it is salutary to reconsider teaching methods and procedures which are familiar, and which in the opinion of many teachers function in a satisfactory manner. One way of approaching them with fresh eyes, and possibly of getting them into a different perspective, is to relate them to the components of communicative competence and the learning processes that have been identified. Figure 17 lists some well-tried procedures under "activity types". In separate columns across the page are listed the components of communicative competence (I) and processes in foreign languages learning (II).

Activity types	I Communicative competence						II Learning			
	Linguistic competence	Pragmatic competence	Fluency	Strategic competence	Metacommunicative awareness	Social/cultural knowledge	Hypothesis formation	Hypothesis testing	Automatization	Consciousness raising
Teacher-controlled discussion of text	2	1	1	1	1	3	1	2	1	1
Reading aloud	3	1	2	0	1	1	1	3	2	1
Group discussion about text, teacher not present	1	2	3	1	1	2	2	1	3	1

Fig. 17: Activity types, communicative competence and learning

The idea is that each activity type can be analysed into its communicative and learning potential by deciding on a value for each component. We have illustrated this by providing one possible analysis of three activity types. The following rates have been used:

3: the activity is expected to focus on the component in question (therefore only one '3' in I and one in II)
2: the activity is fairly important for the component in question
1: the activity has some relevance for the component in question
0: it is inconceivable that the activity will be relevant for the component in question.

We suggest that teachers and learners add activities to the list, and experiment with allocating values to them. This could lead to an increased awareness of the utility of various classroom procedures for reaching specific aims.

Footnotes to chapter 14

1. We prefer the term 'linguistic syllabus' as this provides a direct link to linguistic competence. Other terms commonly used are 'grammatical' or 'structural' syllabuses. See for example *Handbook to Longman's Structural Readers*, Longman 1968.
2. See Alexander/Allen/Close/O'Neill 1975.
3. In the teacher's book, speech acts are referred to as "functions". These are learned in combination with "topics", this link stressing that the speech act operates in relation to something, ie a topic. Sometimes "notion" is used interchangeably with "topic", and many syllabuses which are described as being "notional" or "functional" correspond to what we are referring to as pragmatic syllabuses.
4. See Andersen/Risager 1977.

Chapter 14. Sources and further reading

On principles of syllabus design, see Johnson 1982, Brumfit 1981, Paulston 1981, Wilkins 1981a and b, and Widdowson/Brumfit 1981.

Experience with thematic syllabus design in the Danish context is often reported in *Ekstrameddelelser fra Gymnasieskolernes Engelsklærerforening*. Danmarks pædagogiske bibliotek has a considerable collection of reports on pedagogical experimentation, particularly of experience in syllabus design and implementation in the upper classes of the Folkeskole.

242

On the selection and structuring of teaching content see Breen/Candlin 1980, Brumfit 1980, and the contributions in Candlin 1981.

On language teaching methodology see Andersen/Fredberg/Vestergaard/Østergaard 1978 for a summary of traditional approaches, Stevick 1976, 1980, and British Council 1982 for presentation of more recent approaches. Comprehensive bibliographies on relevant books and journals are obtainable from the English-Teaching Information Centre, The British Council, 10 Spring Gardens, London SW 1A 2BN.

Chapter fifteen:
Evaluation

In all teaching, feedback on the outcome of learning is essential, both to the parties directly involved in the process (learners and teachers) as well as to society at large. In our coverage of evaluation, we concentrate on feedback obtained through tests, and address the question of what constitutes a good language test.

15.1 Achievement and profiency testing

A major distinction, reflecting different purposes of testing, can be made between achievement and proficiency testing. ACHIEVEMENT TESTING tests to what extent a student has learnt what has been taught. The test is closely linked to course work. Achievement testing can therefore be described as back-pointing. PROFICIENCY TESTING tests the extent to which the student's mastery of the foreign language is adequate for future needs, and can therefore be characterized as forward-pointing. A clear example of this would be a language test for a Danish nurse who has applied for a job in voluntary service in Africa. Among other things, the oral language test requires her to carry out certain nursing instructions in English.

Many exams contain elements of both testing aspects, for instance when students are examined on the basis of prepared texts (achievement) as well as unseen texts (proficiency). Sometimes exams are biassed towards achievement, even when one might expect the profiency aspect to be of primary importance. This is the case with the test of oral expression taken on leaving the Folkeskole. The exam usually restricts the learner to giving short answers to questions on a text which has been studied in class. The learner is given little scope to demonstrate her communicative competence. An attempt to devise a reform of this examination, making it more of a proficiency test, is described at the end of the chapter.

15.2 Norm-referenced and criterion-referenced testing

There has been extensive discussion among educationalists about norm-referenced and criterion-referenced testing, this distinction touching a political nerve because tests often serve the purpose of selecting and streaming students.

In NORM-REFERENCED testing one student's proficiency in English is compared to that of the other students in the group, or those at the same educational level nation-wide. Focus is on a particular student's proficiency compared to an average, which means that assessment is relative.

CRITERION-REFERENCED testing concerns itself with the extent to which each individual student lives up to the aims set for the studies in question. It is an absolute assessment, which leaves out considerations of the group and focusses entirely on the individual's mastery of the set tasks. Criterion-referenced testing has received much support in theory, but there are several obstacles to its implementation. A major one is that this approach presupposes precise descriptions of the criterion used, ie in the case of a final exam, of the educational aims. And as we pointed out in chapter 3, neither the Folkeskole nor the Gymnasium have precise descriptions of aims.

In a recent Danish research project on the Folkeskole leaving exam in English, a set of criteria were proposed for the assessment of learners' free oral production.[1] The proposed criteria were language functions, vocabulary and communication strategies. This focus on pragmatic and strategic competence is in line with the official aims for English in the Folkeskole.

15.3 Formative and summative evaluation

The distinction between formative and summative evaluation also has to do with the purposes of testing. The main purpose of FORMA-TIVE EVALUATION is to provide for feedback on the teaching/learning *process*. SUMMATIVE EVALUATION takes place on completion of a course, and focusses on the *outcome* of teaching/learning exclusively. It is typically in the form of an exam, on the basis of which marks are allocated. Exams represent a societal check on the teaching/learning in question.

As a support for formative evaluation, teachers may have recourse to *diagnostic* tests. A diagnostic test is not necessarily a different type of test from the ones introduced earlier. It may be an achievement test which is utilized for diagnostic purposes. In the marking the teacher identifies problem areas which are then followed up carefully with individual learners or groups. Good tests can be extremely useful for such purposes.

15.4 Validity and reliability

It is now important to consider the test instrument itself and ask the question: what is a good language test? To answer this it is necessary to present the concepts reliability and validity.

RELIABILITY means the precision with which a test measures. Essay-marking is notoriously unreliable, firstly because teachers who do the marking often operate with different criteria for what constitutes a good essay or weight the criteria differently, secondly, even if there is agreement on the criteria, individual teachers may apply them idiosyncratically, some being stricter than others. This inter-scorer reliability, or rather the lack of it, is also a central point of criticism of most oral exams, where it is extremely difficult to disentangle language factors and personality factors.

A good example of a reliable test is a multiple choice test, which has only one correct answer to each item. For this reason it is commonly referred to as an objective test. This, however, is a misleading term, since the objectivity applies only to the marking phase of the test. The selection of the content of the test is just as subjective as that for other tests.

The VALIDITY of a test is the extent to which it measures what it intends to measure. Validity is first and foremost concerned with *what* is tested, ie the content of the test, whereas reliability focusses on *how* one tests. True validity presupposes reliability.

It is possible to distinguish between several types of validity, but we shall restrict our attention to three, namely predictive validity, content validity and face validity. A test has PREDICTIVE VALIDITY if the test results, eg marks in English at one educational level, effectively predict success in English at higher educational levels.

A test may by said to possess CONTENT VALIDITY if it assesses

246

precisely the skills or knowledge described in the aims of the particular course or teaching sequence in question. One reason why it is so difficult to give Danish learners tests developed elsewhere, for instance in North America, is that they lack content validity with respect to the specific aims of foreign language teaching in the Danish education system. Content validity is also the issue when students, often justly, complain that the content or form of an exam does not reflect the stated aims of the course in question.

The third type of validity is FACE VALIDITY, which means the extent to which a test *appears* to test the right things. In orther words whether the test looks valid to learners, teachers, parents and administrators, as opposed to expert test constructors. When cloze tests, for instance, were introduced in the Folkeskole written exam in English and German, they caused heated debate because it was in no way obvious that filling in gaps in a text is directly related to communicative competence. The fact that there is empirical evidence to support this, at least for well constructed cloze tests, and for certain proficiency levels, does not solve the immediate problem of lack of face validity.[2] A test which does possess face validity is the oral interview, but with this there are problems, particularly with reliability.

15.5 Discrete point tests and integrative tests

In DISCRETE POINT tests, communicative competence is broken down into its smallest constituent elements. Traditionally a discrete point test is one that focusses on one point of linguistic competence at a time, either phonology, syntax or lexis. The test items are often presented with little contextual support. What is tested is discrete elements of discrete aspects of discrete components of discrete skills (Oller 1979, 172). A typical example of a discrete point test uses the written medium, singles out grammatical competence (one component of communicative competence), focusses on one area of grammatical competence, for instance the word class of adverbs, and has a large number of items covering adverbs with two forms:

Choose the right alternative:
1. We had to dig (deep/deeply) to find gold.
2. She was (deep/deeply) in debt.
...

247

Discrete point tests are often multiple choice tests. They can consequently be marked objectively. When the test consists of a large number of items, this also increases reliability, which is the main virtue of discrete point testing.

INTEGRATIVE TESTS are tests of language use in actual communicative events or in tasks that mirror normal discourse. Examples are free production tests such as the oral interview and composition writing, in which many components of communicative competence are activated and where an assessment of how they interact can be made.[3] While discrete point testing is based on the principle of taking language apart, integrative tests put it back together again. Cloze procedure (see chapter 5) is considered an integrative test, mainly because items are context-embedded and because cloze taps the learner's knowledge of several components of communicative competence, notably discourse, lexical and syntactic knowledge, both in reception and production.

Translation tests, such as the translation of a piece of Danish prose into English, are widely used in Danish exams at intermediate and advanced levels. It might be thought that translation tests are integrative tests, but this is not necessarily the case. Sometimes the "texts" are specially constructed to test specific grammatical and lexical problems, and are therefore in reality discrete point tests in disguise, especially if they are evaluated in a way that focusses on linguistic competence only.

In Danish foreign language exams within general education, discrete point tests are only used at few educational levels. Scepticism about them is justified at least so long as the contribution of the individual components to overall communicative competence is so unclarified. When one sees how often relative pronouns, for instance, have been chosen in tests in Denmark, one cannot help wondering whether the test writers really believe that this area is particularly important for communication, or whether it just happens to be an easy one to test!

Ideally we would like to see exams challenge the students' use of all relevant components of communicative competence in integrative tests. This implies that exams should consist not of one but of a number of communicative events. This is, however, difficult to implement. If we sum up the state of the art in language testing, there are, on the one hand, discrete point tests that are reliable but weak on content and face validity, and, on the other, integrative tests that are unreliable but strong on content and face validity.

Two lines of approach have been followed to try to solve this dilemma. The first broadens the scope of discrete point tests to include aspects of pragmatic competence and to contextualize testing items much more than previously (see for instance Morrow 1977). The second insists on integrative tests, but works seriously to improve their reliability, for instance by offering precise information about the components of communicative competence to be assessed. Integrative tests have dominated the Danish scene, which we think is as it should be, but much more attention needs to be paid to increasing the reliability of these tests.

15.6 Towards a reform of school language examinations

The research project on the *Folkeskole* exam mentioned above covered all areas of the oral exam, reading, listening and oral expression. We shall limit ourselves to describing the oral expression test and the attempts at improving its content validity and reliability.

According to the official regulations for the Folkeskole, learners are expected to be able to *use* the language ("brugssprog") and participate in a dialogue or conversation. The research team interpret this as meaning that the learner should be able to participate as a full partner in a dialogue, to take some initiative and to contribute a fair amount of language. The team therefore introduced a new communicative task into the exam, namely a simulation between the teacher and learner, based on one of the topics studied. The simulation might involve the learner applying for a part-time job at the local baker's, with the teacher playing the role of the baker. Or the learner could be in the role of a spokesperson for the whole class discussing the planning of a party with the teacher. Both participants are given cue cards as prompts, these mainly serving the purpose of ensuring that the learner not only responds to language from the teacher but can take some initiative. Such a task challenges the learner to produce a wide range of speech acts, informative, attitudinal and ritual, and it involves the learner in the opening and closing phases of a communicative event. The traditional exam is text-based and tests only a very restricted range of speech acts (see 15.1), so the experiment improves the content validity of the test of oral expression.

The reliability of the test was tackled by the explicit formulation of a set of criteria for the assessment of oral expression. These focus on pragmatic competence (including a range of speech acts, speech act modality and discourse knowledge) and strategic competence. With the emphasis on role simulation and strategic competence, the team wants to promote risk-taking, to encourage learners to use achievement strategies rather than reduce or give up. The proficiency aspect of testing is strengthened by letting learners show how well they are able to stretch their language to meet the demands of new situations.

It is hoped that this testing experiment will have a backwash effect on classroom practice and that the proposed criteria, together with explicit descriptions of performance levels, may help teachers to come to grips with the "new" components of communicative competence, pragmatic and strategic competence.

There is also a strong case for reform of the examinations at the *Gymnasium* level. It is striking that there is a total absence of explicit and precise criteria for the evaluation of students' oral expression. And that listening comprehension is only tested in relation to the familiar teacher's familiar English.

In an experiment in foreign language teaching at the Gymnasium, in which new exams have been developed, some of the innovation is in accordance with the principles we have advocated.[4] The proficiency aspect of the exam is strengthened by giving more emphasis to unseen texts than is usually the case. The students have two days in which to work on these texts, which are related to a topic they have been investigating. Teaching notes and reference works can be used in preparing for the oral exam. The examination also includes a listening test based on a three minute tape.

We suggest that readers as a follow-up to this chapter analyse exams at the educational level(s) they are familiar with, and compare the aims, official guidelines, exam regulations, and their own experience of exams. In this analysis it should be feasible to include the test parameters introduced in this chapter, notably validity and reliability.

250

A prerequisite for designing more appropriate exams is that teaching and learning aims are well defined. This makes it possible to decide which components of communicative competence are to be in focus, and consequently to include in the exam the types of communicative tasks (integrative tests) that make it possible to assess these components. The proficiency aspect can be strengthened at all levels by selecting unrehearsed tasks, so that students can demonstrate how they can apply their knowledge in new situations. Based on precise aims it will be possible to develop descriptions of target level performances, which will increase reliability and facilitate an approximation to criterion referenced testing.

Footnotes to chapter 15

1. The project was financed by "Folkeskolens Forsøgsråd" and is described in Brick-Hansen/Engel/Haastrup/Gregersen 1983.
2. We express reservations about the validity of cloze tests because in the case of German we know of no empirical evidence with respect to cloze tests at this fairly low proficiency level.
3. What we here call integrative tests are sometimes referred to as "tests of integrated skills", "tests of global proficiency", and "communicative tests".
4. See Herlev Statsskole 1982, 178–179.

Chapter 15. Sources and further reading

Our introduction to basic parameters in language testing is in accordance with Allen/Davies 1977, a standard work on fundamental concepts in testing, test construction and statistics, and with Oller 1979, a strong advocate of integrative tests.

For surveys of test development in the 70s, see Carroll 1980, Morrow 1977 and Jones/Spolsky 1975. Alderson/Hughes 1981 gives a vivid impression of the ongoing debate.

As practical handbooks for the classroom teacher we recommend Heaton 1975 and part III of Oller 1979.

Chapter sixteen:
Innovation

In this chapter we relate the principles and theories expounded so far in the book to trends in foreign language teaching in Denmark. There is no attempt at an exhaustive coverage of ways in which one might innovate in foreign language teaching. Rather, we have been very selective in what we present, and focus on trends that reflect how we would like to see foreign language teaching in Denmark develop. We have ignored present limitations as regards teacher education and resources available – our description therefore has a certain utopian quality.

We first consider a number of influential general pedagogical principles, learner-centredness, learner consciousness, negotiation of content and methods, collaboration across subjects, and project work, and discuss how each of these relates to foreign language teaching. We then discuss various types of innovation, developed specifically within foreign language teaching. The final topic covered in the chapter is teacher education and how this can live up to the challenge of the principles we elaborate.

16.1 Differentiation

DIFFERENTIATION involves organizing teaching so that the different needs and abilities of learners are catered for. In unstreamed, comprehensive education, there is a clear need for differentiation. This is the case in the Danish Folkeskole and, increasingly, also in the Gymnasium, which now has a broad intake of learners with a wide range of interests, abilities and learning styles.

Differentiation exists in several forms in the classroom. An extreme form is totally individualized teaching, each learner working with her own topic and materials at her own speed. Reading and listening comprehension are appropriate for individual work, in that texts and accompanying activities can be chosen to suit the individual learner's level.

In the age of the micro-processor it is necessary to be aware of both the potential and the dangers of computer-assisted foreign language learning. Given the materials available commercially so far, such work is confined to mechanical exercises which only practise few of the components of communicative competence.

As learning a foreign language includes learning to engage in communicative interaction with other individuals in a range of social contexts, one highly appropriate form of differentiation is learning in small groups. Interacting with teaching materials cannot substitute for real-life communication. Moreover, group work contributes to furthering one of the primary goals of general education, namely socializing pupils to cooperate, to accept other opinions and draw on varying abilities, in short to work together towards solving common problems.

A precondition for differentiated teaching is awareness on the part of both teacher and learner of learning needs and goals, of the utility of the materials available and of how they can be exploited, of the function of different learning activities. But consciousness is not enough. Differentiated foreign language teaching should be undertaken in rooms which lend themselves to a wide range of activities, preferably with small group rooms available. Ideally, there should be access to videotapes, cassette-recorders, books, newspapers and magazines, cardboard and crayons, etc. Finally, it is less than likely that the teacher is in a position to provide individual guidance if the class of learners exceeds 20 – indeed the maximum size of a foreign language class should be considerably smaller.

16.2 Consciousness

One of the goals of education is to develop independence of thought in the individual, to encourage a critical consciousness. If one considers the specific contribution of foreign language school subjects in relation to this general goal, it is possible to identify three types of knowledge which could contribute to achieving it. These are metacommunicative knowledge, knowledge about language learning, and socio-cultural knowledge.

16.2.1 Metacommunicative knowledge

We have already stressed the importance of metacommunicative awareness in relation to communicative competence (cf chapter 10). We indicated that knowledge of the rules governing linguistic form could be directly relevant for the development of learners' proficiency, as such metalinguistic knowledge can provide short-cuts to learning or can monitor language production and increase correctness. Conscious knowledge therefore has a direct utility value in relation to the development of language proficiency.

We also made the point in chapter 10 that metacommunicative awareness is a valuable goal in itself in a school subject a central aspect of which is communication. Metacommunicative knowledge in relation to a foreign language can increase the individual's awareness of communication in the mother tongue as well as provide an informed basis for insight into the conventional nature of language and the different forms that it assumes in different cultures.

It is the last-mentioned function of metacommunicative knowledge that we find particularly important. We should therefore like to see greater cooperation between teachers of Danish and teachers of foreign languages, studying in depth specific features of communication, for instance speech act realization in the relevant languages, discourse structure, forms of address, strategy use, etc.

16.2.2 Knowledge about learning

For learners to be able to participate actively in establishing teaching goals and selecting activity types and materials for study, they need a certain amount of knowledge about foreign language learning. In particular they should be aware of the relationship between the development of specific aspects of communicative competence and such factors as classroom organization, textual input, feedback and language rules as formulated in reference works or by teachers. What mediates between these factors and the development of communicative competence is learning processes, as described in chapter 11. In addition to being equipped to identify their own learning needs, learners should therefore be able to pinpoint areas of their communicative competence which are most in need of improvement.

Furthermore, they should be able to relate these learning needs to processes of language learning and to select appropriate learning "strategies". This last step would involve negotiation with the other learners in the class as well as with the teacher, in order to reach a procedure which not only suits the individual learner's personal needs and learning style but also coordinates this with the needs of other learners in the class.

When teachers are offered this idealised scheme for negotiating a syllabus with learners, a common reaction is that it is unrealistic. Our response to this is that if the teacher genuinely wants learner participation in planning teaching content and methods, then learners have to be in possession of the necessary metaknowledge, including knowledge about learning. Pupil participation without such metaknowledge can easily lead to pseudo-democratic decisions, with the teacher manipulating the pupils. Or to pupils opting for a course of action which can lead to only some of their learning goals being met. This is the case, for instance, if the only factors which are considered seriously in the negotiation phase are themes and texts, to the neglect of metacommunicative or language learning goals.

16.2.3 Socio-cultural knowledge

All examples of English which learners meet, whether literary products, newspaper articles or video-taped conversations between native speakers, are anchored in a socio-cultural context. Learners of English develop their communicative competence in relation to this socio-cultural reality, especially their pragmatic competence, as we pointed out in chapter 10.

Traditionally, there has been a tendency to identify the concept of "content" in foreign language teaching with socio-cultural knowledge, often with an emphasis on the historical dimension. On the other side was language, which was considered to be primarily proficiency-related. We would argue that a central area of the content of foreign language teaching is linguistic, in the sense that it deals with communication (in a broad sense) in the foreign language. Therefore, when we argue for the importance of metacommunicative knowledge and knowledge about language learning, we are not arguing for an increase in the proficiency side of foreign language education, at the cost of socio-cultural knowledge. What we would like to strengthen is *knowledge* about what we consider to be the core of all foreign language subjects: communication in the foreign language, including learning to communicate in the language.

16.3 Negotiation of syllabus

The concept of negotiating a syllabus implies that teacher and learners together establish the teaching sub-goals, the route to be followed in order to reach these goals, as well as the types of activities needed, including the selection of texts.

For learners to be able to participate in such negotiation, they need to have metacommunicative knowledge, knowledge about language learning, and socio-cultural knowledge. As learners cannot be expected to acquire such knowledge in other school subjects, it is essential that foreign language teachers convey this knowledge to the learners at a fairly early stage. In one Folkeskole in which this is done systematically, the goals for pupil awareness are that the pupil is to understand:[1]

- why English is being learned
- what is being learned
- how learning takes place
- her own role and that of her fellow pupils in the teaching/learning situation
- how she can help fellow students to learn.

In addition to strong pedagogical arguments in favour of learners taking responsibility for what they are learning, we can advance three further reasons. The first is that no description of potential learner needs, however comprehensive, can anticipate all the needs of a specific set of individuals. The second is that there is a risk of teaching materials and elaborate syllabuses giving the impression that foreign language learning is exclusively a question of assimilating a given, normatively-defined content and a set of rules, a complete package. Negotiating a syllabus stresses the learner's active role in construing and creating meaning in the foreign language, as preparation for dialogue and contact with the new language. A third reason is that learners must be prepared to continue their foreign

256

language learning on their own after completing general education. They must therefore learn to plan language learning.

16.4 Inter-subject collaboration

We use the term *inter-subject* rather than *inter-disciplinary* because we are referring to collaboration between two or more school *subjects*. Disciplines such as economic theory, phonetics and text analysis are of relevance to many subjects, and most problems need to be analysed with the help of more than one discipline.

There are many points at which school subjects overlap and support each other, and the increasing trend towards collaboration across subject boundaries is a recognition of this. Collaboration can consist of an agreement between a couple of teachers to cover parallel ground in different subjects, with each subject pursuing the topic independently. Or collaboration can consist of much more integrated work.

An example of such integrated work is a first-year Gymnasium collaborative venture involving English, Mathematics and Physics, running over a period of three months.[2] The topic was energy, and fundamental principles of Mathematics and Physics were studied in relation to specific aspects of the topic. The contribution of English was not merely to read texts which were only available in English, but to take up problems which are exemplary for an understanding of the Anglo-American world and how it relates to the third world. The particular theme chosen was technology and industrialisation and the forms of energy which are relevant to the economy of a particular African country. The English texts were read with more understanding because of the insights into the topic from the natural sciences, and the natural science coverage of energy benefitted from the reading of texts which put the issues into a wider perspective.

We would not wish to minimise the very considerable demands that such collaboration makes on the teachers involved. This example comes from an experimental Gymnasium, but a great deal of inter-subject collaboration takes place at many other institutions, both at the Gymnasium and, to a lesser extent, in the top forms of the Folkeskole.

One worry which has led to a resistance to inter-subject collabo-

257

ration is a feeling that the identity and goals of English may not be respected, for instance that the foreign language becomes downgraded to being a tool for other subjects. As a communication subject, English has "content" of the three kinds that we have outlined above, quite apart from proficiency development, and it is essential that inter-subject collaboration takes this into consideration. If this is done, there is every reason to encourage learners and teachers of English to collaborate with other subjects.

16.5 Project work

By PROJECT WORK is understood a specific way of organizing learning so that the participants, typically working in small groups, are actively involved in:

1. selecting topics
2. formulating the problem(s)
3. selecting working procedure, including choice of methods and materials
4. processing texts, data, etc.
5. producing a report or an equivalent product
6. evaluating the product and the working process.

Occasionally, the term "project work" is used to refer loosely to any thematic approach to teaching, eg working with Northern Ireland for a period of 3 weeks. For this to be project work proper, the *process* has to reflect the six steps enumerated above: project work is as much a way of organizing learning as it is a question of studying a specific theme.

One reason why project work has been evolved at school and higher education levels is that it provides a means of reconciling some of the problems discussed in the preceding sections. Project work allows for differentiation without leading to complete individualization. It enables learners to develop consciousness and to negotiate a syllabus. It lends itself to collaboration across subject boundaries.

When project work is used in foreign language learning, there is the problem of how to ensure that the participants not only develop consciousness but also proficiency in the foreign language. This is a

258

difficult problem which to our knowledge has not been tackled in a satisfactory manner yet. If project work is decided on for a restricted period of time, one might accept that the learners use their mother tongue when working in the group as long as they produce a report in the foreign language and that they primarily use materials written/recorded in the foreign language. In this way there is an element of proficiency training within some of the four skills at least. But for obvious reasons it would be desirable if learners would accept using the foreign language *in the groups*. In order to achieve this, it is necessary for the teacher to spend a good deal of time discussing the issue with the learners before they embark on their project, pointing out to them what benefits will accrue from using the foreign language and giving them advice on how to handle the problems which will often arise.

Project work is hardly feasible if the traditional pattern of foreign language teaching in schools is preserved, namely dividing up the available time into periods of 45 minutes or 90 minutes. For project work to operate in a satisfactory way it is necessary to introduce phases in which the learners work intensively with one subject (or a few if the project is carried out in collaboration with other subjects). Working intensively with a foreign language for a certain period of time, rather than spreading out the time thinly over a long period has been recommended, eg by Hawkins/Perren 1978. Intensive work can provide a qualitative leap, particularly as regards language proficiency, which may not otherwise occur. In particular, less successful learners can develop a sense of achievement in foreign language learning. One could therefore consider reorganizing the time-table in Danish schools so as to allow for more intensive work at different phases of the school year, and correspondingly less intensive ones at others. As alternatives to project work can be mentioned trips to the foreign country or the production of a fairly major report (a "speciale").

16.6 Communicative foreign language teaching

The major goal of COMMUNICATIVE FOREIGN LANGUAGE TEACHING is to build up competence which can be used for a variety of communicative purposes in non-educational contexts, and to do so by upgrading communicative activities in the classroom.

The extreme case of communicative foreign language teaching is to abandon the subject as such and to use the language as a medium of instruction in other school subjects. This is what happens in IMMERSION PROGRAMMES in North America, in which children receive a substantial part of their early school instruction in a language which is not their mother tongue (eg French in the province of Ontario in Canada). Although such programmes have led to very positive results, immersion children reaching a higher proficiency level in the foreign language than traditionally taught children and still doing as well or even better in other school subjects including the mother tongue (cf Swain/Lapkin 1982), it is unrealistic to expect foreign language teaching in Denmark to become reorganized along such lines.[3]

A mild variant of immersion education would be teaching a single non-language subject like geography through the medium of English. Provided teachers could cope, this would undoubtedly be effective for the development of proficiency in English. But as there would still be a need for other aspects of communicative competence and all the types of knowledge associated with English to be developed, English would remain as a distinct subject on the time-table.

We turn now to the *present* situation in Denmark, with foreign language learning taking place in classes specifically established for this purpose. How can such lessons be made to approximate to varieties of communication outside school?

Many types of communicative activity are in use in order to achieve this. Typical examples are:

- GAMES and PROBLEM-SOLVING ACTIVITIES of various sorts, in which fairly restricted goals are set for the communicative interaction
- ROLE PLAYS and SIMULATIONS, dialogues or small group interaction in which the pupils act out or simulate roles that they have been assigned or can imagine themselves in.

Most of these activity types not only practise aspects of linguistic competence, they also develop learners' pragmatic and strategic competence. There are examples of simulations and role plays at the end of chapter 11 and 15, and the extracts from the exercise typology in chapter 14 demonstrate how both production and reception development can be built up by activities which gradually stretch the learner's proficiency, providing enough support initially, and setting up freer, more creative situations later on.

Activities like role playing are often employed with a view to developing learners' productive skills. A focus on production skills has characterised most communicatively oriented language teaching, this in part reflecting the behaviouristically based assumption that something is only learned when the learner is able to *produce* utterances in the foreign language. With cognitivist views on comprehension, which see this as an active process (cf chapter 8), there is now a clear tendency to upgrade listening and reading activities.

Especially at the beginning levels of foreign language learning, it has been suggested that a COMPREHENSION APPROACH has significant advantages. According to this, learners are not required (or in some cases even allowed) to *speak* the language for a period of perhaps several months, the idea being that learners' receptive competence should be well developed before they start using the language for productive purposes. This has obvious affective advantages, as much of the pressure and anxiety associated with beginning to speak a foreign language is removed.

A strong case can be made for strengthening listening skills, not just as part of a comprehension approach but generally, at all levels of education. The listening comprehension test introduced in 1978 as part of the school leaving examination at the end of Folkeskole was one move in this direction. At Gymnasium level, authentic listening materials can serve similar purposes to written texts in providing stimulating source material which can be analyzed for metacommunicative and socio-cultural knowledge. Both receptive competence and the kinds of conscious knowledge that can be built up in connection with such listening activities will be relevant for the subsequent development of the learners' productive competence, and can be linked up with participation in the kinds of communicative activities mentioned above.

261

16.7 Language teacher education

Some teachers are already putting into practice many of the principles presented in this chapter and in the book as a whole, although they may never have encountered them in their studies. The evaluation and discussion of such experience would benefit from systematic analysis of it, within an explicit foreign language pedagogical framework. This can provide the concepts and a metalanguage for knowledge about the teaching and learning of foreign languages.

While the ideal state of affairs is for teachers to be trained in all these areas in the course of their studies, this is not the case for those teaching today. There is therefore a real need for extensive programmes of in-service training which can relate the experience of teachers to theoretically explicit principles of foreign language pedagogy.

In concluding this part of the book we shall describe the qualifications that foreign language teachers should ideally have. We begin by considering in what ways the demands made on teachers of foreign languages differ from those made on teachers of other subjects.

In the first place, foreign language learners are already communicatively competent, to a greater or lesser extent, in their mother tongue. The proficiency side of foreign language teaching therefore involves learners in doing things that they can already do, but in a different code. Although other subjects can also draw upon experience from outside the classroom, it is only foreign language teachers who have to "re-teach" or re-formulate what the learner already knows.

Secondly, foreign language learners are learning something that others, namely the native speakers of the language, have not had to "learn" at all but have assimilated naturally in interaction with their environment. The foreign language teacher has to lead learners to a similar kind of proficiency, possibly by quite a different route.

Thirdly, language use is intimately related to personality, social identity, to the ability to perform cognitively demanding operations. Learning a foreign language can be psychologically very demanding, and the teacher must know how to alleviate anxiety and linguistic insecurity.

Fourthly, whereas in many school subjects the insight and knowledge that learners develop is the main concern, in foreign language learning, in a very real sense, the medium is the message. Many of the activities are important in themselves as they represent the communication which is the essence of the subject.

These factors mean that it is no exaggeration to state that foreign language teaching is qualitatively different from other types of teaching and that teachers require special qualifications and training. We would claim that these are as important for teachers of beginners as for teachers of more advanced learners. When learners are meeting the pronunciation and rhythm of the language for the first time, are exploring the relationship between L1 and L2 and building up their learning styles, there is a need for teachers with expert knowledge of the language and the processes of learning it, just as there is at more advanced levels. Unfortunately, it is not uncommon to meet the erroneous belief in the Folkeskole that the teaching of beginners does not require special qualifications.

What then are the *essential requirements* of these professional qualifications? In the first place, *proficiency* in the language, in all the areas of communicative competence discussed in part I of the book. Lack of proficiency can result in, for instance, over-dependence on teaching materials and a tendency to be rigid in assessing learner language.

The second requirement is a solid grounding in all the 3 areas of knowledge discussed earlier in this chapter. We shall briefly consider each of these. As regards *metacommunicative knowledge,* students today generally acquire a training in grammar and phonetics, some awareness about vocabulary, and very little if any familiarity with pragmatics, discourse, strategies or fluency. While there is a natural resistance and reluctance to adding "new" areas to an already crammed study programme, with perhaps a feeling that even less grammar and phonetics would be the result, the phenomenon of a knowledge explosion is a real one. It is true, for instance, in medicine, where no-one would argue that doctors should only be trained in a selection of the areas necessary for their profession. If foreign language teachers are to be qualified to critically assess and utilise teaching materials and the methodological suggestions of "experts", then the issue of what they should know and be able to do cannot be side-stepped. Future teachers need an up-to-date introduction to all relevant aspects of knowledge and a training which permits them

263

to follow up the issues during their professional lives, and means have to be found for achieving this.

Socio-cultural knowledge is generally well-represented today in teacher education, especially at university level. There has been an important re-orientation within this area towards contemporary social phenomena, at the cost of more traditional cultural knowledge. What could perhaps be strengthened is the cross-cultural dimension, developing knowledge about significant similarities and differences between the native and the target language culture.

Knowledge about foreign language learning and teaching and general pedagogy is part of the obligatory syllabus of colleges of education, but only sporadically found in university degree programmes. One consequence of this is that many university graduates experience a mismatch between their professionalism as regards socio-cultural and metacommunicative knowledge and their language proficiency on the one hand, and their amateurism and lack of relevant knowledge with respect to foreign language learning and teaching on the other. Overcoming this problem involves ensuring that foreign language departments in the universities are obliged to cover foreign language pedagogy.

Again, it is only fair to ask how foreign language pedagogy can be fitted in. How do we find room, without cutting down on other important areas of study? The approach to foreign language pedagogy presented in this book helps to solve some of these problems, in that the study of the subject as traditionally defined and the study of the learning and the teaching of the subject are combined in dialectic interaction. For instance, in an integrated programme of study of learner language and the grammar of English, the student not only develops metalinguistic knowledge of grammar but an ability to improve her own correctness. Relevant constituents for such a programme could include the following: ways in which grammatical rules may be simplified for different purposes, the adequacy of different grammatical descriptions, error correction, the contribution of grammatical knowledge to learners' proficiency development, etc. In working with learner language analyses and language learning systematically, the student's knowledge will be put to use in ways which help to relate theoretical description to practice.

The learner language approach to foreign language pedagogy

represents an integrative solution to the problem of how both to qualify students in specific subject areas and to prepare them for teaching. The approach therefore differs from the one traditionally adopted at *colleges of education.* Here one department is responsible for the subject English, including foreign language pedagogy, and other departments cover general pedagogy, didactics, educational psychology and teaching practice respectively, so that there is a risk that the different areas of study never form a coherent whole. Even though the organisational framework is not ideal and more collaboration between departments is desirable, it is possible to achieve many of the goals of foreign language pedagogy in teacher training by adopting a learner language approach.

At *universities,* as opposed to the university centres, students can seldom supplement their study of the foreign language with the study of general didactics or educational psychology. In this situation, the responsibility of the foreign language pedagogy teachers becomes even greater than at colleges of education. They have to ensure that the study of foreign language pedagogy does not stop at the level of learner language analysis but also relates this to a wider didactic, educational and socio-political framework.

Footnotes to chapter 16

1. See Dam 1983.
2. For a more comprehensive description of this, and other examples of inter-subject collaboration, see Herlev Statsskole 1982.
3. Immersion programmes in North America have involved a range of foreign languages and are well documented (Lambert 1983, Lambert/Taylor 1983). The factors which have contributed to the success of the programmes are that parents and learners are aware of the advantages of bilingualism, both for general cognitive development and for job prospects; that the mother tongue of the learners is not threatened (as is the case for immigrant ethnic minorities); that trained teachers exclusively use the target language but understand the children's L1; and that the schemes are an optional alternative to conventional education.

Chapter 16. Sources and further reading

For the pedagogical principles referred to, see the coverage in Muschinsky/Schnack 1981. Danish innovation in English teaching is mostly reported in *Sproglæreren* and *Ekstrameddelelser fra Gymnasieskolernes Engelsklærerforening*. For a polemic on reform of schooling for 16–19 year-olds, see Harsløf 1983.

The role of metacommunicative knowledge and knowledge about learning in foreign language education is discussed in Piepho 1974, Breen/Candlin 1980.

A readable basic introduction to communicative language teaching is Littlewood 1981, the main focus being on classroom activities. The book includes an annotated 'further reading' section which covers a wide range of teaching materials and relevant theoretical works. On role play, see Livingstone 1983. On games, see Wegener/Krumm 1982, Wagner 1983. On the use of authentic listening materials, see Poulsen 1981. On radically different approaches such as suggestopedia and the silent way, see Stevick 1976 and 1980, and a specialised bibliography from Danmarks Pædagogiske Bibliotek, 1982.

Part IV
Principles and methods of interlanguage studies

This part of the book is particularly intended for those who are interested in the theoretical bases of IL studies or who are considering undertaking research work. Part IV can be read as a self-contained methodological section explaining principles which are drawn on in many of the examples presented in parts I and II.

Chapter 17 describes how interlanguage studies developed from an interest in learner errors and the need to see these in a wider linguistic and psychological perspective. Some of the characteristic formal properties of IL are summarised, in particular its systematicity, IL as a reduced system, and as a dynamic system. There is also a summary of the functional properties of IL systems as compared with native languages.

Chapter 18 gives a fairly detailed description of the range of types of study that come under the heading "performance analysis", and exemplifies quantitative and qualitative methods. The steps involved in error anlysis are described, including error identification and the classification of errors on the basis of their causes. Contrastive analysis is related not only to linguistic systems but also to learner performance. Tolerance testing and interaction analysis are presented as examples of approaches to the study of the effects of IL.

Chapter 19 presents the data base from which most of the examples of learner language used in this book are taken. It describes the various types of text, spoken and written, that can be used in IL studies, and their suitability for specific types of study. Finally there is some practical advice on the recording and transcription of learner language.

Chapter seventeen:
Interlanguage

One approach followed in the study of foreign language teaching and learning rests on the principle that decisions about teaching necessarily presuppose an understanding of what is involved in *learning*. It is assumed that the primary source of knowledge which can lead to such an understanding is the language produced by learners when they use their own version of the foreign language. This "learner language" can be described as an INTERLANGUAGE, a language which is between two languages, the learner's L1 and an L2. Research in which the point of departure is an analysis of IL is referred to as INTERLANGUAGE STUDIES. This chapter begins with a short historical presentation of the background to IL studies. It then presents some central assumptions about the formal properties of IL systems and about ways in which IL functions in communication situations in which at least one of the speakers uses an IL.

17.1 Historical background to interlanguage studies

The boom in foreign language learning and teaching research, prompted by specific needs during World War II, particularly in the US, was for a long time strongly associated with developments in general linguistics. There was a well-established tradition, going back to the turn of the century, of systematically comparing two or more languages as a means of reconstructing prehistoric stages of the same languages. This approach was utilized for a different purpose during the 50s and the 60s: to describe areas of similarity and difference between two languages, namely the mother tongue of a group of learners, and the language they are to learn. The underlying assumption, based on behaviourist psychology, which was widely accepted at the time, was that learning would be easy in those areas where the two languages were similar, whereas problems were to be expected in areas of difference. Large-scale projects were initiated in the early 60s by the Center for Applied Linguistics in Washington, D. C., and contrastive analyses of English in relation to German, French, Spanish, Italian and Russian were produced. Contrastive analysis projects were established in a number of European countries in the late 60s, and contrastive linguistics became one of the most flourishing areas of linguistic research.[1]

That contrastive analysis is not capable of handling all the problems of foreign language learning was brought out clearly when the results of analyses of learner language became available.[2]

In the first place, many predictions about ease and difficulty in FL learning, based on a contrastive analysis of learners' L1 and L2, were not confirmed by analyses of the errors of foreign language learners in speech and writing. There was no simple one-to-one correlation between linguistic difference and learning difficulty. Areas which were assumed to be difficult sometimes turned out not to lead to errors, and vice versa.

Secondly, foreign language learners were observed to commit errors which could not be accounted for by contrastive analysis. These errors seemed to indicate that foreign language learning was in important respects similar to the process of L1 acquisition. For example, errors like *comed,* which are caused by a generalisation of a regular pattern, can be found both in children's L1 and in the language of some foreign language learners.

Dissatisfaction with contrastive analysis, and a shift in psychology from behaviourist to cognitivist theories, resulted in the emergence of a completely different type of research, which took as its point of departure not the two linguistic *systems* in general but three "languages" as they meet in the learner: that part of the L1 that learners know and master; the parts of the L2 that learners are actually exposed to; and, as something new, the learners' own version of the L2, their interlanguage. These are the essential components identified for analysis in Selinker 1972. Dealing with learner language as a language in its own right had already been advocated by Corder 1967.

This shift of focus from contrasting linguistic systems in general to languages actually present in the 'contact' situation (Nemser 1971) was greatly inspired by research in L1 acquisition. A number of research projects in the 60s and early 70s had carefully recorded and analysed the language produced by children and their caretakers, in order partly to outline the development of child language,

270

partly to assess how caretakers' language shapes the development of child language.[3] It was felt that the progress of learners of foreign languages could be analysed in similar ways.

The most important methodology within IL studies in the early 70s was ERROR ANALYSIS. This involves studying those elements in the learner's interlanguage which are considered to be erroneous in relation to a target language norm. A primary objective of such analyses was to decide what psycholinguistic processes may be responsible for the errors. A second aim was to describe the relationship between these processes and the social context in which the IL has been learned or produced. In later developments, studies were carried out which related errors to correct parts of learners' IL. Usually these studies were restricted to a certain field, eg use of the expanded tense (see Zydatiss 1976). Such 'performance analyses' (Svartvik 1973) provided a useful check on conclusions based on an analysis of errors only. Towards the end of the 70s, a number of researchers extended the scope of interlanguage studies in the direction advocated by Selinker in 1972, by relating interlanguage to the L2 to which the learner has been exposed, primarily in the foreign language classroom. This resulted in a number of studies of "teacher talk", the language used by teachers when addressing the class, as well as in studies of the interaction in the classroom between learners and teachers (see Seliger/Long 1983, Sinclair/Brazil 1982). Furthermore, a number of studies have appeared reporting on how learners perform in communication outside school (see eg Kasper 1981, Edmondson/House/Kasper/Stemmer 1982, Færch/Kasper 1983b).[4]

17.2 Interlanguage: definition and characterisation

One way of defining an IL might be as follows: an IL is a variety of language which is both formally and communicatively reduced when compared to languages used as native languages by adults. As well as applying to the language of foreign language learners, such a definition would cover child language, pidgin languages and, possibly, reduced varieties of native languages like "foreigner talk" (ie the way native speakers sometimes address foreigners by simplifying their L1).[5]

271

This definition has primarily been adopted by researchers who have been concerned with analysing the similarities between these various types of language. An alternative definition would be: an IL is a variety of language which exists in a contact situation between a learner's L1 and an L2. According to this, an IL typically has features in common with both a learner's L1 and with the L2, which means that the other varieties covered by the first, broader definition are excluded from consideration. It is this narrower definition of interlanguage that we have adopted in this book, as this is the variety we are specifically concerned with. This practical decision, however, does not exclude insights of a theoretical or methodological nature in parallel work on any of the other varieties of language.

Interlanguage can be looked at from two angles:

- in terms of *formal* characteristics, which have to do with interlanguage seen as a linguistic system
- in terms of *functional* characteristics, which specify how the interlanguage system is put to communicative use.

17.2.1 Formal characteristics

Probably the most important assumption of interlanguage studies is that interlanguage shares important characteristics with native language (cf Adjemian 1976). Interlanguage is therefore *not* seen as a distorted and amputated variant of a native language, but as a linguistic system in its own right.

This means that IL is assumed to be *systematic,* ie governed by rules. If one did not expect to find systematicity, there would be no point in describing learner language linguistically. There are two important points to be aware of, however, in connection with IL systematicity.

First of all, IL rules which account for such systematicity may differ considerably from native language rules. L2 rules are in principle of no relevance when describing IL systematicity. Put differently, whether or not IL rules are in accordance with L2 rules is not a relevant issue when describing their systematicity.

Secondly, systematicity may be different for different learners, even if these belong to the same group and have received teaching in

272

common. In descriptions of a native language, a certain amount of idealization of the data is needed when the objective is a description of rules observed within a certain speech community.[6] By contrast IL descriptions cover individual variation within groups of learners, because an important objective, beyond describing their language, is to clarify the role of psychological and social processes in FL learning. Systematicity is therefore typically of a much less general nature in IL studies than in descriptions of a native language.

A second feature of ILs, which they share with native languages, is that they are assumed to be *systematically variable,* ie that a language user may use different rules for expressing the same content, depending on the context in which the language is used. Stylistic variation by a native speaker might involve using "intoxicated/inebriated" in formal contexts and "drunk/tight/sloshed/..." in informal ones. Similarly, learners vary their performance systematically, not in the sense of using stylistic variants like native speakers, but regressing at times to previous stages of learning in more informal situations. A learner might write "he wants his parents to leave" in an essay but say "he want that his parents leave" in a group discussion with other learners.

Stressing similarities between interlanguage and native language in terms of systematicity should not obscure the fact that interlanguage differs from native language in important respects.

Interlanguage systems are typically *reduced systems,* compared to native language systems, both as regards the number and complexity of rules (pragmatic, syntactic, phonological, etc.) and the number of words they contain. An important concern of IL researchers has been to compare the IL of foreign language learners with other types of "simplified systems" (eg child language and pidgin languages), in order to find similarities, assumedly of a universal nature.

The following example is one of "teacher talk", observed in an English language class in California (Hatch 1978b, 416):

(Teacher (native speaker of English) explaining how to take telephone messages:)
"I want speak other person. He not here. What good thing for say now".

273

Foreign language teachers in Denmark are very unlikely to simplify grammatical structures in this way, and they often hesitate to acknowledge any similarity between pidgins and the language of their learners. Some degree of syntactic simplification is, however, a characteristic trait of learner language. Many Danish intermediate learners tend, for instance, to express futurity exclusively by using one of the following: *shall/will*/present tense + adverbial. In many contexts a different form *(to be to/going to/be about to/...)* would be more appropriate. This means that compared with native speakers, such learners use only part of the available repertoire: they have a simplified system.

Interlanguages are typically *dynamic systems* in the sense that they are likely to change, both by incorporating new rules and words and by revising already existing rules. This is an essential aspect of IL systems in the context of FL teaching. An alternative way of characterizing the dynamic nature of IL systems is to describe them as "permeable", as opposed to being "fossilized" (see chapter 11).

In specific cases, it would be an oversimplification to characterize an IL system as such as either dynamic/permeable or as static/fossilized. A more precise characterization would be to describe specific areas of the system as more or less permeable/fossilized. A particular IL speaker may have a fossilized phonological system but have a relatively permeable lexical or pragmatic system.

When an IL is not kept active, there is a risk of it neither progressing nor fossilizing but regressing to a less developed stage. In spite of the fact that this is familiar to anyone who has given up using an L2, there have been few analyses of IL regression (but see Lambert/Freed 1982).

When interlanguage is looked at as a system in its own right, it is a contradiction in terms to talk about *erroneous* aspects of the system. The concept of error implies the presence of a linguistic norm, and as discussed above, an interlanguage sets its own norms. However, as norms play an essential part in education, there is a clear need to characterize parts of IL systems as erroneous relative to an educationally-defined norm. Although the notion of error is therefore not consistent with the internal logic of the interlanguage system, the analysis of errors serves an important function when interlanguages are described within specific, norm-oriented situations.

274

17.2.2 Functional characteristics

As compared to native language communication, IL communication for most individuals serves a more restricted range of purposes. It is typically used for communication in certain types of event only, and even within these events, communication may be reduced at the pragmatic, the referential and the modal level (see chapter 9). In this respect, IL communication is comparable to communication in pidgin languages (cf Todd 1974), which are typically used for restricted commercial transactions.

The native language serves an important function in creating group identity. ILs do not generally serve this function as they are not used for communicative purposes within social groups. Furthermore, there is a close link between native language and personal identity, established through primary socialization, whereas ILs do not usually attain the same affective or social significance for individuals.[7]

One of the reasons why IL communication is often reduced, compared to L1 communication, is that IL users may have difficulty in achieving their communicative goals because of limitations in their communicative resources. IL users sometimes experience this as having to function with a "reduced personality" (Harder 1980).

The pressures in IL communication are not on the IL user exclusively. The native speaker has to assess the level of the IL user's competence and adjust her language accordingly. Furthermore, the native speaker may become distracted (cf chapter 10) by the form of the IL user's speech, having difficulty in attending to content as a result. Such distraction may be triggered off by foreign accent, by frequent or salient errors, or by the production difficulties already referred to. Finally, native speaker and learner alike often have to resort to repairs and to use the language metacommunicatively in order to ensure mutual comprehension. This accounts for the sometimes tortuous and often demanding nature of IL communication.

Footnotes to chapter 17

1. For a general introduction to the history, purposes and methods of contrastive analysis see James 1980. The classic example of this approach is Lado 1957. Examples of the results of contrastive analysis are Stockwell/Bowen/Martin 1965, and Moulton 1962. For studies of the application of contrastive analysis to language teaching, see Fisiak 1981.
2. See Richards 1974 for a collection of papers.
3. See Brown 1973, Snow/Ferguson 1977. Hatch 1983 summarises input-studies in second language acquisition research.
4. For collections of articles reflecting these developments, see Richards 1974, Richards 1978, Hatch 1978c, and Corder 1981.
5. See Corder 1981 and Meisel 1980.
6. For a summary of these principles see Corder 1973, chapter 8.
7. But see Börsch 1982, which documents instances of learners experiencing foreign language learning and IL communication as emancipatory, when compared to communication in their L1.

Chapter eighteen:
Some methods of analysis in IL studies

As explained in chapter 17, IL studies focus on language which is present in the learner's mind or language which learners encounter and which they attempt to process in order to reconstruct their addressers' communicative intentions. The term "language" is here used with two distinct meanings:

(1) language as a *system*, either as described by linguists or as cognitively present in individuals (cf the discussion of linguistic and psycholinguistic rules in chapter 6)

(2) language as *observable behaviour*, physical signs and noises functioning as communicative signals by using the code of a linguistic system.

In the following we shall restrict the term *language* to the first of these two, the system, and use the term *performance* to refer to the physically present manifestation of language.

Performance represents one, very important, source of information about language. Describing language on the basis of linguistic performance will be referred to as PERFORMANCE ANALYSIS. All the methods described in this chapter are variants of this type of analysis. One alternative to performance analysis is to ask individuals to introspect, ie to state what they know, or how they believe that they process language. Unfortunately, introspective methods have not yet been developed to such a degree within IL studies that one can have great confidence in them. It therefore needs emphasizing that although it is often advisable to supplement a performance analysis with introspective techniques, it is problematic to use introspection as the only method in an IL analysis.

18.1 Performance analysis

The primary linguistic data in IL studies are of three types:

(a) learners' native language (L1) performance
(b) learners' interlanguage (IL) performance
(c) performance in the target language (L2) which learners are exposed to in and outside the classroom.

In the book we have concentrated on performance analysis of learners' interlanguage, ie on (b). In the crudest form of such analyses, learners' performance is described without any attempt to relate this to other types of performance (eg to the IL performance of other learners, or to learners' L1 performance) or to a target language norm. In such an analysis there are no "errors" in learner performance. But as soon as IL is seen in a norm-related context like an educational situation, the notion of error is indispensable. Performance analyses of IL therefore usually include analyses of both errors and non-errors. We shall first exemplify the basic principle of performance analysis of learners' IL by giving two examples which do not contain any analysis of errors, and delay coverage of performance analysis which includes error analysis until error analysis has been described in 18.2.

Both the following examples illustrate ways of *quantifying* results. The first (in 18.1.1) calculates the frequency of occurrence in data of specific forms or functions. The second (in 18.1.2) investigates how many individuals belonging to certain groups of learners use specific forms or functions. Both examples presuppose that the analyst has already delimited the area to be investigated. This choice may be based on previous experience, eg knowledge that learners often have problems in creating cohesion in their written texts (cf chapter 4). Often the precise formulation of research goals is the result of preliminary *qualitative* investigations, in which the analyst selects phenomena for further study. Whether the researcher then decides to proceed with qualitatively oriented methods exclusively or also uses quantitative methods will depend on the objectives of the analysis. But it is probably the case that quantitative considerations cannot be

278

completely ignored even in qualitative investigations. Methods of analysis are often neither purely qualitative nor purely quantitative but a combination of the two (for a discussion of these, and related issues, see Hatch/Farhady 1982).

18.1.1 Example 1: Description of IL vocabulary

The aim of this part of a more extensive investigation into the development of learners' vocabulary is to describe the frequency of different words in texts written by a group of Gymnasium learners. The texts are essays on 'violence', referred to in chapter 19. One way of describing the vocabulary is to classify the words into word classes. Table 14 shows one of the results from this analysis: conjunctions used by the learners in the group, ordered according to frequency.

Table 14: Frequency of conjunctions in essays written by twelve 1gs learners

	Frequency	
	Total number	%
AND	117	37,38
THAT	39	12,46
BUT	38	12,14
OR	35	11,18
IF	22	7,02
BECAUSE	17	5,43
WHEN	13	4,15
AS	7	2,23
SO	5	1,59
BEACOURS	4	1,27
THAN	4	1,27
BEFORE	2	0,63
EITHER	2	0,63
EXEPT	2	0,63
A	1	0,31
BECAUS	1	0,31
EVENTHOUGH	1	0,31
TO	1	0,31
UNTIL	1	0,31
WHILE	1	0,31
	313	99,67

As can be seen from the list, different orthographic variants of the same conjunction have been listed separately. It would be a simple matter to conflate those at a later stage of the analysis. What can *not* be seen from the description is whether the conjunctions listed have been used appropriately, how the learners supplement the use of conjunctions by other means for creating cohesion (eg adverbials, pronominalization, lexical variation, cf chapters 4 and 5), or whether the relative frequency of each conjunction is what one would also find in the learners' L1 or in essays written by a group of native speakers of English. These comments illustrate the obvious, but important, fact that although a limited performance analysis like the one just described is often a necessary first step in IL studies, it does not in itself provide much insight into foreign language learning. To attain explanatory power, the description has to be supplemented by further studies, such as:

- comparisons between the results from groups of learners representing different educational levels, to find out whether learners at different levels have different preferences in choosing conjunctions
- analyses of the ways in which the conjunctions are used in the learner texts, in order (1) to relate conjunction use to other means of creating cohesion in texts, and (2) to analyse whether some of the conjunctions are used erroneously
- comparisons between the learners' use of conjunctions in IL and in Danish essays, to investigate whether their IL repertoire matches their repertoire in the L1 or not. Learners' problems in using conjunctions in a foreign language might reflect insecurity in writing cohesive texts in any language.

18.1.2 Example 2: Description of use of different types of noun phrase

The aim of this investigation is to describe how many learners within two groups (grades 8 and 3gs) use different types of complex noun phrases (NP) in writing an essay (the task also studied in 18.1.1).[1] A complex NP is defined as a NP that contains either a qualifying premodifier or a postmodifier or various combinations of these. This

280

means that *the beautiful lake* and *the paper I lost on the train* are both complex NPs, whereas *that rhinoceros* is not. Table 15 gives the result for NPs in subject position (excluding embedded NPs like *the train* in the example just quoted).

Table 15: Proportion of learners using complex NPs of different types

	Proportion of learners	
Types of complex NP	Grade 8	Grade 3gs
head + 1 postmodifier	100 %	100 %
1 premodifier + head	67 %	100 %
premodifier + head + postmodifier	50 %	73 %
2 premodifiers + head	25 %	9 %
head + 2 postmodifiers	17 %	36 %
others	8 %	36 %
	(N = 12, total sum of NPs = 436)	(N = 11, total sum of NPs = 700)

The description shows that learners at grade 3gs generally use a wider repertoire of complex NP types than learners at grade 8 (the only exception being the type "2 premodifiers + head", eg "the sweet little pussycat", which only one learner at grade 3gs uses). But the analysis itself clearly cannot be used to conclude anything about whether or not learners at grade 8 do not *know* the more complex types of NP, or whether these learners in fact know them but *avoid using* them. Performance analyses like the two we have described (more precisely, "performance descriptions") only scratch at the surface of IL learning and communication.

18.2 Error analysis

Error analysis concentrates on those parts of learners' performance that diverge from whatever norm this performance is compared with. Especially in interlanguage studies concerned with foreign language learning in educational contexts, error analysis is an important research tool because errors may provide direct insight into the learning – teaching process.

The main stages in error analysis are:

(1) error identification
(2) classification of errors into linguistic categories
(3) classification of errors according to the causes of errors.

18.2.1 Error identification

As was emphasized in chapter 17, errors are only errors relative to a norm. Error identification therefore presupposes the selection of a norm. In theory, *any* norm could be chosen for this purpose, including norms that differ from those holding for native speakers of the foreign language. For instance one might identify as errors only those items which are undesired at a particular level. Such "pedagogical" screening of errors is carried out every day by teachers and serves an important function in giving learners feedback. But in descriptive error analysis it is advisable to operate with norms which do not vary relative to the data in question, for instance by adopting native speaker norms as described in grammars and dictionaries. In this way one has a fairly constant norm against which different types of performance can be described (eg texts from both grades 8 and 3gs), and one can avoid questions of the sort "could we expect a learner at level ... to know ...?" or "is it fair to consider ... an error?". However, deciding on a native speaker norm for the identification of errors raises a number of problems in itself.

Firstly, native speakers also make errors, in particular when they are under stress or tired. But since they are usually able to correct themselves, "errors" like these are of a different type from errors

282

typically produced by a learner of a foreign language. A learner who produces a sentence like "can I English can I "lidt" [æmərikænsk]" (= 'if I know some English, then I also know a little American'), is unlikely to be able to correct the use of *can* as a main verb, or the word order. These errors are not the result of performance disturbances but are produced on the basis of the learner's interlanguage system. Both types of error ("slips" and interlanguage errors) are of considerable interest to the IL researcher as they provide complementary information on the underlying representation of language and on processes in speech production.

Second, as anybody with experience of error identification is aware, the native language norm is not always that clear. Particularly with vocabulary, native speakers may disagree as to whether a certain word is correct or appropriate in a given context. Reference to authoritative works provides a useful check on acceptability, but may not always decide the issue. Error identification is therefore best done by a team consisting of both native speakers and people with a good knowledge of the L1. The latter are needed particularly in order to spot COVERT ERRORS. These occur when on the surface of it there is no error, but the utterance does not convey the learner's intention. This can easily happen with "false friends". A learner who says "it is an actual problem" might well mean 'current' or 'topical' rather than 'real'. This might escape the notice of a native speaker, but not someone with a good familiarity with both languages. Even so, there may be cases where it is difficult to decide whether something is to be counted as an error because it is difficult to decide what the learner is trying to say. To be able to handle such cases, it may be instructive to consult the learner as soon as possible after the event, to ask her to introspect about what she intended to say, what she was conscious of, and whether she could have produced a more correct version.[2]

Finally, one should not expect 100% consistency between error identifiers. In one of the PIF pronunciation analyses all our texts were listened to by three people. When a form was noted by two out of the three as being an error we classified it as such for the purpose of the analysis. Another procedure often adopted is that if either of two error identifiers does not identify a form as an error, it does not count as an error in the analysis.

18.2.2 Linguistic classification of errors

The aim of the linguistic classification of errors is to specify in which areas of language errors occur. Whether one is satisfied with a fairly rough classification, for instance into orthographic, syntactic, morphological and lexical errors, or tries to achieve a more delicate analysis of errors into many subtypes will depend on the specific aim of the analysis as well as on the size of the corpus. In the PIF project, one objective was to trace the development of learner language on the basis of errors identified in 240 texts written by 111 learners from 11 different groups. This called for a detailed classification into more than 300 error types (see Færch/Grindsted 1982). By contrast, an analysis of essays written by a class of learners could be successfully conducted on the basis of a much simpler error classification system.

It is practical to classify errors in two phases. In the first, errors are grouped into very broad categories, like errors of orthography, punctuation, lexis and grammar. In the second phase, each of these categories is further subdivided into as many error types as is feasible.

The first phase of the error classification process can be integrated into the task of error identification. When errors are identified in the text, they can be slotted into different error categories by means of different symbols. This is illustrated by the extract from a PIF text printed below. The following conventions have been used:

└───	lexical error	In addition the following symbols have been used for:	
───	grammatical error		
	word order		
S	spelling	V	omission
|	word division	( )	excess
o	punctuation	──→	line run over

MOSTLY THE POLICE AND THE ARMY -(THE)SOCIETY -

~highjackers~

WIN THE "GAME", BUT THE HIGH|JACKERS ARE OFTEN

~get~

GETTING THE THINGS THEY WANT - FOR EXAMPLE SOME

OF THEIR FRIENDS(,) WHO ARE IN PRISON. SOMETIMES

~try~

|ARE| THE POLICE TRYING AN ATTACK AGAINST THE HIGH|

~highjacked aeroplanes~ ~of~

JACKED AEROPLANS AND BECAUSE OF THAT A LOT∨PEOPLE

~highjackers~

GET KILLED BY HIGH|JACKERS, WHO WANT TO DEFEND

THEMSELVES. IT'S VERY OFTEN A VERY IMPORTANT DE-

CISION |TO TAKE| FOR SOME "LEADER" WHEN HE HAS TO

~innocent~

ORDER AN ATTACK BECAUSE SO MANY INE∫ENT PEOPLE

~But~

CAN GET KILLED. |BESIDES IT'S NECESSARY TO TRY TO

~kills~

STOP THE VIOLENCE. ANOTHER THING THAT OFTEN |MAKES

~a lot of people~ ~bomb attacks~

A LOT∨PEOPLE DIE IS BOMB|ATTACKS. IT'S A VERY COM-

~especially~ ~Every~

MON THING IN IRELAND - ESPECIAL IN BELFAST. |THE

~day the news reports on fresh cases of~

DAILY NEWS|TELLS ABOUT|NEW BOMBS PLACED IN CARS

AND HOUSES. YESTERDAY A BOMB WAS PLACED IN A RE-

STAURANT AND MORE THAN 10 PEOPLE WERE KILLED AND

~badly~

ABOUT 20 WERE|HARDLY WOUNDED.

As can be seen, the person doing the error identification has suggested corrections of the errors identified. This is important for the second phase of error classification, as it is sometimes difficult to reconstruct why something was identified as an error.

In the subsequent, more detailed analysis, each of these groups of errors is further subclassified. Lexical errors could be grouped on the basis of which word classes they belong to. A simple classification of grammatical errors would be into errors in the noun phrase, in the verb phrase, in adverbial phrases, as well as word order and concord errors. The errors identified in the text above could be classified as follows:

Lexical errors:
— verbs: tells about, make ... die
— adjectives: new
— adverbs: hardly
— conjunctions: besides

Grammatical errors:
— noun phrase: the society, a lot people
— verb phrase: are getting, are trying
— adverbial phrase: especial
— word order: sometimes are the police trying,
  decision to take for some "leader"

Orthographical errors:
— spelling: aeroplans, inesent
— word division: high jackers,
  high jacked, bombattacks

Punctuation errors:
— comma before restrictive relative clause:
  some of their friends, who are in prison.

18.2.3 Classification of errors on the basis of error causes

The last stage in error analysis is the classification into different causes of errors. There are two major dimensions along which errors are usually explained. First there is a distinction between *learner-internal* and *learner-external* causes. Errors may be the result of "internal" cognitive procedures like transfer from the learner's native language or generalization to new contexts of IL rules which the learner already knows (transfer and generalization were discussed in chapter 11). Alternatively, errors may be the result of factors external to the learner such as misleading teaching or teaching materials, or faulty instructions in a research context. In these cases the errors are often labelled "induced" errors (cf Stenson 1975, Kasper 1982).

The second dimension for accounting for errors distinguishes between *direct* and *indirect* causes. This can be demonstrated by an example, namely the familiar overuse of the expanded tense in the IL of Danish learners of English. The direct cause of the error is generalization, a learner-internal factor. The indirect cause might be learner-external factors such as infelicitous teaching, for instance in relation to sequencing (introducing the expanded tense before the simple tense), or to presentation and practice (the teacher using the expanded tense for a series of events).

Another factor which can indirectly influence whether learners produce errors is such psychological traits as an individual's willingness to take linguistic risks rather than concentrating on being correct. A further factor could be a learner's assumptions about which parts of their L1 can be freely transferred to their IL.

Identifying the internal causes of errors in specific cases as being either transfer or generalization is not straightforward. We can explore this issue by attempting to identify the psycholinguistic processes which account for the errors in text 22. The table below lists the errors in the text which have exact formal translation equivalents in Danish. Such errors could therefore be attributed to transfer.

Interlanguage	Danish
aeroplans	(svæve)plan
some of their friends, who are in prison	nogle af deres venner, som er i fængsel
tells about	fortæller om
hardly wounded	hårdt såret
the society	samfundet
a lot people	en masse mennesker
sometimes are the police trying	nogle gange har politiet forsøgt at ...
decision to take for some "leader"	beslutning at tage for en "leder"
bombattacks	bombeangreb

These errors amount to less than half of the total number of errors originally identified. The other psycholinguistic process, IL generalization, can account for virtually all the errors in the text, including those having formal translation equivalents in Danish. Some of these are listed in figure 18.

IL performance	IL rule	example
tells about	verb + preposition	talk about
the society	determiner + noun	the army
a lot people	determiner + quantifier + noun	a few people
hardly (wounded)	adjective + ly = adverb	badly wounded

Fig. 18: Examples of IL generalization

There are two ways of approaching these apparently contradictory results. If one assumes that errors can only have one direct cause – meaning that, for instance, *a lot people* must be attributed to either L1 transfer or generalization – the problem is one of "causal ambiguity". The implication of this view, which was until recently very widespread, is that if only we had more direct access to the psycholinguistic processes, we could allocate errors to one of the two internal causes.

An alternative way of handling the problem is to assume that errors can have more than one direct cause, meaning that transfer and generalization can function together. A consequence of this is that it is not possible to quantify exactly the proportion of errors due to one cause rather than another, which was precisely what some of the early error analysis projects set out to do. Researchers then have to adopt a more qualitative approach and try to characterise the intricate and complex ways in which the various causes of errors interact with each other.

One of the ultimate goals of educationally related error analysis must be to detect external causes of errors, as these provide information about foreign language teaching itself. To be able to do so, more information is needed than what is to be found in learner language texts, eg information about what parts of L2 the learner has been exposed to ((c) in 18.1 above) and how the learner has been exposed to this. Such information may be gathered through analyses of teaching materials used, observations of teaching in the classroom, and interviews with learners and teachers.

To simplify the presentation of methods in this chapter, we first introduced some basic principles of performance analysis and then described error analysis. There is a danger that this is understood to mean that performance analysis and error analysis are mutually exclusive. Although for certain purposes one may prefer performance analysis without analysing errors or analyse errors without relating these to the performance as a whole, it is often the case that an analysis of IL will contain both an analysis of errors as well as an analysis of non-erroneous parts of performance. Thus the example in 18.1 of a performance analysis of the frequency of occurrence of conjunctions in a corpus of learner texts could be extended so as to cover correct and incorrect use of conjunctions. Chapters 6 and 7 contained examples of this type of analysis within grammar and pronunciation.

18.3 Contrastive analysis

Error analysis is implicitly contrastive. Learners' IL is compared to an L2 norm, and differences between the two are identified. However, the term contrastive analysis involves more than this. It implies either the contrasting of two linguistic systems or limited parts of them (the way we used the term in the historical section of ch. 17), or contrasting the performance of two groups of learners in comparable situations ("contrastive performance analysis"). Both types of contrastive analysis are relevant for interlanguage studies.

18.3.1 Contrastive analysis of linguistic systems

Learners' L1 and L2 are contrasted in order to generate hypotheses or to explain already analysed data. In the first case, contrastive analysis (CA) is used in a similar way to open-ended data (cf ch. 19) and has to be followed up by more controlled investigations. The hypotheses are based on the assumption that systematic differences between L1 and L2 will lead to greater difficulty than similarities (an assumption which is not without problems, as mentioned in ch. 17). We can illustrate this type of CA by the following example, taken from pronunciation.

A comparison of stops (plosives) in Danish and English reveals that each language has six (/p,b; t,d; k,g/), but that they differ in both their distribution and articulation (the glottal stop does not have phonemic status in RP). The English sets (/p,t,k/ and /b,d,g/) contrast word initially, medially and finally. The Danish sets (the same) only contrast initially, which means that in word medial position, and in word final position followed immediately by another word, only /b,d,g/ occur, in final position before a pause /p,t,k/ occur. One can therefore hypothesize (Phillipson/Lauridsen 1982) that Danes will pronounce

1) English medial unaffricated plosives as [bdg]
    eg both rapid & rabid as [ræbɪd]
             waiting & wading as [weidɪŋ]
             vicar & vigour as [vɪgə]

2) final unaffricated plosives occurring utterance finally, eg before silence, as [ptk], ie lenis with aspiration,
    thus both rip & rib as [rɪp]
               cat & cad as [kæt]
               leek & league as [li:k]

3) word-final unaffricated plosives in other contexts, ie before another vowel or consonant, as [bdg]

thus both rip   &   rib   as   [rɪb]

bought &   bored   as   [bɔːd]

leek   &   league   as   [liːg]

Rather than use CA for the purpose of hypothesis formation in research, it has been suggested that the major function of CA is to explain data in a late phase of the analysis of IL (cf Wardhaugh 1970). This function of CA was implied in section 18.2 above, when we referred to errors which could have been caused by L1 transfer. But as we also stated, it is often difficult unambiguously to apply the results of CA to the results of an error analysis of IL.

No matter whether the CA of linguistic systems is *used* in a hypothesis creating or an explanatory way within interlanguage studies, there are a number of theoretical as well as practical problems which need solving before an analysis can be carried out: the problem of deciding what counts as "the same" in the two systems; the problem of "directionality", deciding whether the contrastive analysis is mono-directional (eg going from L1 to L2) or bi-directional; and finally the problem that different languages may have different formal means for expressing identical content. For a detailed discussion of these problems, see James 1980.

18.3.2 Contrastive performance analysis

There are three ways in which contrastive performance analysis is used within interlanguage studies.

1. Contrasting the performance of a group of native speakers of one language with the performance of a group of native speakers of a different language.
2. Contrasting the performance of learners using their L1 with the performance of the same learners using their IL.
3. Contrasting the performance of learners using their IL with the performance of native speakers of the L2.

In all cases, it is crucially important for the situations to be comparable to make sure that instructions and objectives are identical, and to attempt to control subjective factors. For example, there exists a real risk that a learner doing the same task a second time in a different language may vary performance to avoid repetition. This is difficult to control but has to be taken into consideration when planning the sequence of tasks as well as when analysing data.

The PIF corpus (ch. 19) contains material which can be utilized for contrasting learners' written proficiency in Danish and in English. The example of types of NP quoted in 18.1.2 is taken from a study which contrasts the interlanguage performance of Danes with the performance of native speakers of English doing the same written task (Grindsted/Rechnitzer 1982). There is also an example of this type of contrastive performance analysis in chapter 4, section 4.3, which has been taken from an extensive corpus that lends itself to all three types of performance analysis. It was collected in an interlanguage project at Bochum University, Germany. The data collection technique used was role-play. The informants were German students not studying English, German students of English, and native speakers of English (students and academics). On the basis of the corpus a number of pragmatic and discourse areas were investigated contrastively, resulting in both descriptions of differences between German and English native language communication as well as in descriptions of interlanguage-specific features, as compared to both L1 and to L2 (see Edmondson/House/Kasper/Stemmer 1982 and Kasper 1981).

Contrastive peformance analysis has the principal function of providing quantitatively based information of a kind which cannot be obtained through a contrastive analysis of linguistic systems. For instance in the Bochum investigation it was found that learners generally overused *yes/yeah/yah* and underused *I mean, look, exactly* and *good* when used as "gambits" (cf ch. 4) (Kasper 1981, 269–70).

18.4 Tolerance testing

Tolerance testing is a method of analysis for assessing the effect of learner language in communication. 'Effect' is usually understood as native speakers' comprehension of and reaction to samples of

292

learner language.

Tolerance testing is a variety of performance analysis in that it is still learners' IL performance which is the object of analysis. It differs from other types of performance analysis described so far in that learner language is analysed from the perspective of the receiver in a communicative event.

We shall briefly discuss one example of a tolerance test, using a method developed by Engh 1971. It was employed in an investigation at Odense University (Jakobsen/Larsen 1977), the objective of which was to assess to what extent errors in learners' written texts affected native speakers' comprehension. The corpus consisted of essays written by Danish teenagers on their plans for the future. A set of sentences containing various types of error was presented to British informants who were asked to rewrite the sentences so as to express what they thought the writer had intended.

One of the learner language sentences was as follows:

It is good if you have been out working in the trade, therefore I will a year in a house.

This was interpreted by three of the British informants as follows:

It is an advantage to have worked in the trade and I therefore intend to work a year in the job.

It is good if you have been out working in a job so I'll do that for a year at home.

It is good if you have been out working in the trade, and therefore I will spend a year with a firm.

It is probable that the Danish learner was in fact contemplating spending a year working as an au pair, that "trade" is a lexical error and the "a year in a house" is a literal, word-for-word translation from Danish.

The main reason for choosing the above method as an example of tolerance testing is that it is simple to carry out. There are, however, limitations to it, because the object of study is isolated sentences rather than continuous discourse, and because it focusses exclusively on the comprehensibility of learner language. In chapter 10, we discussed a more comprehensive tolerance study which covered comprehensibility as well as "distraction".

18.5 Analysing interaction

Most of the methods discussed in this chapter have described learner language in isolation from the interaction learners engage in. One exception to this was the analysis of pragmatic and discourse features in role-play between German learners and native speakers of English. A further step towards including the interlocutor was taken with tolerance testing in the section above.

However, tolerance testing in its existing forms puts the native speaker into the role of an outside arbiter or expert, and does not describe actual interaction between learners and native speakers. One method of investigating the interaction itself is to make recordings of learners talking to native speakers, and then analyse whether learners can put across what they want to say, when and why there are breakdowns in communication, and how learners, with or without the assistance of their native speaker interlocutors, solve their communication problems. An approach which tackles some of these issues is the study of communication strategies, discussed in chapter 9. A different way of investigating learners involved in communicative interaction is to analyse classroom language, whether among the learners themselves or between learners and their teacher. Such analyses are essential in order to clarify the impact of teaching on the development of learners' IL.

Although with interactional data there is a large number of variables to control, and the interplay between participants' contributions is difficult to assess, IL studies will have to refine ways of analysing genuinely interactional data since the main objective of foreign language learning is to develop learners' communicative competence.

Footnotes to chapter 18

1. The results in table 15 are from Grindsted/Rechnitzer 1982
2. See Corder 1974.
3. PIF informant no. 28, 1gs.

Chapter 19:
Learner language data, collection and transcription

A necessary preliminary to studies of learner language is the collection of good samples of it. This chapter has three purposes: to present the corpus of learner language drawn on in this book; to state what sort of texts, of the written or spoken language, in addition to other types of data, are suitable for the kinds of analysis that we have described in part I; and finally to provide some guidelines for how to collect and process data.

19.1 The learner language corpus drawn on in this book

Linguists, sociologists and psychologists acquire their expertise, just as ordinary people do, by reading, by pondering, by observing people going about their business or performing a specific task. Unlike ordinary people, they may also wish to set up experiments in order to test a particular hypothesis. The information collected by researchers in order to shed light on a problem is referred to as DATA. The label CORPUS is used to describe a collection of samples of language, generally a rather extensive one, which has been compiled as a resource for use in scientific studies.

The project to which the authors of this book are attached is PIF, *P*roject *I*n *F*oreign Language Pedagogy, Copenhagen (see Færch 1979). The project has collected an extensive corpus of learner language, consisting of samples of the written and spoken English of 123 Danes who span a range from near-beginner (after 1 year of instruction) to near-native (higher education students). Participants in a research experiment of this kind are called SUBJECTS or INFORMANTS. As we have drawn on texts from this corpus throughout the book we shall present the various text types in some detail.

With the one exception that the 12 learners at the lowest level did not provide written texts, each of these texts was elicited from all our informants. So as to hold as many factors constant as possible,

Table 16. The PIF Corpus

Spoken texts

Video-recordings	A 20 minute conversation between a native speaker of English and each informant. The native speaker was about the same age as the informant, and knew no Danish. The two of them were free to talk about anything they liked, but had a list of suggested topics in case they got stuck.
Sound-recordings	In a language laboratory: Text 1: The reading aloud of a passage of English prose. Text 2: After watching twice a 5-minute film, a description or summary of the film.

Written texts

Film summary	Informants were asked to write a précis or interpretation of the film they had watched in the language laboratory.
English essay	Informants were asked to write an essay on "Violence". Photos showing scenes of violence were offered as a source of inspiration.
Danish essay	The same as for the English essay on the topic "Work".

learners with different ages, experience and personalities were given the same tasks. Most of these tasks were familar from school, eg reading aloud and writing an essay, whereas the video-taped conversation was novel and represented an attempt to place the learner in a real communicative situation. In very general terms one could say that our intention was to test how well English, developed in the classroom, could function in the context of talking to an unfamiliar native speaker.

When planning the collection of our corpus we considered three important factors, namely the geographical origin, social class, and sex of the informants. For practical and financial reasons, however, we could not establish a corpus with these three factors as controlled variables. We were obliged to limit ourselves to the greater Copenhagen area. As this conurbation covers a wide range of social backgrounds, our informants reflect this. With regard to the sex of informants, we have equal numbers of males and females at "Folkeskole" level and a larger proportion of females at higher levels, which in almost all cases reflects the actual composition of English classes at such institutions. Thus what we have is a corpus which represents some of the learners in the Copenhagen area, including learners from varying social and economic backgrounds. We are not in a position to make generalisations specifically about the relationship between the social class or sex of our learners and their English learning.

When compiling a corpus designed to reveal the development of learner language, a choice has to be made between two approaches, one 'longitudinal', the other 'cross-sectional'.

In LONGITUDINAL studies data is collected from the same subject or group of subjects over a period of time. This approach is often used in studies of child language acquisition. Here researchers observe the linguistic and cognitive development in the same child or group of children over time, for instance making tape-recordings every month from birth to two years. The same method can be used in learner language studies: in an Odense project on the learning of German, for instance, researchers have monitored the performance of a group of learners at twelve-monthly intervals.[1]

In a CROSS-SECTIONAL study data is collected from a range of learners at different levels at the same time. The method is also referred to as 'pseudo-longitudinal', the idea being that data from the least advanced learners is hypothesized to represent data collected first, and data from the most advanced learners the data collected last in a longitudinal study.

The PIF corpus covers a cross-section of Danish learners of English, all our data being collected at one point of time, ie in the space of a couple of weeks in 1978.[2] As our informants range from twelve-year-old beginners to university students in their twenties, a longitudinal study would have required ten years of data collection! So for this practical reason, the PIF project collected a cross-sectional corpus.

It is important to stress that the PIF project was in no way concerned to *evaluate* the language proficiency of our informants in the way that official examinations or standardised tests do, putting people in rank order or giving them a mark of some kind. In fact we went to considerable lengths to assure our subjects that we were not assessing them. The PIF corpus was collected in order to facilitate research into many aspects of learner language, both along traditional paths (vocabulary, grammar, pronunciation) and along less well-trodden ones (conversational interaction, communication strategies).

The PIF corpus is a collection of learner language texts which lends itself to many sorts of analysis. It has indeed already been used for several purposes by students of English both at colleges of education and universities, though we should stress that this can only be done under the supervision of researchers involved in the project. Naturally people who have spoken freely about personal matters were assured that what they said and wrote would be treated in confidence. The PIF corpus can therefore not be borrowed. In any case we believe that institutions or groups of learners will benefit most by collecting and analysing their own data.

The rest of this chapter is devoted to a description of a number of ways of collecting samples of learner language or information about learner English.

19.2 Learner language data types

When planning an empirical study many possibilities can be envisaged. One can go to the nearest school and observe what happens in a classroom, one can study a set of written exercises, or one can set up a minor research experiment. The approach adopted will reflect the immediate research goals one is pursuing. For example if one is interested in obtaining good samples of authentic learner language, in order to generate hypotheses which will be followed up later, one will collect open-ended types of data. On the other hand, if one is focussing on a specific aspect of learner performance, because hypotheses have already been formulated, the data collected will generally be more controlled. Examples of open-ended data would be essays written by learners or tape-recordings of role-play where learners can choose what to say. An example of highly controlled data would be a text read aloud, a sentence completion task specifically designed to test how learners cope with particular lexical or grammatical phenomena, or a questionnaire, asking learners to describe the learning strategies they pursue. Methods used to collect controlled types of data are usually referred to as ELICITATION TECHNIQUES because their function is to prompt or "elicit" specific information from the informant. All of the data types collected in the PIF corpus (listed above) are of a more open-ended kind, with the exception of the reading aloud passages.

The data types presented below do not constitute an exhaustive list. We have chosen to focus on data types which are immediately available in the classroom or which can be collected without expensive equipment or research experience.

Written language. This is accessible in the form of written work provided by learners: essays, group reports, picture compositions etc. There are considerable practical advantages in working with written language: unlike spoken language, it does not need transcription before analysis can begin; linguistic norms are generally better described for written than for spoken language, which facilitates error analysis.

Spoken language. This may be collected on sound- or video-tape. *Spontaneous* speech may be obtained by, for instance, individual students describing pictures or objects, or pairs or groups of students participating in role-plays, simulations, or communication tasks. These involve students in giving and receiving instructions, for instance for building a lego model, without recourse to non-verbal communication, or sketching in a route on a map (for a discussion of such tasks, see Wagner 1983). Such problem-solving activities can be designed to suit learners at many proficiency levels. *Prepared* speech may be elicited by students giving a short talk on a topic chosen by themselves, or reading aloud a text they have studied in advance.

Working with spoken language data is generally more time-consuming than working with written language. However, some issues can only be studied in speech. In the first place, some aspects of language only occur in spoken language communication, eg certain parts of discourse (cf chapter 4) and fluency (cf chapter 8). Secondly, speech more directly reflects the language production process than does writing. Thirdly, speaking spontaneously reduces the amount of monitoring (cf chapter 8) and, as a result, spoken language provides access to automatized and implicit IL knowledge (cf chapter 11).

Interviews. Informants can be interviewed or asked to complete questionnaires, in order to clarify questions of motivation and attitude. Interviews have also been used in foreign language pedagogy research in order to tap people's introspection, to find out more about people's intuitive awareness of the way they tackle learning problems, why particular language forms are used or avoided, and so on.

Observation. Classroom activities can be studied, with observers noting down things as they occur and possibly making a tape-recording. In order to get beyond a general awareness of classroom interaction patterns, analysis can specifically focus on such matters as question/answer patterns, teacher talk, error treatment, amount and type of learner contributions.

Diary studies are a record made by an individual of progress in learning a foreign language, involving systematic noting down of items learnt, how the learner believes things are learnt, in what order, etc.

When planning empirical work, it is imperative to select a suitable data type, as this will have a decisive influence on the sorts of result that can be obtained. A useful way of checking one's predictions about the suitability of a particular data type for a particular analysis is to undertake a *pilot project*. This might involve collecting and analysing data from just one or two learners before deciding on the form of the investigation proper.

19.3 Recording and transcribing learner language

Recording. It is a relatively simple matter to make recordings of the spoken language on sound tape. In principle any activity in the classroom can be taped, but naturally it is easier to get good quality recordings when students are in small groups or speaking on their own (as in a language laboratory). For the study of grammar, vocabulary or pronunciation, sound-tapes are perfectly adequate, and much simpler to work with than video-tapes. For pronunciation studies really good quality tapes are necessary.

Video-taping is more demanding, but is increasingly available in educational institutions. There are incontestably big advantages in working with a video-taped corpus. Sound recordings capture only a fraction of the communication going on between people in face-to-face interaction. A picture which records the multiplicity of signals through gesture, smiles, eye contact and body movements, together with the visual and oral production and reception of words, quite obviously enables one to put language into a wider perspective. There is a risk of too much information being recorded, but video-tapes are invaluable for the analysis of speakers misunderstanding one another and of communication strategies.

Transcribing. At an early stage of the analysis a spoken corpus needs writing out. Writing out exactly what has been recorded on a sound track is generally an eye-opener: there are surprises in sentence structure, the degree of repetition and incoherence, in the many ways expression is put into the voice. Such work is excellent listening training which is guaranteed to provide insight into the nature of the spoken language.

In the extracts reproduced in transcription in the examples in this book, pauses have been noted with a system of dashes, and vocal hesitations (*er, erm*) put in, but we have chosen not to supply punctuation. The reason for doing so is that in a spoken language transcript it is important to think in terms of the units of speech rather than the conventions of the written language.

The job of transcribing is made more complicated by the fact that at times more than one person is speaking at the same time. We have found that, assuming one can puzzle out what has been said and by whom, a system of tramlines with one line per voice provides a practical framework which shows visually voices following on from one another and occasionally overlapping. Additional lines can be used for noting down anything of interest at the point at which it occurs: this could be errors, communication disruptions, or interpretations of unclear passages.

Speaker 1	bla bla bla
Speaker 2	bla
Notes	2 smiles

A further example shows how the tramline system can be used for a pronunciation analysis, in this case of the [ɒ/ʌ] problem (the *rot/rut* pair). In the top lane the learner's speech has been transcribed in conventional orthography; in the second, the required target sounds have been filled in; in the third, errors are noted; in the fourth, there is room for comments and interpretation.

text	she said she'd love a cup of coffee, Mum
target	ʌ ʌ ɒ ʌ
error	ɒ ʌ ɒ
notes	

A system like this with 1 or 2 extra lines is practical during the stages of an analysis when observations are being recorded. Textual extracts can finally be presented in a form appropriate for the particular purpose.

This last example shows how the tramline format lends itself to the analysis of a limited number of phonemes. Other studies of pronunciation might need a phonetic transcription of all the sounds in short extracts. If one is analysing the interaction between speakers, it may be necessary to mark intonation: from the transcribed words only it may not be apparent whether an utterance is to be regarded as a statement or a question, which a falling or rising intonation respectively might help to clarify. Intonation can be regarded as the equivalent of punctuation, in that one of the functions of pitch modulation is to mark whether a speaker intends to continue speaking, or to surrender the floor to someone else. There are many ways of transcribing intonation, the simplest being those used in introductory phonetics textbooks (eg Davidsen-Nielsen 1981). More sophisticated transcription systems have been evolved to record tempo, loudness and other features of voice modulation as well as intonation.[3]

The purpose of transcribing is to make the analysis phase more manageable and effective. Transcribing is very time-consuming, and for many purposes only small extracts of a tape need to be transcribed. The amount will always depend on *what* particular problems it is that are to be investigated.

Footnotes to chapter 19

1. ISAK, *In*ter*s*proglig *a*rbejds*k*reds, Department of German, University of Odense.
2. For details of the PIF corpus including a detailed description of informants see Færch 1983b.
3. See Crystal/Davy 1969.

References

Abbs, Brian / Freebairn, Ingrid (1979a), *Building Strategies, Students' Book*. London: Longman.

– (1979b), *Building Strategies: Teacher's Book*. London: Longman.

Abercrombie, David (1956), *Problems and Principles in Language Study*. London: Longman.

– (1972), *"Paralanguage"*. In Laver/Hutcheson (1972), 64–70. (Originally published 1968).

Adjemian, Chris (1976), "On the Nature of Interlanguage Systems". *Language Learning* 26, 297–320.

Albrechtsen, Dorte / Henriksen, Birgit / Færch, Claus (1980), "Native Speaker Reactions to Learners' Spoken Interlanguage". *Language Learning* 30, 365–96.

Alderson, J. Charles / Hughes, Arthur (1981), *ELT Documents 111 – Issues in Language Testing*. London: The British Council, Central Information Service.

Alexander, Louis G. (1967), *First Things First, Teacher's Book*. London: Longman.

Alexander, Louis G. / Allen, W. Stannard / Close, R. A. / O'Neill, Robert J. (1975), *English Grammatical Structure*. London: Longman.

Allen, J. Patrick B. / Corder, S. Pit (eds.) (1974), *Techniques in applied linguistics*. The Edinburgh Course in Applied Linguistics, vol. 3. London: Oxford University Press.

– (eds.) (1975), *Papers in Applied Linguistics*. The Edinburgh Course in Applied Linguistics, vol. 2. London: Oxford University Press.

Allen, J. Patrick B. / Davies, Alan (1977), *Testing and Experimental Methods*. The Edinburgh Course in Applied Linguistics, vol. 4. London: Oxford University Press.

Andersen, Erik / Fredberg, Morten / Vestergaard, Torben / Østergaard, Frede (1978), *Temaer i anvendt lingvistik*. Copenhagen: Akademisk forlag.

Andersen, Helga G. / Risager, Karen (1977), "Samfunds- og kulturformidling". In Glahn/Jakobsen/Larsen 1977, 27–55.

– (1981), *Kommunikativ kompetens*. Serie om fremmedsprog nr. 20. Aalborg: Aalborg Universitetsforlag.

Austin, John L. (1955), *How to Do Things with Words*. Oxford: Clarendon Press.

Baldegger, M. / Müller, M. / Näf, A. / Schneider, G. (1980), *Kontaktschwelle: Deutsch als Fremdsprache*. Strasbourg: Council of Europe, 1981. München: Langenscheidt.

Bausch, Karl-Richard (ed). (1979), *Beiträge zur didaktischen Grammatik*. Königstein/Ts.: Scriptor.

Bencke, Jens / Hansen, Hans Henrik / Wahlgren, Bjarne (1981), *Gymnasiedidaktik*. Copenhagen: Gyldendal.

Bialystok, Ellen (1982), "On the relationship between knowing and using linguistic forms". *Applied Linguistics* 3, 181–206.

Bialystok, Ellen / Fröhlich, Maria (1980), "Oral Communication Strategies for Lexical Difficulties". *Interlanguage Studies Bulletin Utrecht* 5, 3–29.

Blum-Kulka, Shoshana (1982), Learning to Say what you Mean in a Second Language. *Applied Linguistics* 3, 29–59.

Blum-Kulka, Shoshana / Levenston, Eddie A. (1983), "Universals of Lexical Simplification". In Færch/Kasper 1983b, 119–139.

Börsch, Sabine (1982), *Fremdsprachenstudium – Frauenstudium? Subjektive Bedeutung und Funktion des Fremdsprachenerwerbs und -studiums für Studentinnen und Studenten.* Tübingen: Stauffenberg.

Bolinger, Dwight (ed.) (1972), *Intonation.* Harmondsworth: Penguin.

Breen, Michael P. / Candlin, Christopher N. (1980), "The Essentials of a Communicative Curriculum in Language Teaching". *Applied Linguistics* 1, 89–112.

Brick-Hansen, Aase / Engel, Merete / Gregersen, Jørgen / Haastrup, Kirsten (1983), *Forsøg med mundtlige prøver i engelsk ved folkeskolens afgangsprøver.* Copenhagen: Danmarks Lærerhøjskole.

The British Council (1982), *Humanistic approaches: an empirical view.* ELT Documents 113. London: The British Council, Central Information Service.

Brodersen, Dorthea / Gibson, Kirsten M. (1982), "Kommunikationsstrategier i folkeskolen – en undersøgelse af 12 elevers intersprog før og efter undervisning i kommunikationsstrategier". *Sproglæreren* 7, 26–36.

Brown, Gillian (1977), *Listening to Spoken English.* London: Longman.

– (1981), "Teaching the spoken language". In Sigurd/Svartvik (1981), 166–182.

Brown, Gillian / Currie, Karen / Kenworthy, Joanne (1980), *Questions of Intonation.* London: Croom Helm.

Brown, Penelope / Levinson, Stephen (1978), "Universals in Language Usage: Politeness Phenomena". In Goody, Esther N. (ed.), *Questions and Politeness.* Cambridge: Cambridge University Press, 56–289.

Brown, Roger (1973), *A First Language.* Harmondsworth: Penguin.

Brumfit, Christopher J. (1980), *Problems and Principles in English Teaching.* Oxford: Pergamon.

– (1981), "Notional Syllabuses Revisited: A Response". *Applied Linguistics* 2, 90–92.

– (ed.) (1982), *English for International Communication,* Oxford: Pergamon.

van Buren, Paul (1975), "Semantics and Language Teaching". In Allen/Corder 1975, 122–153.

Burstall, Clare (1975), "Factors affecting foreign language learning: a consideration of some recent research findings". *Language Teaching and Linguistics Abstracts* 8, 5–25.

Burstall, Clare / Jamieson, M. / Cohen, S. / Hargreaves, M. (1974), *Primary French in the balance.* Slough: National Foundation for Educational Research.

Canale, Michael (1983), "From communicative competence to communicative language pedagogy". In Richards/Schmidt 1983, 2–28.

Canale, Michael / Swain, Merrill (1980), "Theoretical Bases of Communicative Approaches to Second Language Teaching and Testing". *Applied Linguistics* 1, 1–47.

Candlin, Christopher N. (ed.) (1981), *The communicative teaching of English: Principles and an exercise typology*. London: Longman.

Carroll, Brendan J. (1980), *Testing Communicative Performance, An Interim Study*. Oxford: Pergamon.

Carroll, John B. (1981), "Twenty-five Years of Research on Foreign Language Aptitude". In Diller 1981, 83–118.

Carton, Aaron S. (1971), "Inferencing: a process in using and learning language". In Pimsleur, Paul / Quinn, Terence (eds.), *Papers from the Second International Congress of Applied Linguistics, Cambridge 1969*. Cambridge: Cambridge University Press.

Chafe, Wallace L. (1982), "Integration and Involvement in Speaking, Writing, and Oral Literature". In Tannen, Deborah (ed.), *Spoken and Written Language: Exploring Orality and Literacy*. Norwood, N. J.: Ablex, 35–54.

Chatman, Seymour (1966), "Some intonational crosscurrents: English and Danish". *Linguistics* 21, 24–44.

Chomsky, Noam (1965), *Aspects of the theory of syntax*. Cambridge, Mass.: MIT press.

Clark, Herbert H. / Clark, Eve V. (1977), *Psychology and language*. New York: Harcourt Brace Jovanovich.

Clark, Ruth (1975), "Adult Theories, Child Strategies and their Implications for the Language Teacher". In Allen/Corder 1975, 291–347.

Corder, S. Pit (1967), "The Significance of Learners' Errors", *IRAL* 5, 161–170. (Reprinted in Richards 1974, Corder 1981).

– (1973), *Introducing Applied Linguistics*. Harmondsworth: Penguin.

– (1974), "Error Analysis". In Allen/Corder 1974, 122–154.

– (1981), *Error Analysis and Interlanguage*. Oxford: Oxford University Press.

Coste, Daniel / Courtillon, Janine / Ferenczi, Victor / Martins-Baltar, Michel / Papo, Eliane / CREDIF/Roulet, Eddie (1976), *Un niveau-seuil*. Strasbourg: Council of Europe. (Paris: Hatier, 1981).

Coulthard, Malcolm (1977), *An Introduction to Discourse Analysis*. London: Longman.

Council of Europe (1981), *Modern Language Programme 1971–1981*. Strassbourg: Council of Europe.

Criper, Clive / Widdowson, Henry G. (1975), "Sociolinguistics and Language Teaching". In Allen/Corder 1975, 155–217.

Crystal, David (1969), *Prosodic Systems and Intonation in English*. Cambridge: Cambridge University Press.

Crystal, David / Davy, Derek (1969), *Investigating English Style*. London: Longman.

– (1975), *Advanced Conversational English*. London: Longman.

Cummins, Jim (1980), "The entry and exit fallacy in bilingual education". *NABE (= National Association for Bilingual Education) Journal* IV: 3, 25–59.

– (1981), "The Role of Primary Language Development in Promoting Educational Success for Language Minority Students". In *Schooling and Language Minority Students: A Theoretical Framework*. Los Angeles: Evaluation, Dissemination and Assessment Center, California University, 3–49.

Dalton, Peggy / Hardcastle, W. J. (1977), *Disorders of fluency and their effects on communication*. London: Arnold.

Dam, Leni (1983), "En eksperimenterende undervisning med vægt på elevernes egen tilrettelæggelse af undervisningen". SELF 3, 17–29.

Davidsen-Nielsen, Niels (1970), *Engelsk Fonetik*. Copenhagen: Gyldendal.

– (1975), *Engelsk udtale i hovedtræk*. Copenhagen: Gyldendal. (Second edition 1983).

– (1981), *Engelsk Intonation*. Anglica et Americana 14. Copenhagen: Department of English, Copenhagen University.

Davidsen-Nielsen, Niels / Færch, Claus / Harder, Peter (1982), *The Danish Learner*. Tunbridge Wells: Antony Taylor.

Davies, Alan / Widdowson, Henry G. (1974), "Reading and Writing". In Allen/Corder 1974, 155–201.

Dechert, Hans W. / Raupach, Manfred (eds.) (in press), *Transfer in Production*. Norwood, New Jersey: Ablex.

van Dijk, Teun A. (1977), "Context and Cognition: Knowledge Frames and Speech Act Comprehension". *Journal of Pragmatics* 1, 211–232.

Diller, Karl C. (ed.) (1981), *Individual Differences and Universals in Language Learning Aptitude*. Rowley, Mass.: Newbury House.

Dirven, René (ed.) (1977), *Hörverständnis im Fremdsprachenunterricht: Listening comprehension in foreign language teaching*. Kronberg: Scriptor.

Dittmar, Norbert (1976). *Sociolinguistics*. London: Arnold.

Edmondson, Willis J. (1981), *Spoken Discourse. A Model for Analysis*. London: Longman.

Edmondson, Willis J. / House, Juliane (1981), *Let's Talk and Talk about It*. München: Urban & Schwarzenberg.

Edmondson, Willis J. / House, Juliane / Kasper, Gabriele / Stemmer, Brigitte (1982), *Kommunikation: Lernen und Lehren. Berichte und Perspektiven aus einem Forschungsprojekt*. Manuskripte zur Sprachlehrforschung 20. Bochum: Seminar für Sprachlehrforschung, Ruhr-Universität Bochum.

Edwards, John R. (1982), "Language attitudes and their implications among English speakers". In Ryan, Ellen B. / Giles, Howard (eds.), *Attitudes towards language variation*. London: Arnold.

van Ek, Jan A. (1975), *The Threshold Level*. Strasbourg: Council of Europe. (Published 1980 as *Threshold Level English*, Oxford: Pergamon.).

– (1976), *The Threshold Level for Modern Language Learning in Schools*. Strasbourg: Council of Europe. (Published 1977 by Longman.)

Ekstrand, Lars (1980), "Sex Differences in Second Language Learning? Empirical studies and a discussion of related findings". *International Review of Applied Psychology*, 29, 205–259.

Ellegård, Alvar (1982), *Språket och hjärnan*. Värnamo: Hammarström and Åberg.

Engh, Bertil (1971), "En toleransundersökning: tyska elever tolkar svenska elevers språkfel". *Pedagogisk-psykologiska problem*, nr. 137. (Notiser och rapporter från pedagogisk-psykologiska institutionen, Lärarhögskolan, Malmø). Malmø: Lärarhögskolan.

Færch, Claus (1977), "Pædagogisk grammatik". In Glahn/Jakobsen/Larsen 1977, 118–137.

– (1979), *Research in Foreign Language Pedagogy – the PIF Project*. Anglica et Americana 7. Copenhagen: Department of English, Copenhagen University.

– (1983a), "Inferencing procedures and communication strategies in lexical comprehension". In Breen, Michael P. / Candlin, Christopher N. (eds.), *Interpretive strategies in language learning*. Oxford: Oxford University Press.

(1983b), *A Corpus of Learner Language*. Copenhagen: Department of English, Copenhagen University.

– (1983c), "Giving Transfer a Boost". *Scandinavian Working Papers on Bilingualism* 2.

– (1983d), "Rules of thumb and other teacher-formulated rules in the foreign language classroom". In Kasper, Gabriele (ed.), *Learning, teaching and communication in the foreign language classroom*. Århus: Arkona.

Færch, Claus / Grindsted, Per (1982), Error Coding Manual. *PIF Working Papers* 7 (revised version). Copenhagen: Department of English, Copenhagen University.

Færch, Claus / Kasper, Gabriele (1982), "Phatic, Metalingual and Metacommunicative Functions in Discourse: Gambits and Repairs". In Enkvist, Nils Erik (ed.), *Impromptu Speech: A Symposium*. Åbo: Åbo Akademi, 71–103.

– (1983a), "Ja und – og hva' så? A contrastive Discourse Analysis of Gambits in German and Danish". In Fisiak, Jacek (ed.), *Contrastive Linguistics*. The Hague: Mouton.

– (eds.) (1983b), *Strategies in Interlanguage Communication*. Harlow: Longman.

Fisiak, Jacek (ed.) (1981), *Contrastive Linguistics and the Language Teacher*. Oxford: Pergamon.

Florander, Jesper / Jensen, M. (1969), *Skoleforsøg i engelsk*. Copenhagen: Danmarks pædagogiske institut.

Fraser, Bruce (1982), "The domain of pragmatics". In Richards/Schmidt (1983), 29–60.

Freudenstein, Reinhold (ed.) (1978), *The role of women in foreign language textbooks*. Brussels: AIMAV.

Gårding, Eva (1981), *Contrastive prosody: a model and its application*. In Sigurd/Svartvik (1981), 146–165.

Gardner, Robert C. / Lambert, Wallace E. (1972), *Attitudes and motivation in second language teaching*. Rowley, Mass.: Newbury House.

Giglioli, Pier P. (ed.) (1972), *Language and Social Context: Selected Readings*. Harmondsworth: Penguin.

Gimson, A. C. (1980), *An introduction to the pronunciation of English*. London: Arnold (3rd edition).

Glahn, Esther / Jakobsen, Leif Kvistgaard / Larsen, Fritz (eds.) (1977), *Fremmed-sprogspædagogik*. Copenhagen: Gyldendal.

Goffman, Erving (1972), "On face-work: an analysis of ritual elements in social interaction". In Laver/Hutcheson 1972, 319–346.

Gregersen, Frans / Hermann, Jesper (1978), *Gennem sproget*. Copenhagen: Gyldendal.

Grewer, Ulrich / Moston, Terry K./Sexton, Malcolm E. (1981), "Developing communicative competence: An Exercise Typology". In Candlin 1981, 63–229.

Grindsted, Per / Rechnitzer, Vibeke (1982), *En sammenlignende analyse af nominalfrasekompleksiteten i 81 danske og engelske elevers stile*. Copenhagen: PIF, Copenhagen University.

Haastrup, Kirsten / Phillipson, Robert (1983), "Achievement Strategies in learner/native speaker interaction". In Færch/Kasper 1983b, 140–158.

Haastrup, Niels (1981), "Ferie i udlandet og færdighed i fremmedsprog, rapportering om bearbejdelse af to statistiske undersøgelser". *Rolig-papir* 25. Roskilde: Roskilde University Centre.

Halliday, Michael A. K. (1973), *Explorations in the Functions of Language*. London: Arnold.

– (1978), *Language as Social Semiotics*. London: Arnold.

Halliday, Michael A. K. / Hasan, Ruqaiya (1976), *Cohesion in English*. London: Longman.

Harder, Peter (1980), "Discourse as self-expression and the reduced identity of the L2 Learner". *Applied Linguistics* 1, 262–270.

Harms Larsen, Peter (1977), "Snak i klassen – om klasseundervisningen som samtalesituation". *Meddelelser fra Dansklærerforeningen* 1977, 206–21.

Harsløf, Olav (1983), *Fremtidens gymnasium*. København: Borgen.

Hartoft, Birgit (1980), "A comparative analysis of Danish and American English intonation". *Meddelelser fra gymnasieskolernes engelsklærerforening* 89, 21–31.

Hatch, Evelyn M. (1978a), "Acquisition of Syntax in a Second Language". In Richards 1978, 34–70.

– (1978b), "Discourse Analysis and Second Language Acquisition". In Hatch 1978c, 401–435.

– (ed.) (1978c), *Second Language Acquisition*. Rowley, Mass.: Newbury House.

– (1983), *Psycholinguistics. A Second Language Pespective*. Rowley, Mass.: Newbury House.

Hatch, Evelyn M. / Farhady, Hossein (1982), *Research Design and Statistics for Applied Linguistics*. Rowley, Mass.: Newbury House.

Hawkins, Eric / Perren, George (1978), *Intensive language teaching in schools*. London: Centre for Information on Language Teaching and Research.

Heaton, J. Brian (1975), *Writing English Language Tests*. London: Longman.

Høedt, Jørgen (1980), "The Study of Needs Analysis". *Unesco ALSED–LSP Newsletter* 4:1, 14–20.

Holmstrand, Lars (1980), *Effekterna på kunskaber, färdigheter och attityder av tidigt påbörjad undervisning i engelska*. Pædagogisk Forskning i Uppsala 18.

Hornby, A. S. (1974), *Oxford Advanced Learner's Dictionary of Current English*. Oxford: Oxford University Press (third edition).

House, Juliane / Kasper, Gabriele (1981), "Politeness Markers in English and German". In Coulmas, Florian (ed.), *Conversational Routine*. The Hague: Mouton, 157–185.

Howatt, Anthony (1974), "The Background to Course Design". In Allen/Corder 1974, 1–23.

Hughes, Arthur / Trudgill, Peter (1979), *English Accents and Dialects: An Introduction to social and regional varieties of British English*. London: Arnold.

Hymes, Dell (1972a), "On Communicative Competence". In Pride/Holmes 1972, 269–293. (Originally published 1971.)

– (1972b), "Towards Ethnographies of Communication: The Analysis of Communicative Events". In Giglioli 1972, 21–44. (Originally published 1964.)

Jakobsen, Leif Kvistgaard / Larsen, Fritz (1977), "Sprogfærdighed: Forståelighed og korrekthed". In Glahn/Jakobsen/Larsen 1977, 74–95.

Jakobson, Roman (1973), "Functions of Language". In Allen, J. P. B. / Corder, S. Pit (eds.), *Readings for Applied Linguistics*. The Edinburgh Course in Applied Linguistics, vol. 1. London: Oxford University Press, 53–57. (Originally published 1960.)

James, Carl (1980), *Contrastive Analysis*. London: Longman.

Jensen, Lillian (1982), *En undersøgelse af begrebet "fluency"*. Copenhagen: Department of English, Copenhagen University (MA thesis).

Johansson, Stig (1973), "The Identification and Evaluation of Errors in Foreign Languages: A Functional Approach". In Svartvik 1973, 102–114.

Johnson, Keith (1982), *Communicative Syllabus Design and Methodology*. Oxford: Pergamon.

Jones, Randall L. / Spolsky, Bernard (1975), *Testing Language Proficiency*. Arlington: Center for Applied Linguistics.

Kasper, Gabriele (1981), *Pragmatische Aspekte in der Interimsprache*. Tübingen: Narr.

– (1982), "Teaching-Induced Aspects of Interlanguage Discourse". *Studies in Second Language Acquisition 4, 99–113.*

Kellerman, Eric (1978), "Giving learners a break: Native Intuitions as a source of predictions about transferability". *Working Papers on Bilingualism 15, 59–92.*

– (1983), "Now you see it, now you don't". In Selinker/Gass 1983.

Kellerman, Eric / Sharwood Smith, Michael (eds.). (in press) *Cross-Linguistic Influence in Second Language Acquisition and Performance*. London: Pergamon.

Kennedy, Chris (1982), "Language Planning". *Language Teaching 15/4, 264–284.*

Knapp-Potthoff, Annelie / Knapp, Karlfried (1982), *Fremdsprachenlernen und -lehren*. Stuttgart: Kohlhammer.

Kramsch, Claire J. (1981), *Discourse Analysis and Second Language Teaching*. Washington, D. C.: Center for Applied Linguistics.

Krashen, Stephen (1981), *Second Language Acquisition and Second Language Learning*. Oxford: Pergamon.

– (1982), *Principles and Practice in Second Language Acquisition.* Oxford: Pergamon.

Krashen, Stephen D. / Long, Michael H. / Scarcella, Robin C. (1977). "Age, rate and eventual attainment in second language acquisition". *TESOL Quarterly* 13, 573–582.

– (eds.) (1982), *Child-Adult Differences in Second Language Acquisition.* Rowley Mass.: Newbury House.

Kristiansen, Bo (1981), *Fremmedsprogsstatus og uddannelse.* Odense: Department of English, Odense University (MA thesis).

Labov, William (1972), "The Study of Language in its Social Context". In Giglioli 1972, 283–307.

Lado, Robert (1957), *Linguistics across Cultures.* Ann Arbor: The University of Michigan Press.

Lambert, Richard D. / Freed, Barbara F. (eds.) (1982), *The Loss of Language Skills.* Rowley, Mass.: Newbury House.

Lambert, Wallace E. (1983), "Deciding on languages of instruction, psychological and social considerations". In Husén, Torsten (ed.), *Multicultural and multilingual education in immigrant countries.* Oxford: Pergamon, 93–104. (Swedish version in *Indvandrare och Minoriteter* 3, 1983, 2–7.)

Lambert, Wallace E. / Taylor, Donald M. (1983), "Language in the education of ethnic minority immigrants: issues, problems and methods". In Samuda, R. J. / Woods, S. L. (eds.), *Perspectives in immigrant education.* New York: University Press of America; and in Homel, P. / Paliz, M. (eds.), *Childhood bilingualism: Aspects of cognitive, social and emotional development.* New Jersey: Erlbaum Associates, 1983.

Lambert, Wallace E. / Taylor, Donald M. (forthcoming), "Language in the education of ethnic minority immigrants: issues, problems and methods".

Larsen, Fritz / Jakobsen, Leif Kvistgaard (1977), "Om fremmedsprogssprogsundervisning". In Glahn/Jakobsen/Larsen 1977, 9–26.

Larsen, Kirsten / Nielsen, Harriet Bjerrum (1982), "Pigerne i klasseoffentligheden". In Drastrup, J. (ed.), *Pigeopdragelse/Pigeliv,* Forlaget Emmeline, Brordrup Bygade 1, 4621 Gadstrup, 25–42.

Lautrop, Marianne (1980), *Kønsroller og franskbøger.* Copenhagen: Undervisningsministeriets udvalg vedrørende kønsroller og uddannelser.

Laver, John (1970), "The production of speech". In Lyons, John (ed.), *New Horizons in Linguistics.* Harmondsworth: Penguin, 53–75.

Laver, John / Hutcheson, Sandy (eds.) (1972), *Communication in Face to Face Interaction.* Harmondsworth: Penguin.

Leech, Geoffrey N. (1980), *Explorations in Semantics and Pragmatics.* Amsterdam: John Benjamins.

– (1983), *Principles of Pragmatics.* London: Longman.

Leeson, Richard (1975), *Fluency and Language Teaching.* London: Longman.

Lenneberg, Eric (1967), *Biological Foundations of Language.* New York: Wiley.

Leontiev, Alexei A. (1971), *Sprache, Sprechen, Sprechtätigkeit.* Stuttgart: Kohlhammer.

– (1974), *Psycholinguistik und Sprachunterricht.* Stuttgart: Kohlhammer.

Linnarud, Moira (1975), *Vocabulary and Sentence Connection in Written Free Production.*

Some comparisons between student performance in Swedish and English. Malmö: Lärarhögskolan i Malmö.

– (1976), "Lexical Density and Lexical Variation – An Analysis of the Lexical Texture of Swedish Students' Written Work". *Studia Anglica Posnaniensia* 7, 45–52.

– (1978), "Cohesion and Communication in the Target Language". *Interlanguage Studies Bulletin Utrecht* 3/1, 23–34.

Littlewood, William T. (1981), *Communicative language teaching*. Cambridge: Cambridge University Press.

Livingstone, Carol (1983), *Role play in language learning*. London: Longman.

Looms, Peter O. (1981), "Behov for fremmedsprog i Danmark". In *Sproglæreren* 1, 31–38.

Lyons, John (1977), *Semantics,* vols 1–2. Cambridge: Cambridge University Press.

– (1981), *Language and Linguistics*. Cambridge: Cambridge University Press.

Maegaard, Bente / Ruus, Hanne (1981), *Hyppige ord i danske børnebøger*. Copenhagen: Gyldendal.

McDonough, Steven H. (1981), *The Psychology of Foreign Language Learning*. London: George Allen and Unwin.

McLaughlin, Barry (1978), *Second Language Acquisition in Childhood*. Hilsdale, New Jersey: Laurence Erlbaum.

Meara, Paul (ed.) (1983), *Vocabulary in second language*. London: Centre for Information on Language Teaching and Research.

Meisel, Jürgen M. (1980), "Linguistic Simplification". In Felix, Sascha W. (ed.), *Second Language Development*. Tübingen: Narr, 13–40.

Morrison, Donald M. / Low, Graham (1983), "Monitoring and the second language learner". In Richards/Schmidt 1983, 228–250.

Morrow, Keith (1977), *Techniques of evaluation for a notional syllabus*. London: Royal Society of Arts (mimeo).

Moulton, William G. (1962), *The Sounds of English and German*. Chicago: University of Chicago Press.

Munby, John (1978), *Communicative Syllabus Design*. Cambridge: Cambridge University Press.

Muschinsky, Lars Jakob / Schnack, Karsten (eds.) (1981), *Pædagogisk Opslagsbog*. Copenhagen: Christian Ejlers Forlag.

Mylov, Peer (1972), *Skoleforsøg i engelsk*. Copenhagen: Munksgaard.

Naiman, Neil (1974), "The Use of Elicited Imitation in Second Language Acquisition Research". *Working Papers on Bilingualism* 2, 1–37.

Naiman, Neil / Fröhlich, Maria / Stern, H. H. / Todesco, Angela (1978), *The Good Language Learner*. Toronto: The Ontario Institute for Studies in Education.

Nemser, William (1971), "Approximative systems of foreign language learners". *IRAL* 9, 115–123.

Oller, John W., Jr. (1979), *Language Tests at School*. London: Longman.

Palmer, Frank R. (1976), *Semantics, a new outline*. Cambridge: Cambridge University Press.

Paulston, Christina Bratt (1981), "Notional Syllabuses Revisited: Some comments". *Applied Linguistics* 2, 93–95.

Phillipson, Robert (1978), "Prosody errors in English spoken by Danes". In Gårding, Eva / Bruce, Gösta / Bannert, Robert (eds.), *Nordic Prosody*. Lund: Department of Linguistics, Lund University, 271–278.

Phillipson, Robert / Lauridsen, Hanne (1982), *Danish Learning of English Obstruents: A PIF Report*. Anglica et Americana 16. Copenhagen: Department of English, Copenhagen University.

Piepho, Hans-Eberhard (1974), *Kommunikative Kompetenz als übergeordnetes Lernziel des Englischunterrichts*. Dornburg-Frickhofen: Frankonius.

Poulsen, Erik (1981), "Brug af autentiske tekster i 8.–10. klasse. Hvorfor? – Hvilke? – Hvordan?". *Sproglæreren* 7, 9–15.

Pride, John B. / Holmes, Janet (eds.) (1972), *Sociolinguistics*. Harmondsworth: Penguin.

Quirk, Randolph / Greenbaum, Sidney / Leech, Geoffrey / Svartvik, Jan (1972), *A Grammar of Contemporary English*. London: Longman.

Richards, Jack C. (ed.) (1974), *Error Analysis*. London: Longman.

– (ed.) (1978), *Understanding Second and Foreign Language Learning, Issues and Approaches*. Rowley, Mass.: Newbury House.

Richards, Jack C. / Schmidt, Richard W. (eds.) (1983), *Language and Communication*. London: Longman.

Rogers, Carl R. (1969), *Freedom to learn*. Ohio: Merrill P. C.

Savignon, Sandra J. (1983), *Communicative Competence: Theory and Classroom Practice*. Reading, Mass.: Addison-Wesley.

Saville-Troike, Muriel (1982), *The ethnography of communication*. Oxford: Blackwell.

Schegloff, Emanuel A. / Jefferson, Gail / Sacks, Harvey (1977), "The Preference for Self-Correction in the Organization of Repair in Conversation". *Language* 53, 361–382.

Scollon, Ron / Scollon, Suzanne B. K. (1983), "Face in interethnic communication". In Richards/Schmidt 1983, 156–190.

Searle, John R. (1969), *Speech Acts*. Cambridge: Cambridge University Press.

– (1972), "What is a Speech Act?". In Giglioli 1972, 136–154. (Originally published in 1965).

– (1976), "A Classification of Illocutionary Acts". *Language in Society* 5, 1–23.

Seliger, Herbert W. (1979), "On the Nature and Function of Language Rules in Language Teaching". *TESOL Quarterly* 13, 359–369.

Seliger, Herbert W. / Long, Michael (eds.) (1983), *Classroom Language Acquisition and Use: New Perspectives*. Rowley, Mass.: Newbury House.

Selinker, Larry (1969), "Language Transfer". In *General Linguistics* 9, 67–92.

– (1972), "Interlanguage". In *IRAL* 10, 219–31. (Reprinted in Richards 1974).

314

Selinker, Larry / Gass, Susan (eds.) (1983), *Language transfer in language learning*. Rowley, Mass.: Newbury House.

Sharwood Smith, Michael (1981), "Consciousness-raising and the Second Language Learner". *Applied Linguistics* 2, 159–168.

Sigurd, Bent / Svartvik, Jan (eds.) (1981), *AILA 81 Proceedings II. Lectures*. Lund: CWK Gleerup.

Sinclair, John M. H. / Brazil, David (1982), *Teacher Talk*. Oxford: Oxford University Press.

Sinclair, John M. H. / Coulthard, R. Malcolm (1975), *Towards an Analysis of Discourse*. London: Oxford University Press.

Skutnabb-Kangas, Tove (1983), *Bilingualism or not – the education of minorities*. Clevedon: Multilingual Matters. (Originally published in Swedish).

Snow, Catherine / Ferguson, Charles A. (eds.) (1977), *Talking to Children – Language Input and Acquisition*. Cambridge: Cambridge University Press.

Stenson, Nancy (1975), "Induced errors". In Schumann, John / Stenson, Nancy (eds.), *New Frontiers in Second Language Learning*. Rowley, Mass.: Newbury House, 54–70.

Stewick, Earl W. (1976), *Memory Meaning and Method*. Rowley, Mass.: Newbury House.

– (1980), *Teaching languages: a way and ways*. Rowley, Mass.: Newbury House.

– (1982), *Teaching and Learning Languages*. Cambridge: Cambridge University Press.

Stockwell, Robert P. / Bowen, J. Donald / Martin, John W. (1965), *The Grammatical Structures of English and Spanish*. Chicago: University of Chicago Press.

Strevens, Peter (1980), *Teaching English as an International Language*. Oxford: Pergamon.

Svartvik, Jan (ed.) (1973), *Errata, papers in error analysis*. Lund: CWK Gleerup.

Svartvik, Jan / Eeg-Olofsson, Mats / Forsheden, Oscar / Oreström, Bengt / Thavenius, Cecilia (1982), *Survey of Spoken English: Report on research 1975–81*. Lund: CWK Gleerup.

Svartvik, Jan / Quirk, Randolph (eds.) (1980), *A Corpus of English Conversation*. Lund: Gleerup/Liber.

Swain, Merrill/Lapkin, Sharon (1982), *Evaluating Bilingual Education: a Canadian Case Study*. Clevedon: Multilingual Matters.

Tarone, Elaine (1978), "The Phonology of Interlanguage". In Richards 1978, 15–33.

Thomas, Jenny (1983), Cross-Cultural Pragmatic Failure. *Applied Linguistics* 4, 91–112.

Todd, Loreto (1974), *Pidgins and Creoles*. London: Routledge.

Trudgill, Peter / Hannah, Jean (1982), *International English*. London: Arnold.

Wagner, Johannes (1983), *Kommunikation und Spracherwerb im Fremdsprachenunterricht*. Tübingen: Narr.

Wagner, Johannes / Petersen, Uwe Helm (eds.) (1983), *Kommunikation i fremmed-*

sprogsundervisningen. Undervisningsanalyser. Copenhagen: Gjellerup.

Walsh, Terence M. / Diller, Karl C. (1981), "Neurolinguistic Considerations on the Optimum Age for Second Language Learning". In Diller 1981, 3–21.

Wardhaugh, Ronald (1970), "The contrastive analysis hypothesis". *TESOL Quarterly* 4, 123–130.

Wegener, Heide / Krumm, Hans-Jürgen (1982), "Spiele - Sprachunterricht - Sprachlernspiele". In *Jahrbuch Deutsch als Fremdsprache* vol. 8, Heidelbert: Gross, 189–203.

Wells, John C. (1982), *Accents of English.* Cambridge: Cambridge University Press.

Wesche, Marjorie B. (1981), "Language Aptitude Measures in Streaming, Matching Students with Methods, and Diagnosis of Learning Problems". In Diller 1981, 119–154.

Widdowson, Henry G. / Brumfit, Christopher J. (1981), "Issues in Second Language Syllabus Design". In Alatis, James E. / Altman, Howard B. / Alatis, Penelope M. (eds.), *The Second Language Classroom.* New York: Oxford University Press, 197–210.

Wilkins, David A. (1981a), "Notional Syllabuses Revisited". *Applied Linguistics* 2, 83–89.

– (1981b), "Notional Syllabuses Revisited: A Further Reply". *Applied Linguistics* 2, 96–100.

Winburne, J. N. (1964), "Sentence sequence in discourse". In Lunt, Horace G. (ed.), *Proceedings of the Ninth International Congress of Linguists, Cambridge, Mass., 1962.* Janua Lingua, Series maior 12. The Hague: Mouton, 1094–1098.

Wolfson, Nessa (1983), "Rules of speaking". In Richards/Schmidt 1983, 61–88.

Zettersten, Arne (1978), *A word frequency list based on American English press reportage.* Copenhagen: Akademisk Forlag.

Zydatiss, Wolfgang (1976), "Learning problem Expanded Form – a performance analysis". *IRAL* 14, 351–371.

Index

accents   *120*–122, 210
achievement strategies   *154*–156,
    159–161, 164, 250;
    testing   *244*
active vocabulary   *99*, 100
addressee   *24*–*27*, 41, 42, 47;
    direct   *24*, 25;
    indirect   *24*, 25
addresser   *24*–27, 41, 42, 47
adjacency pair   *60*–62
age   *210*–212
analytic languages   *103*
aptitude   208, *213*–215
attitude   *121*, 122, 126, 208–210, 212
automatization   190, 197, *203*–206
availability   *87*, 88

bottom-up processing   141, *148*–149

category width   213, *214*
channel, aural   *26;*
    visual   *26*
closing phase   49, 66, *67*–69
cloze procedure   *95*, 96, 248
code   *27*, 28, 41, 43;
    linguistic   *27*, 28;
    non-linguistic   *28*
code-switching   *28*, 156, 159
cognate words   *90*
coherence   *60*–63
cohesion   62, *63*–65, 176
collocation   *95*, 96, 99
communication, asymmetric   *26*, 154;
    educational   *35*–37;
    face-to-face   26, *28*–32;
    informative   *21;*
    intentional   *21*, 23;
    interlanguage   *21;*
    native speaker   *21;*
    one-way   *32*–35
    symmetric   *26;*
    verbal   *21*

communication strategies   *154*–165,
    167
communicative competence   *167*–179,
    204, 224, 235–41, 247–49, 254, 255;
    efficiency   *121;*
    event   *23;*
    language teaching   *259*–261
competence, communicative   *167*–179,
    204, 224, 235, 241, 247–49, 254, 255;
    linguistic   *168*–170, 178, 247, 248;
    pragmatic   *168*–171, 173, 179, 245,
    249, 250;
    social   68, *171;*
    strategic   *168*–170, 173, 227, 245,
    250
comprehensible input   *187*, 188
comprehension approach   *261*
consciousness   178, 179, 186, 190, 194,
    197, 202, 203, 253–256
consciousness-raising   *203*, 205, 206
contact, direct   *26*, 27, 42–44;
    non-direct   *27*
content words   *84*, 85
context-embedded language   *177*,
    178, 228, 248
context-reduced language   *177*, 178
contextual cues   *96*
contrastive analysis   104, *289*–292;
    performance analysis   290, *291*, 292
core phase   66, *67*, 68
corpus   86, 87, 191, 292, *295*–298
coverage   *87*, 88
covert errors   *283*
criterion-referenced testing   *245*
critical period   *211*
cross-sectional studies   *297*

data   *298*–300
diagnostic tests   *246*
differentiation   *252*, 253
directive function   41, *42*–44
discourse analysis   *60*, 61

317

discrete point tests   *247–249*

educational situation   *186,* 194
eliciation technique   *299*
error analysis   *104–*113, 129–137,
  271, *282–*289
evaluation   244–251
expressive function   41, *42,* 44
extroversion   213, *214*

familiarity   *26*
feedback, delayed   *27, 32;*
  direct   *199;*
  immediate   *26, 32, 35,* 144;
  indirect   *199;*
  negative   *198,* 199;
  positive   *198,* 199
field dependence   213, *214–*216;
  independence   213, *214–*216
fluency   142, *143,* 144–148, 167–169,
  173, 176, 224, 228, 299;
  compensatory   *145,* 146
foreign language   *221*
foreign language pedagogy   *9–*15
formative evaluation   *245,* 246
fossilization   *192,* 274
frequency   80, *86,* 87, 105, 106, 279,
  280
function words   *84–*86, 110

gambits   *71–*75
generalization   157, 158, 162, *193*

hypotheses   190, *191–*201, 204;
  formation   *190,* 200, 201, 203, 205,
  206;
  testing   *190,* 194–201, 203–205

idioms   *79,* 87, 110
imitation   *188–*190, 203–205
immersion programmes   *260*
inferencing   *150,* 151, 162, 187, 188, 192
input   186, *187,* 188, 192, 196;
  comprehensible   *187,* 188
intake   186–*188,* 196
integrative tests   *248–*251
interactional strategies   *158,* 162
interdisciplinary approaches   13, 257
interlanguage   *28,* 68, 167, 269,

271–274;
  communication   *275;*
  studies   *269–*271
interlingual cues   *96–*98
interrules   *114,* 116–118
inter-subject collaboration   *257,* 258
intonation   *123–*127
intralingual cues   *97, 98*
introspection   160, 161, 277

knowledge, explicit   *201–*204;
  implicit   *201–*203;
  metacommunicative   *254,* 255, 263;
  socio-cultural   96, *255,* 256, 264;
  about learning   *254,* 255, 264

language functions   *40–*45
lateralization   *211*
learner English   *7–*9
learner-external factors   137
learner-internal factors   136, 137
learner language approach   *9–*14
learner vocabulary   *88–*96
lexical density   *80,* 84, 85;
  inferencing   *96–*98
  variation   64, *80–*84
lingua franca   120, *221,* 222
linguistic competence   *168–*170, 178,
  247, 248;
  rules   *114;*
  syllabus   *231–*233, 235
longitudinal studies   *297*
long-term memory   *189*

meaning potential   *78,* 90, 99
message   *27,* 32, 41
metacommunicative awareness   69,
  178, 179, 194, 206, 224, 228
metalinguistic function   41, *43*
monitoring   113, *141,* 142, 203, 300
motivation   208, 209, 212, 215

native language   *28;*
  rules   *114*
negotiation of syllabus   *256,* 257
non-educational situation   *186*
non-linguistic strategies   *158,* 159
norm-referenced testing   *245*

opening phase   49, 66, *67*–69

partial comprehension   *151,* 187
participant   *24*–27
passive vocabulary   *99,* 100
pedagogical interrules   *115*–118
performance analysis   131–135, 175, *277*–281, 293
permeable   *192,* 274
permission   44, *46,* 47, 50, 233, 234
phatic function   41, *43,* 44, 47, 68
poetic function   41, *43*
politeness   *54*–58
pragmatic competence   *168*–171, 173, 179, 245, 249, 250;
   syllabus   *233*–235
prefabricated patterns   *79,* 87
proficiency testing   *244,* 250, 251
project work   *258,* 259
prosody   *120*–129
psycholinguistic rules   *114,* 187

qualitative studies   136, 278, 279
quantitative studies   136, 278–281

received pronunciation   121, *137*
reception   27;
   strategies   *162*–164
reduction strategies   69
referential function   41, *42*–44
reliability   *246,* 248–250
repair, interactional   72, 73, 158, 162;
   non-interactional   *72*–75;
   other-initiated   72, 73, 162, 163, 199;
   self-initiated   *72*–75, 142;
   work   *72*–75, 205
request   44, *45*–47, 50–53, 162, 163
role, communicative   *24,* 25, 53, 189;
   social   *25,* 26

second language   *221*
setting   *24,* 41, 42;
   institutional   *24*
   physical   *24*
   psychological   *24*
short-term memory   *189*
social competence   68, *171*
speaker selection   *70*

speech act modality   *54*–58, 124, 125, 139, 227
speech acts   *45*–58, 60, 61, 67, 139, 233;
   attitudinal   *48*–50;
   back-pointing   *48*–52, 54, 62;
   direct   *54*–57;
   directing   *45*–49, 68;
   forward-pointing   *45*–52, 54, 62;
   indirect   *55*–57;
   informative   *47,* 54, 62;
   initiating   60, *62,* 69;
   responding   60, *62,* 69;
   ritual   48, *49,* 50, 62, 67, 68
speech production   *139*–142, 154–162, 203, 205, 300;
   norms   120–122
speech reception   *148*–151, 154, 162–164, 203, 205
status   *25,* 26
strategic competence   *168*–170, 173, 227, 245, 250
strategies, achievement   *154*–156, 159–161, 164, 250;
   communication   *154*–165, 167;
   interactional   *158,* 162;
   non-linguistic   *158,* 159;
   paraphrasing   87, *157*–159;
   reception   *162*–164;
   reduction   154, *161,* 162, 164;
   restructuring   *157;*
   word-coinage   *157*
strategy markers   *160,* 165
stress   *128,* 129
suggestion   *45*–47, 50, 53, 55
summative evaluation   *245,* 246
syllabus   *231*–237, 256
synthetic languages   *103*

text   32, 33, 49, *60,* 66
thematic syllabus   *235,* 236
threshold level   *225*–229;
   functions   *225,* 226
tolerance of ambiguity   213, *214*
tolerance testing   *174,* 176, 292–294
top-down processing   141, 149, *150,* 187
transfer   90, 92, 93, 103, 135, 137, *193,* 194, 291

turn   *49,* 50, 69, 70
turn-keeping   *71*
turn-taking   *69*–71
type-token ratio   *80*–84

uptaking   *72,* 73, 142

validity   *246,* 247, 250;
   content   *246*–247, 249;
   face   *247,* 249;
   predictive   *246*

word tokens   *77*–84, 86, 87;
   types   *78*–87

DATE DUE

DATE DUE			
AUG 27 1987			
AUG 30 1987			
JUN 5 1990			
DEC 1 0 1999			

DEMCO 38-297